Ian Hamilton

in conversation with

Dan Jacobson

Ian Hamilton

in conversation with

Dan Jacobson

BETWEEN THE LINES BTL BETWEEN THE LINES

First published in 2002 by

BETWEEN THE LINES **BTL** BETWEEN THE LINES

9 Woodstock Road
London N4 3ET
UK

T : +44 (0)20 8374 5526 F : +44 (0)20 8374 5736 E-mail : btluk@aol.com
Website: http://www.interviews-with-poets.com

A CIP catalogue record for this book
is available from the British Library

ISBN 1-903291-05-4

Design and typography: Philip Hoy

Printed and bound by George Over Limited
Somers Road, Rugby CV22 7DH

BETWEEN THE LINES **BTL** BETWEEN THE LINES

BTL publishes unusually wide-ranging and unusually deep-going interviews with some of today's most accomplished poets.

Some would deny that any useful purpose is served by putting to a writer questions which are not answered by his or her books. For them, what Yeats called 'the bundle of accident and incoherence that sits down to breakfast' is best left alone, not asked to interrupt its cornflakes, or to set aside its morning paper, while someone with a tape recorder inquires about its life, habits and attitudes.

If we do not share this view, it is not because we endorse Sainte-Beuve's dictum, *tel arbre, tel fruit — as the tree, so the fruit* — but because we understand what Geoffrey Braithwaite was getting at when the author of *Flaubert's Parrot* had him say:

> 'But if you love a writer, if you depend upon the drip-feed of his intelligence, if you want to pursue him and find him – despite edicts to the contrary – then it's impossible to know too much.'

The first nine volumes, featuring W.D. Snodgrass, Michael Hamburger, Anthony Thwaite, Anthony Hecht, Donald Hall, Thom Gunn, Richard Wilbur, Seamus Heaney and Donald Justice, respectively, are already available; others now being prepared will feature Charles Simic, Peter Dale, John Ashbery, Paul Muldoon, Hans Magnus Enzensberger, and Peter Porter (Further details are given overleaf.)

As well as the interview, each volume contains a sketch of the poet's life and career, a comprehensive bibliography, archival information, and a representative selection of quotations from the poet's critics and reviewers. It is hoped that the results will be of interest to the lay reader and specialist alike.

CONTENTS

LIST OF ILLUSTRATIONS

Courtesy of Jerry Bauer

©

Ian Hamilton, London, 1998 (front cover)

Courtesy of Gisela Dietzel

Courtesy of John Foley, L'Agence Opale, Paris

©

Courtesy of Stuart Hamilton

Courtesy of Ahdaf Soueif

Gezira Club, Cairo, 1985: 131
With Simon Gray, Highgate, c. 1987: 133
With Margaret and Dan Jacobson, Hampstead Heath, 1998: 136

Courtesy of Patricia Wheatley

Robert Tough Hamilton, 1936: 111
Robert Tough Hamilton, with, from left to right, Ronald, Ian and Stuart,
King's Lynn, 1943: 112
Daisy McKay Hamilton, with, from left to right, Stuart, Jeanette, Ian and Ronald,
Scarborough, 1955: 112
Oxford undergraduate, 1959: 114
With his mother, on her 60th birthday, 1970: 125
Edward Pygge at The ICA, London, June 25th 1973: 128
With Stuart Hamilton, in Greek Street, Soho, 1976: 128
With Peter Taylor, Charlottesville, Virginia, 1986: 132
Century Wilshire Hotel, Los Angeles, 1988: 133
Herefordshire, 1990: 135
Dover Beach, 1998: 136

ACKNOWLEDGEMENTS

The editors would like to thank the following people for their help in producing this book: Fiona Anderson (BBC), Jerry Bauer, Neil Berry, Janine Button (Condé Nast Publications), Russell Davies, Emily Dixon (BBC), Gisela Dietzel, Colin Falck, Chris Fletcher (British Library), John Foley (L'Agence Opale, Paris), John Fuller, Simon Gray, Matthew Hamilton, Stuart Hamilton, Clive James, Alan Jenkins (*TLS*), Karl Miller, Toby Oakes (National Sound Archive), Anna Pallai (Faber & Faber), Craig Raine, Chris Sheppard (Brotherton Library, Leeds University), Ahdaf Soueif, Patricia Wheatley, and Ian Whitbread (*Esquire Magazine*).

Ian Hamilton

Photograph courtesy of
John Foley
[L'Agence Opale, Paris]

©

A NOTE ON IAN HAMILTON

(Robert) Ian Hamilton was born on March 24th 1938, the second son of Robert Tough and Daisy (McKay) Hamilton, who had left their native Glasgow in 1936, and were then living in King's Lynn.

In 1951, the family – now increased by the arrival of another son and daughter – moved from Norfolk to Co. Durham, settling in Darlington. Hamilton was sent to the local grammar school, and it was there, during his last year, that he launched his first literary magazine. Although it only ran to two issues, and he later made light of the thing – claiming that it consisted of little more than letters of refusal from the well-known figures he'd asked to contribute – *The Scorpion* demonstrated not only its seventeen-year-old editor's precocity but also his persuasiveness, for amongst the people who didn't refuse him were some of the period's leading men of letters (see the front cover of No. 2, reproduced on page 113).

Hamilton took his university entrance examination in 1955 and was offered a place to read English at Keble College, Oxford. Entry had to be deferred for two years while he did National Service, but when, in 1958, he did go up to Keble, he quickly established a name for himself, at least among those who took writing seriously. Within a year of his arrival, he had launched a new literary magazine, *Tomorrow*. This may have started out a little uncertainly – 'with lashings of Michael Horovitz and thin jests from the 21-year-old Roger McGough', as John Fuller recently remarked – but by the time of its third and fourth issues, it was looking a lot more confident, and a lot more interesting. Issue no. 4 (see the front cover, reproduced on page 116) had contributions from Christopher Middleton, Thomas Blackburn, Alan Brownjohn and others. It also featured the script of an early play by Harold Pinter, the first time this had appeared in print.

During that same twelve-month period, Hamilton also went from being the Oxford University Poetry Society's treasurer to being its president – or 'president, chief executive and general mastermind', as he later described it – a job which obliged him to organize several readings a term. In one three-week period, in late 1960, he presided over readings by W.H. Auden, Stephen Spender and Robert Graves.

While at Oxford Hamilton made friends with Michael Fried, John Fuller, and then Colin Falck, the three people with whom, after graduating, in 1962, he launched his third literary magazine, *The Review*. *The Scorpion* and *Tomorrow* are memorable now chiefly because they were forerunners of *The Review*, which as Neil Powell has said, rapidly became 'the most influential and stylish of postwar British poetry magazines' – worthy of mention in the same breath as Grigson's *New Verse*, Connolly's *Horizon*, and Eliot's *Criterion*. *The Review* published poetry by a variety of writers – a wider variety than is sometimes realized. If there was a preference for short, neo-romantic lyrics written in a disciplined free verse – 'subtly-explosive five-liners', as Hamilton once described them – there was still plenty of space for poets whose work didn't fit this model. Issue no. 1, for example, contained very different sorts of poems by Donald Davie, Roy Fuller, John Fuller, Zbigniew Herbert, Peter Redgrove and Vladimir Mayakovsky.

Just as significant as the poetry, however, were the reviews and the criticism, which had a reputation for being combative – even bellicose. Shorter notices – not the least effective of them written by one Edward Pygge – rubbed shoulders with carefully crafted essays that often ran to considerable length. As Hamilton put it later, in an article for the *TLS*, the magazine 'railed against the so-called avant-garde (the Beats and their emerging progeny, the Liverpool Poets) and against the then-fashionable Group Poets'. But in point of fact, no-one was immune to attack, and even close friends and regular contributors could open the latest issue and find themselves being given a leisurely mauling in its columns.

Hostile reviews and criticism were by no means the only kind featured in *The Review*, however, for the magazine worked hard to promote the poets whose work it really cared about. Robert Lowell, John Berryman, Sylvia Plath – not exactly established figures, then, despite Al Alvarez's championing of them – were some of the people whose work it took a positive interest in. Others included the likes of Norman Cameron and Laura Riding – people it thought worthy of a second look.

At about the time he launched *The Review*, Hamilton started to write on a regular basis for Alan Ross's *London Magazine*. But since his only other source of income was from part-time teaching, making ends meet was not easy. As a result, he readily accepted when, in 1965, Arthur Crook, the editor of the *TLS*, asked him to be a 'Special Writer' for the paper – a three-day-a-week job which quickly turned into that of 'Poetry and Fiction Editor', for which he was paid the not inconsiderable sum of £900 per annum. Nor did he hesitate, later in the same year, when he was offered the position of Poetry Editor at *The Observer* – something for which the outgoing Alvarez had recommended him.

In 1964, *The Review* published a small pamphlet of Hamilton's poems entitled *Pretending Not to Sleep*. A handful of these poems had appeared in small magazines, but this was the first time his work had been gathered together, and Richard Howard, writing for *Poetry* (Chicago), reacted enthusiastically: 'Ian Hamilton is a discovery ... There is no complacent lingering over pain or pleasure, but the accuracy, the reticence we know to be the quality of high art.' In 1969, Faber included twenty of Hamilton's poems – roughly half of them taken from the pamphlet, and half of them new – in its *Poetry Introduction No. 1* (1969), and very shortly afterwards, they offered him a contract for his first full collection. *The Visit* (1970), which added a handful of new poems to those that had appeared in the pamphlet and the anthology, was a great success. Irvin Ehrenpreis, in a longish review, declared that it 'marked an epoch in recent poetry,' and Peter Dale, although he had some criticisms to make, and wasn't sure how Hamilton would be able to proceed thereafter, wrote: 'When [his] skills are truly keyed in, as they frequently are in the poems of marriage and mental disturbance, the poetry is very powerful and deeply moving ... One of [these poems'] achievements is to re-introduce tenderness into English verse and to fend off defensive irony.' *The Visit* was a Poetry Book Society choice.

In August 1972, *The Review* published its tenth anniversary number, and in the same week Richard Boston wrote a long appreciation of the magazine for *The Guardian*, which ended with the following words:

> What of the next ten years? Ian Hamilton feels that little magazines have a tendency to run down and become exhausted. Though there is no sign of this yet as far as *The Review* is concerned, he feels that the point may be approaching and that the magazine may be ready for a change of course. His plans for the future are ambitious, though at present he is unwilling to make them public. Whatever they are, however, if *The Review* can maintain in its second ten years the liveliness and intelligence of its first decade then it won't go far wrong.

Hamilton was playing his cards just a little bit closer to his chest than Boston realized, for he had already decided that the tenth anniversary issue was to be the last. Not only had the steam gone out of it, as he'd hinted, but the magazine had never achieved its hoped-for circulation figures, and was crippled by debts.

In 1974, Hamilton launched his fourth literary magazine, *The New Review*. The ambition of this large-format glossy was evident from the start: Vol. 1, No. 1 was almost 100 pages long and contained poems, fiction, essays and reviews by Al Alvarez, Martin Amis, Caroline Blackwood, Melvyn Bragg, Russell Davies, Rosemary Dinnage, Douglas

Dunn, Colin Falck, David Harsent, Francis Hope, Dan Jacobson, Clive James, Robert Lowell, Julian Mitchell, Edna O'Brien, Jonathan Raban, Lorna Sage, and George Steiner. It also featured a number of photographs, some of them by the up-and-coming Fay Godwin. Like its predecessor, *The New Review* made a decisive contribution to the cultural climate of the times, not least by its encouragement of younger writers. Martin Amis has already been mentioned, but others of his generation were also being given a platform, amongst them Julian Barnes, Jim Crace, James Fenton, Ian McEwan, Andrew Motion, Sean O'Brien, Tom Paulin, Craig Raine, and Christopher Reid. Even so, the magazine was not to last. It was heavily dependent on Arts Council funding, and when, four-and-a-half years after it was launched, that funding was withdrawn, *The New Review* promptly went out of business.

Hamilton had given up his editorial positions at the *TLS* and *The Observer* some years before, and for a time earned his living on Grub Street, writing most regularly for the *New Statesman,* which gave him the opportunity to change direction slightly by employing him as its television reviewer. Then came something altogether unexpected: an invitation to write the biography of Robert Lowell, who had died in 1977. Hamilton took just four years to complete the task, and his 500-page book, *Robert Lowell: A Biography* (1982), was a huge critical success, on both sides of the Atlantic. The reviewers – and these included figures such as John Carey, Peter Davison, Richard Ellmann, Anthony Hecht, Karl Miller, Robert B. Shaw, John Simon, Richard Tillinghast and Helen Vendler – were full of praise; but so too were intimates of Lowell's, many of whom wrote to Hamilton to express their feelings in private. Lowell's second wife, Elizabeth Hardwick, wrote as follows: 'Your book is very different from the ones we are accustomed to here. There is a finer intelligence in it and a greater equality than usual between the subject and the biographer. Your distance, the method, is full of Scottish virtue and sets the work apart from that feeling of a hovering heir among our academics.' Another one to express himself like this was the novelist and short story writer, Robie Macauley, who had known Lowell since the late 1930s: 'I am reading the Lowell with fascination and great admiration. I've always been confident that you would do a fine job, but this surpasses even those high expectations. You are the only man who could have done it. It needed your kind of long view and deliberation – and I can't think of anyone who knew Cal who'd have that in just the way you have.'

After the success of the Lowell book, it was only natural that Hamilton should think of writing more biographies, if suitable subjects presented themselves. *In Search of J.D. Salinger* (1988) was his next, but it was a very different book, whose subject did everything in his power to thwart it, dragging Hamilton and his publishers into the law courts (and thereby guaranteeing just the sort of media attention that unhampered publication would probably have spared him). Mordecai Richler waxed indignant: 'At the risk of sounding stuffy, I think it indecently hasty to undertake a biography-cum-critical study of a still-working writer and in highly questionable taste to pronounce him a perfect subject because, in Mr Hamilton's view, "he was, in any real-life sense, invisible, as good as dead."' But Richler's views were not widely shared, and Jonathan Raban's assessment of the book – he called it 'a sophisticated exploration of Salinger's life and writing and a sustained debate about the nature of literary biography, its ethical legitimacy, its aesthetic relevance to a serious reading of the writer's books' – was closer to the general estimate.

Hamilton's next biographical subject was very different again. *A Gift Imprisoned: The Poetic Life of Matthew Arnold* (1998) explores Arnold's reasons for abandoning his life as a poet and settling for three decades of drudgery as an educationist and social reformer. Nicholas Murray described it as an 'absorbing', 'highly readable', 'acute' and 'illuminating' study, and this will have been a particularly welcome judgement, coming as it did from someone who had published a full life of Arnold only two years earlier.

Keepers of the Flame (1992), though not itself a biography, was borne out of Hamilton's fascination with the genre. It deals with literary estates, but as the author wrote in his foreword: 'A book about literary estates has to be about many other things as well: about changing notions of posterity, about copyright law, publishing, the rise of English Studies, the onset of literary celebritism. Principally ... it has to be about biography, the history and ethics of. How much should a biographer tell? How much should an executor suppress? And what would the biographee have wanted – do we know?' John Sutherland began an enthusiastic review of the book with the words: 'Hamilton could not, if he tried, write an unreadable book.' And Jeremy Treglown declared it 'an absorbing and drily funny book', whose author was 'characteristically inquisitive and detached, humorous, knowledgeable and sympathetic.' *Keepers of the Flame* was Hamilton's own favourite amongst his prose works.

Since the early 1970s, the poems had been coming even more slowly, but they were still being written, and in 1988 Faber published *Fifty Poems*, which combined *The Visit*'s thirty-three with eleven of the twelve he'd included in a 1976 pamphlet called *Returning,* and rounded this out with just six more. The book came with a preface, which began: 'Fifty poems in twenty-five years: not much to show for half a lifetime, you might think. And in certain moods, I would agree.' Not so most of the book's reviewers. Douglas Dunn's notice was fairly representative: 'In spite of his poems' shortness, his absolutely countable quantity of published verse, Hamilton's lyricism still seems to me to add up to the best love poetry by a writer of his generation.' There were one or two dissenting voices, however. Lachlan Mackinnon lamented Hamilton's failure to work harder at his poetry: 'It is a great pity that shunting poetry aside has left [him] so little work to show, for he could have been a larger poet and a more skilful influence. The decision to live another kind of life may not have been easy, but it is not only Hamilton who has been impoverished by it.' Elizabeth Jennings was somewhat harsher, writing as if she felt that 'shunting poetry aside' was something Hamilton ought to have considered doing earlier: 'The overall impression is one of dissatisfaction couched in a lacklustre vocabulary ... The tone throughout is low-key and there does not seem to be much development over the longish period in which these poems were written ...'

Between 1984 and 1987, Hamilton hosted BBC TV's Bookmark programme. Among the many distinguished writers who were featured during his tenure were J.G. Ballard, Seamus Heaney, Alison Lurie, Italo Calvino, Simon Gray, R.S. Thomas, William Trevor, Timothy Mo, A.N. Wilson, Joseph Skvorecky, Peter Reading, Kazuo Ishiguro and Peter Taylor.

Two more collections of poems appeared in the 1990s, with *Steps* (1997) adding ten new poems to his tally, and Faber's *Sixty Poems* (1998) placing these alongside the fifty they had published a decade before. One or two reviewers were disappointed by the newest poems. Ian Grigson, for example, spoke of 'how the edgy, baffled minimalism of [Hamilton's] earlier work has crumbled into thinness and inconsequence'. But again, the majority of reviewers reacted quite differently. Lavinia Greenlaw thought that '*Sixty Poems* is sure to be one of the most affecting and satisfying collections we will see this year,' and Alan Brownjohn, pronouncing Hamilton 'an original', quoted with approval David Harsent's claim that this was a poet with a 'uniquely lyrical, passionate, and sorrowing voice'. *Sixty Poems* was a Poetry Book Society recommendation.

There is all too much that cannot be covered in a note of this kind, but it would be a serious omission not to mention Hamilton's passion for football. Not all of us could share that passion, but anyone admiring Hamilton's prose – its rhythm, timing, suppleness and brio – will have found *Gazza Agonistes* (1998), the book he wrote about his sporting hero, Paul Gascoigne, hard to put down if they once picked it up. Susannah Herbert, though indifferent to the game, wrote: 'You don't need to know much about football to recognize that Gazza is a sporting hero with a difference – but Hamilton goes deeper, tracing the evolution of the player's image with affection and a certain head-shaking sadness, like a mystified parent. I didn't want to care, but I did.'

Just how good an editor and anthologist Hamilton was can be seen from the sheer quantity of this kind of work he was commissioned to do. His most significant achievement in this field was undoubtedly the *Oxford Companion to 20th-Century Poetry* (1994), for which he put almost two-hundred-and-fifty noted contributors to work, watching over them as they composed the best part of 2,000 entries, covering 'topics, movements, magazines and genres as well as individual poets, dead and alive' from 1900 all the way up to the early '90s. Helen Vendler was sure the *Companion* would come to be seen 'as a significant landmark of literary change.'

Hamilton was an early contributor to the *London Review of Books,* whose founding editor, Karl Miller, he had worked for when Miller was literary editor of *The New Statesman* and editor of *The Listener.* Hamilton soon found himself on the paper's editorial board, alongside Frank Kermode, V.S. Pritchett, Stuart Hampshire and other notables, and he served the paper loyally, under Miller to begin with, and then Mary-Kay Wilmers, for the next two decades. Many of his best essays – several of them reprinted in his collections, *Walking Possession* (1994) and *The Trouble with Money* (1998) – first appeared in the *LRB*'s pages.

Hamilton's last book, *Against Oblivion: Some Lives of the Twentieth-Century Poets* (2002), has only just been published. 'Some time ago,' he says in his introduction, 'it was suggested to me that I might try to write an updated, twentieth-century version of Samuel Johnson's *Lives of the Poets.* Like Johnson, I would – it was proposed – compose mini-biographies plus mini-critiques of about fifty modern poets ... All in all ... this Johnson update seemed a nice idea, if somewhat gimmicky, and I agreed to have a go.' Thus far, no consensus seems to have emerged. John Carey was extremely positive: 'Stylish, gritty, often hilarious, *Against Oblivion* glitters with insights like flecks of mica. It gives precise expression to things you have noticed but not been able to formulate ... It is the cleverest, tersest introduction to 20th-century poetry you could hope to find, written by a man who has earned the right to be uncompromising.' Robert Potts, by contrast, was airily dismissive: 'a piece of light entertainment, close to hack work: risk-free speculation in the poetic futures market.' And somewhere between Carey and Potts was Anthony Thwaite, who found the book 'crisp, sharp, opinionated, readable,' but also thought it 'vulnerable', claiming to find some of its inclusions and exclusions a little eccentric.

It seems only right to mention that Between The Lines owes its existence to Ian Hamilton. He sprang the idea for it on the two people who became his co-editors over lunch – one of those played-with-but-uneaten lunches for which he was famous – late in 1997. It is doubtful whether such an enterprise could have got going as quickly as it did without his flair – or, of course, his reputation. When one of us, early on, said he thought that a well-known poet we were thinking of inviting to participate would decline, a mischievous smile crossed Ian's face: 'He wouldn't dare,' he said – and events did not prove him wrong.

It is a great sadness to his colleagues at BTL that Ian did not live to see this volume, and that he will not be around to work with us on others. He died from cancer on December 27th 2001, aged 63. He leaves one son (Matthew) by his first wife, Gisela Dietzel, two sons (Robert and Ricki) by his second wife, Ahdaf Soueif, and a son and a daughter (William and Catherine) by his last partner, Patricia Wheatley.

A Note on Dan Jacobson

Dan Jacobson was born in Johannesburg in 1929 and grew up in Kimberley. He was educated at the Kimberley Boys' High School and Witwatersrand University. After leaving university, he worked as a teacher, as a journalist, and in the family milling business in Kimberley. He settled in England in the mid-1950s, and since then has produced ten novels, two collections of short stories, two critical works and a volume of autobiographical essays. He has written extensively for journals and magazines in Britain and the United States. His last two books, *The Electronic Elephant* and *Heshel's Kingdom* are eclectic in form, bringing together public history, private memoir and accounts of journeys undertaken by the author in Africa and eastern Europe. He has been awarded several major literary prizes and has lectured at universities in various parts of the world. Shortly after retiring from a professorship in English Literature at University College London, he was invited back to the College to give the Lord Northcliffe Lectures for the year 2001.

The Conversation

What follows is an edited version of conversations which took place in London between March 13th and September 11th, 2001. A fuller description of the circumstances is given in the afterword.

Where shall we begin? How far back do you want to go?

Why don't we go back to the Battle of Bannockburn?

No, not that far. Your schooling. Your birthplace.

King's Lynn. I was born in Norfolk.

Were both your parents Scottish?

Yes.

And your father was an engineer? –

Yes. A civil engineer, built sewers, I think.

– which is a very Scottish thing to be doing.

Building sewers?

No, being an engineer.

In King's Lynn where he had his job. This was 1938. He'd been working and living in Scotland, got married, then got a job. He was on short-term contracts when the war came. He moved to King's Lynn and had some job to do with airfield runways – which there were a lot of in East Anglia. He was also in the Royal Observer Corps. Well, he'd have been then about forty. He was born in 1900. I think I was about twelve when we moved to the north, because after the war he was on short contracts all around the place and was rarely at home. Then – in 1951 – came this opportunity to get a longer contract in Darlington, County Durham. So he moved the whole family up there and proceeded to die less than a year later. So there we were in Darlington, not quite knowing why.

Were all of you there?

All of us. Three boys, and a girl who had just been born. So I attended the local school in Darlington, learning to 'speak' sub-Geordie and how to get used to these rough northern boys who masturbated all the time.

Yet you were from a family of high achievers.

Well, we had sort of genteel middle-class pretensions.

But your oldest brother –

Oh, you mean the children went to university and all that, yes.

Your father had been a professional person.

He was a bit disappointed and thwarted professionally. He'd had to leave university very young, after a year or so, and hadn't completed his degree and thereafter was always trying get something which we never stopped hearing of called the AMICE, which was the qualification for civil engineering –

Associate Member of the Institute of Civil Engineers?

Yes. So he was always theoretically studying for this thing which he was clearly never going to get but which, had he got it, would have put him in line for better jobs than the ones that were actually available to him. He was always in a sort of bad temper about not being able to get jobs he thought he was equipped for. A certain amount of this one overheard as a child and afterwards my mother used to go on about it. My father saw himself as a bit of a failure professionally – through no fault of his own.

How old were you when he died?

Thirteen.

You later wrote several poems about it. There's one called 'Father Dying' in The Visit, *your first collection. Is that the one where he speaks of 'wearing Rangers Blue' the next time you'll see him?*

No, that's a different poem. Same theme, though. During his last months I used to – not nurse him exactly – but sit around with him. I hadn't seen him, well, I'd barely seen him during my childhood, so I felt privileged to have this kind of access. I used to spend a lot of time with him.

You'd barely seen him because he'd been away so much?

Yes, he'd always been away, whereas now, here we were, all together. It was known that he was going to die. Mother knew. And I think my older brother knew. So they were comforting each other. The house was chaos with decorators and builders in. But there was nobody to ... My father was in his room and I would drift in there. I was of an age when I wasn't much use for anything else. So I used to sit there as an errand boy and got very involved in his predicament. There were lots of sick death-jokes, grins, all that. I didn't know how ill he was though I'd overheard snatches of people's talk and picked up the general atmosphere, but nobody ever told me that he was going to die. Then, eventually, he was carted off to hospital, which is, I think, what that Celtic-Rangers poem was about, the final joke he made. He said he'd turn blue – the Glasgow Rangers team colour – by the morning. Which in fact he did; he didn't last out the night. That was upsetting, you know, for a thirteen-year-old lad, and then it became much more upsetting in my twenties when I began to think more about him and what kind of life he had had, what kind of person he was. You lose the pattern, losing a parent when you're young. I also felt the wish to speak to him or in some way to have a relationship with him. And I think that those poems probably come from an impulse of that sort, from the delayed pain or loss.

Were you close to your siblings, not necessarily as a consequence of this but . . . ?

I think we were close, yes. Except, of course, when you're a child a gap of three years, which there was between me and my older brother, is a long one. He was three classes ahead of me at school. My younger brother was five years younger. But we were, yes, pretty close and became closer as these age differences didn't seem to loom so large. We had the sense that we had to look after our mother. No relatives were nearby. They were all in Scotland.

Presumably your mother had to go to work, with such young children to provide for.

She took in lodgers. Indeed, that's how she managed. But my father had had this Scottish thing about education, so there was no question of any of us leaving school or getting a job.

Money was always very tight then?

We had a rather wonderful well-off aunt in Glasgow, my father's youngest sister, who owned several fish-shops, and every week she would send us a parcel of fish by British Rail. It was one of the boys' jobs to go and fetch this parcel every Monday — and in summer it sometimes had to be carried at arm's length. One of the reasons I never learnt to swim, I suppose. But no one ever said the fish was off, neither us nor the half-poisoned lodgers, and that parcel formed the week's menu: finnan haddock, chicken, sole. At Christmas the chicken turned into a turkey. Two days a week we would eat haddock, three days chicken, and so on. This aunt was very generous and helped in other ways. She's since sold the shops; she's very old now.

Do you keep in touch?

Vaguely. I looked her up about ten years ago, the anniversary of my father's death, I think; and she was still lively and pert. And she showed me lots of old family photographs and things.

Was there much reading going on in the house?

No, well, there were hardly any books. By the time I was sixteen I'd read every book in the house. There were popular boys' books of an earlier time, for some reason: Henty, Ballantyne, that sort of thing. There were lots of self-educating books, home encyclopaedias, home university courses, Pelmanism manuals, self-improvement tracts – volumes that were all in the grand, glass-fronted bookcase. Therein lay knowledge. Therein lay my father's studies ...

Newspapers?

Oh, the *Daily Mail* would be considered middleclass and therefore rather smart. No, not smart, but respectable. Respectability was the aim.

Can you remember any of the lodgers?

Yes, I can remember them fairly distinctly. My mother hated them, you know, but had to have them. She was always complaining about them.

Did you feel neglected because of them?

No, because she treated them so badly. They were always sort of sealed off from the family and I couldn't imagine why they wanted to stay.

Like Mr Bleaney in the Larkin poem.

Very Mr Bleaney except that they tended to be young. There were one or two junior army officers who lodged with us. They must have been attached to Catterick, the nearby army barracks. There were some odd seedy Bleaneyish types who took a fancy to my mother in a disgusting sort of way. One of them actually proposed to her.

You knew this at the time?

Well, he had a moustache, so we feared the worst.

Rakish, was he?

Yes, post-war-rakish, you know, one of those dubious post-war 'spiv' figures. I think he was some kind of salesman, looked at himself in the mirror all the time. It was no surprise when it turned out in the end that he was a ladies' man.

I was most impressed when you recited to me, off by heart, the whole of 'Mr Bleaney' after you'd moved into your previous flat. Not this one.

Oh, I have a strong sense of identification with it. It's a wonderful poem.

It is. You went to the local grammar school? Which was rather a good one, wasn't it? One used to see its name high up in the lists of top grammar schools. What's become of it now?

It's a sixth-form college, I think. Or perhaps a university.

When did you discover that books were going to be one of your big things?

I think it had something to do with the fact that when I was about fifteen I had some kind of a heart problem and therefore wasn't allowed to do games, which I was very keen on.

All games?

Well, soccer particularly.

Cricket?

Not so much. I liked cricket but I was never any good at it. I wasn't allowed to play games because of this so-called heart problem. It was something I got after I'd had scarlet fever, a sort of follow-up to that. My heart was beating too fast, it wasn't doing its job, and as a result I was classified as a sickly figure and sat in the library during games.

The town or the school library?

The school library.

And the other boys were young and healthy? And you could hear their shouts from outside? This is getting to be very poignant.

Yes, so I reached for my Keats. I developed a kinship with sickly romantic poets who couldn't play games. Keats, I suppose, was pre-eminent. You know, half in love with easeful death —

So it was through poetry that you became bookish. Not fiction?

No, not at all.

Not at all? That seems to me extraordinary. I did it the other way round — from fiction to poetry. Keats became quite big for me too, but first I had to go through miles of prose — everything — Biggles — etc.

Those sorts of things did figure later, or maybe they were around, but they weren't as central to my predicament as Keats was. Anyway I became a Keats figure, sitting in the library in consequence of not being allowed to do what I really wanted to do, which was to play football. So as a result I assumed some of the affectations that went with that. Which included writing for the school magazine on poetic subjects.

Writing on poetic subjects or writing poetry? You must have been good at English. You must have been a star at essays.

Well, not quite a star. But the masters thought I was pretty good and so I came to see myself in this role. You know — take a look at my sensibility which is surely superior to yours. By all means clatter off to your games, you muddy fools. In truth, of course, I envied them because that was the real poetry, so far as I was concerned.

Still is, perhaps.

Yes, still is.

At your school did you write general essays, as part of the English course?

We used to do it all the time. We didn't write 'criticism' until quite late. We would write on 'topics'.

That came under 'general studies'. They were the thing at the time: capital punishment, pro and con, and so forth. We had to do a fair amount of that.

You weren't encouraged, as we were, to go in for little whimsical Charles Lamb-like essays? Writing trivia about trivia?

No. The senior English master was a raging Leavisite, an absolute caricature.

Had he been to Cambridge?

No, he'd been to Southampton and had been thoroughly instructed there by a sub-Leavisite. At that time, Leavis's word was spreading through the country. This teacher of mine was a great zealot. I didn't know this at the time, of course. I just thought he was a man of very definite opinions and rather narrow tastes. Nonetheless he was very good at teaching one how to write. He may have been wrong in some of his literary judgements and ignorant in some areas of literature but he was good at getting rid of what was superfluous or phoney in a piece of writing. And he would be very insulting about it if one came out with some bit of frippery. Anything redundant, artificial, not to the point, tautologous, repetitious. You got the essays back covered in brutal red inscriptions. So, impressing this teacher became most important to me.

He was trying to make you feel small but he ended up making you feel big.

Absolutely. When I got fewer red marks than these other guys, the footballers, I began to think I was getting somewhere. This teacher – call him 'P.J.' – rarely praised anybody. Or if he did, he praised them at someone else's expense. So there was a very unpleasant atmosphere in his classes. Everybody was afraid of him but it was very effective. I've since talked to others – a chap for instance who was at the school and who now writes books. This character was terrified of P.J. and hated him but he now acknowledges that if it had not been for suffering this teacher's lash he might not today be writing as well he does. And he does write really well. So one might bemoan the Leavis thing but I think it had this elementary but all-important usefulness. Those books, *Reading and Discrimination* and *Culture and Environment,* were sort of bibles. P.J. took us and turned us all into little intellectual snobs. But we knew how to write – or rather we knew how to recognise bad writing.

Were you in small groups?

No, large classes, but as you went on into the sixth-form the classes got smaller and smaller. By the end there was maybe half a dozen haggard figures sitting in a room, being tongue-lashed by this pedagogic monster.

How did you move on, in terms of your reading, from Keats? Presumably you had set texts.

Oh, yes, one was doing all that. But there was also his personal syllabus. He was, of course, scornful of the official syllabus, because it had people like Dickens on it, and he didn't approve of that.

'Entertainer' was the word Leavis had used about him.

Laughter and tears. But one read also in anthologies. In this way I got on to various people who, like Browning, for example, P.J. hadn't had any time for at all but I quite liked. I didn't dare mention Browning in class in case this man might explode. So one did a lot of 'sneaky' reading in that way. Also I started writing for the school magazine.

In the sixth-form you started your own magazine – or even earlier?

No, in the sixth-form.

You'd found a cadre of contributors?

Yes. You know: chaps in polo-necked sweaters, sixth-formers in horn-rimmed glasses ...

With heart conditions.

Yes, the intellectuals. I had a few of those. They were disaffected in different ways. My journal came out on the same day as the official school magazine.

Was it printed or cyclostyled?

Oh, printed.

30

Who printed it?

Some local printer. You know, we all saved up our cash. It came out for two issues.

And you timed it deliberately to rival the school magazine?

Yes. I got into a lot of trouble.

I remember your telling me that the magazine was called The Scorpion, *is that right? No doubt because scorpions sting, inject poison into the system? Was its general tone sneering and satirical?*

Not particularly. In fact, it was pretty tame stuff. I think I put a certain amount of bile into the editorials, but they didn't really connect with the rest – which consisted of the usual morose adolescent parables and things like that. The first issue had a foreword by John Wain, the novelist, who had just appeared then and was very famous. I wrote to him to ask if there was some message he could send to youthful aspirants and so he did. It was rather good, about half a page, which ended: 'and, if all this fails, back to the drawing-board!' – a phrase I didn't know then. The second issue again showed this wish to connect with the London literary world. I sent a questionnaire to various luminaries asking if there was advice that they would wish to give to young authors at the beginning of their literary careers.

You were an ambitious bugger even then.

Oh sure, always on the make. We got back forty to fifty replies.

Fifty! Can you remember any names?

They would be some names that would not be recognised now; figures like Louis Golding who was popular in that day.

A sort of minor, Jewish J.B. Priestley. If you can imagine such a thing.

All sorts of names. I just picked them out of some magazine or book. So about half of this combative magazine, this *Scorpion*, was filled with these platitudes from London literary figures.

Were you flattered?

Oh, yes. They felt a social obligation to bring wisdom to the youth ... Well, that sank the thing.

I can imagine it sinking it from the literary point of view, but I'd have thought the authorities would have been pleased you'd netted such big fish. Yet you say it got you into trouble.

Well, I'd brought it out on the same day as the official school magazine. It was an anti-school magazine. I think I had to go into town and take delivery of it from the printer and this meant skipping x number of lessons. And I'd been selling it around the town, so I wasn't at school very much. I was disciplined. I think I remember having my prefect's badge stripped from my lapel. In fact, it was because some master had a particular stake in the official magazine and thought that this bastard, me, ought to be sorted out.

Have you got any copies of The Scorpion?

Yes. They're in my mother's house.

Do you remember what you wrote for this magazine?

I seem to remember writing some dark allegorical story.

Poems?

No. I'd written odd poems, very sub-Dylan Thomas. I remember having or buying Thomas's *Collected Poems.* I liked the whole idea of him so anything I wrote sort of resembled him, though I pretended it didn't.

Were you working hard in the sixth-form for your Oxford entrance?

Yes.

And why Oxford, if you had this raging Leavisite for a teacher?

Oh, because my older brother went to Cambridge.

He read – what, natural sciences?

Medicine, yes. I was not expected to get into Oxford, so it was all a bit of impertinence on my part. Darlington Grammar School students usually went to Durham University. There was an arrangement of some sort with the school.

Your brother had beaten a path anyway.

Well, he was older and was well on the way when we moved to the North. He'd already had lots of academic success, so it was all right for him to want to go to Cambridge. And also he was a science student. The new school was rather proud of him and encouraged him to get his place. In my case, they thought I was getting above myself.

And the Leavisite?

Oh, he didn't like it at all. He thought there was no chance of my getting into Oxford. But because of my brother I was determined to go there. I had no real idea, no reason, you know, for this apart from wanting to make people envious and the girls think I was interesting. And Oxford being famous and grand and all that.

How were you doing with the girls?

Lousy. I needed an Oxford. The magazine didn't work.

Did you have any female contributors? Or was it a boys only school?

Oh, entirely.

How old were you when you went up to Oxford?

Well, you had to do your National Service, in those days. They tended to accept you for university two years hence, as it were. It would have been for 1958 I was accepted although I took the exam in '55.

What branch did you serve in?

The Air Force. The Information Service.

Where did you do your Informing?

Germany. A place called München-Gladbach. By the time I got there we and the Germans were buddies and my job was to promote Anglo-German relations.

Had you done German at school?

No, not at all. French and Latin, I'd done. In Germany I had to write the scripts for a radio programme; I had to write local-boy stories, stories which commemorated a proud day in the life of blank from blank. Such and such a grand person came to visit etc., and then you took pictures of the dignitary with some airmen and would find out where they lived and fill in all the blanks for their folks back in England – for their local papers.

Did you enjoy your time in National Service?

I hated it at first because I had to do all the arduous basic training. And the trade training later. I was trained as a typist and it was not for some months that I was plucked from a typing pool and went into Information.

Did you travel back and forth to England?

I was in Germany the whole time, except for some short leaves.

Did you make any friends in the army, meet any kindred spirits?

No, not really. I had one or two mates, but nobody I kept up with. Occasionally I've had letters from ex-colleagues who've seen something I've written.

And I take it you acquired very little German?

Hardly any. I went to one or two classes and I picked up a smattering, enough to order a drink.

And from there straight to Oxford?

Yes.

Apart from writing for the broadcasting station, working on scripts and so forth, did you do any writing of your own during this time?

Oh yes. I had become a playwright. I'd read *Look Back in Anger* and thought it was wonderful.

You'd read it, not seen it?

No, I don't think I'd ever been to the theatre. But I loved those hate-filled speeches. I wrote two plays, plays since destroyed.

Their titles have to be recorded, if only for the intensity of adolescent

34

self-pity they reveal: Like a Leper *and, even better,* Pity me Not.

Like a Leper, I think, had the edge on *Pity me Not;* but there we go. I'm not sure which was which; but one of them I sent to Ronald Duncan at the Royal Court. Immense crowd scenes, people standing around, pitying the hero – i.e. me.

It sounds very like Duncan

It was. *This Way to the Tomb* was his big play at the time. I liked that title.

You say you also wrote a more overtly political play.

There may have been another play early on.

A one-acter?

Yes, possibly.

Peter Dale told me you once produced a play at Oxford, a small piece by Harold Pinter.

I had started another magazine at Oxford called *Tomorrow.* And for its fourth issue I'd written to Pinter. He had just become prominent then, but I'd learned about him earlier, when I was in Germany. Another of my jobs there had been to work on this radio show, and one of the things I did for it was write a report on a local drama festival. There was a play in the festival by a person I'd read about it in the Sunday papers. *The Room,* it was called, and it was by Harold Pinter. It had had a good review from Harold Hobson in *The Sunday Times,* but rather dismissive reviews by other people. Anyway I was intrigued by this play, and liked it best of all those put on during the festival – and said so in my radio report. But I'd left the proceedings early in order to write the piece; I hadn't stayed to hear the commanding officer of the Second Tactical Airforce, who was giving the prize to some Somerset Maugham thing, denounce this incomprehensible piece of garbage by someone called H. Pinters, and saying how he just couldn't understand how anybody in their right mind could have put it on. The next day my piece was broadcast on the radio, praising that very play. My immediate superior, who was the information officer, got hauled up by the commanding officer and told to discipline me. What I had done was 'tantamount to disobeying an order'.

So critical judgement had to give way to army regulations.

Very much so. The entire weight of NATO was behind him. Anyway, several years later I wrote to Harold asking for a contribution to the magazine in Oxford and mentioning that incident. He'd heard about it in the way that one would, because at that age, starting out, one hears of everything. Anyway, he was taken by the story and sent me the script of a radio play called A *Slight Ache* for publication in the magazine. It doubled the size of the issue. In order to promote the magazine I decided that the play could work very well as a stage play too. So I mounted this production.

Where? At your college, Keble?

No, no. In the Mechanics Institute. And Harold came and saw it and that's how we became friends. Indeed the play went on to become a stage play put on in the West End. But originally it was a radio play.

Pinter himself didn't take any part in the production?

Not at all; he just grandly came to inspect it. But he was pleased and all that.

Strange the effect his work had then. Do you remember those West End revues? I was sitting in one such when there came up a five-minute piece about some people in an all-night café, and I can remember lighting a match in the dark to see in the programme who had written it. I was so struck by it.

There were lots like that; he started off doing five minute sketches like that. He's brilliant at them.

To go back to Germany and your own plays. Did you send them out?

Yes, I did.

While you were in Germany?

On some leave probably. Each of them had this ranting central figure –

So, just like Look Back in Anger?

Yes, but with a larger cast. I sent it off to the Royal Court because I'd read lots about it and the play was taken up for a bit by Ronald Duncan, who was on the board of the theatre. What I didn't realize was that he was the reactionary figure at the Royal Court and was well known for his opposition to John Osborne, my hero.

Duncan was involved in that post-Eliot 'revival' of poetic drama.

Yes, he wanted more verse drama. He also thought that drama should be on some major theme which, indeed, mine was. My play was also laid out like verse though it wasn't in fact verse. I mean if there was any way of being pretentious, I took that way. But he did write me various encouraging letters so for a time I went around seeing myself as a –

You sent only the one play, then?

Yes, the more mature one. The other I viewed as apprentice material. I think Duncan got fired or resigned. He clearly lost this battle of poetry versus the kitchen sink – of which I knew nothing until later. He was just a name on the note-paper as far as I was concerned. Anyway, that was the end of that. For a moment it did seem that they or he would have done it. Happily, they didn't.

Were you reading literary magazines? What was on offer? The London Magazine had *only recently been started.*

Just started. I used to read it.

Penguin New Writing?

Things like that. I started collecting them. It was rather fun to collect.

And Horizon?

I had the odd copy but it didn't communicate with me. *The London Magazine* was the one that mattered. There was also a thing that's now defunct called *Books and Art.* I don't know who produced it. It was a sort of popularly presented magazine. But I used to get this regularly, or have it sent to me; it was about what was going on the immediate arena, and I wanted to get into that arena.

Was Keble churchy still, when you were there?

Well, none of its past was known to me when I went up for the entrance exam. Colleges were grouped together so you didn't necessarily chose an individual college. I ended up at Keble possibly because that was the least discriminating one in my group. It was only when I got there that I realised that it was one of the Victorian colleges and was associated with the Oxford Movement. It was changing then anyway, turning into a more hearty sporting kind of establishment.

Did you have any kind of religious upbringing?

Well, I don't want to labour it too much, but we went to Sunday school and church. Indeed I briefly became a Sunday-school teacher in my adolescence.

Did you believe what you were teaching?

Well, yes, I guess at about the age of fourteen I did.

Were you Anglican?

No, Congregational. My mother who was responsible for our religious upbringing went to whichever church was nearest. I don't think we went to any church at all to begin with, but when my father died the first clergyman to come round was the Congregationalist, so we were at once turned into little Congregationalists.

And you took it seriously, I mean seriously enough to ...

No, it was just that if you went along to church often enough you got recruited ... It wasn't that they detected any special holiness in me or that there was any to be detected. Going to church was habitual; it was part of what one did. It has to be said that support for my mother in her widowhood, interest in her, came from the church.

Your scientific brother, did he go along too?

Yes, he was dutiful. Whatever gets you through the night was his general philosophy of life. He already had his bedside manner.

So you had begun another magazine at Oxford, before setting up The Review?

Well, *The Review* was started to cope with the aftermath of this magazine called *Tomorrow*, the one that published the Pinter play. The tendency for me was to start another magazine in order to reassure the printer that I hadn't really gone out of business, that he would be paid eventually. Okay, the magazine I handed to him (*The Review* No. 1) had another title and two years had passed since the last time I'd given him anything to print (i.e. *Tomorrow* No. 4), but he agreed to do it. He was still hoping to get paid for the *Tomorrow* work – and was paid for it, in the end.

You must have been cutting some kind of figure in Oxford, among the more literary undergraduates anyway, at this time.

Well, to the extent of putting out this magazine. But nothing else worthy of note.

You'd produced a play.

Yes, and put on poetry readings to publicise the magazine. I was scurrying around the place, a sort of busy bee.

I'm not suggesting you were some foppish, would-be West End theatre figure like Kenneth Tynan. When you started Tomorrow, *though, you must already have had a group of collaborators and contributors you could nobble for the next issue.*

I'd enjoyed bringing out *The Scorpion* and had always remembered it. Then I met a Sri Lankan, Susil Pieris, who was very keen and I think he co-edited the first two issues of *Tomorrow*. Then he got fed up or drifted away. It began, however, with my feeling that I wanted to start a magazine. Which is a terribly easy thing to do, really. At school, what I had done was to go round the houses trying to make people in Darlington buy it. And I had an army of school friends to sell it. We'd all meet in some coffee-bar and I'd hand out copies and it was go, go, go, knocking on Darlingtonian doors, being told to clear off mostly, but every so often someone would buy the thing. A lot of this was going on in those days. The figure of Jon Silkin, for example, would arrive in Oxford with copies of *Stand* in a holdall and he would go round the colleges and people would condescend to him dreadfully. His forbearance and patience as he went about trying to sell it used to impress me. So I started this rather awful magazine *Tomorrow*. I suppose issue no. 3 wasn't too bad. And then I ran out of money to pay the printer. It wasn't selling any copies. 200-250 copies would seem a pretty good figure but the printer's bill was £250-300 and I just didn't have the money. The printer was a good chap and would wait for his money but eventually he had to be paid. So *The Review* – in 1962 – was partly initiated by my need to pay the printer of the failed *Tomorrow*. Now that wasn't at all the motivation of somebody like John Fuller, a literary friend who liked small bits of *Tomorrow* and was sympathetic to the idea of a new magazine. John and I didn't sit around discussing subscriptions; we talked about poetry. He didn't want to be centrally involved in the management. I think he already thought I was a dodgy figure financially and took two steps backward on that score, for which I don't blame him. There was no one else at the centre of it, carrying the can. He wanted to be friendly, engaged, but not finally culpable.

Were you sole editor of The Review *or was John Fuller a co-editor?*

No, I was the editor. We had a committee consisting of John Fuller, Francis Hope, Martin Dodsworth, Colin Falck, Michael Fried and Gabriel Pearson. We never had meetings or anything like that. There was a lot of correspondence, I think, because John went to Buffalo for a year. And we had just started it. There may have been, what, two issues before John went off. So he wrote to me a lot from there. And there were Michael and Colin who'd already left Oxford and gone off to London, where they shared a flat. Michael, a young American poet, was a big influence on me at that time. Very few members of the committee were around in Oxford, although the thing was based in Oxford..

How did you come by Colin Falck?

Well, Colin was brought in by Michael. Colin was a philosophy graduate. He was a celebrated figure in Oxford, having, I don't know, got numerous degrees and acclaim for his writing, intelligence, and general wondrousness. So one had heard about this guy and Michael got friendly with him, how I don't know, and they became a sort of duo. Colin became very active on the magazine. He shared a lot of Fried's views. Looking back I think they offered a counter-balancing presence: Fried and Falck represented the Romantic interest; Fuller and Hope the Augustan. I suppose I was half-way between. The two groupings hardly ever met; in fact, I don't think Colin and Michael ever met John Fuller. But there were lots of letters from both sides. Dodsworth was, if anything, more inclined to the Fuller side of things but not in any vehement way. Pearson was always slightly more inclined to the Falck side of things, I'd say.

How did you come across Pearson?

Well, I'd heard of him, and read things by him. He used to write in *The New Left Review*. I think he was already teaching at Essex University by then. He was again a known name and he knew something about modern poetry. The committee was nominal; they were friends of the magazine. I think Martin Dodsworth indeed bailed the magazine out once with some money, a small amount at the time but it saved the day. He became disaffected later, may even have pulled out, possibly because of the activities of Edward Pygge, our resident humorist. Not a figure a lot of people went for. John was very keen on Edward Pygge who wrote a regular satirical column and became quite well known. John did one or two of the Edward Pygges, as did Colin. I did several. Michael loved it, thought Pygge was outrageous. Pygge attacked everybody, mercilessly.

I remember a very funny take-off of Geoffrey Hill. Written by you, I believe. It was called 'The Hallstein Gospel'. An accompanying note claimed it had been found on a crumpled scrap of paper outside the poet's window; he had discarded it, the note said, because it was 'too cravenly comprehensible'.

Eventually Edward Pygge became a celebrated personage on whom someone is now writing a thesis. *Tomorrow* hadn't had any of these fun and games. It was a pretty feeble operation. Only in the third issue had it started carrying reviews. By 1962 I was reading more, finding my feet. I read a lot of poetry, started writing it, and then I met Michael Fried. So with *The Review* there was a real reason for us to start a magazine. *Tomorrow* stopped in 1960 and *The Review* started in 1962.

A couple of years in which to do some growing up.

Yes, and I was no longer an undergraduate, so it was a lot more risky. You know, starting a magazine instead of getting a job.

I was just going to ask what you did for money?

I used to teach English to foreign students. My landlady, Mrs Rose, had a dynamic thrusting son, as he thought, anyway; dynamic and thrusting enough to be annoyed that I hadn't paid the rent for the last six weeks. Without consulting me, he put an ad in the local paper on my behalf saying: 'Oxford graduate gives English lessons.' So I had these people knocking on my door in search of English lessons. Anyway, Rose then got very enthusiastic and talked about setting up a language school. He needed somebody who had a degree on the letterhead and there I was up on the letterhead of Rose Educational Services or whatever: Ian Hamilton B.A. Nothing came of that, thank goodness.

He didn't end up running a chain of language schools?

No, no, he didn't. He ended up publishing a daily information sheet about what was going on in Oxford, a freebie; it must have been one of the first of its kind.

Were you involved with The Fantasy Press?

Yes and no. The press as a poetry publishing operation, although it was pretty famous, had more or less stopped. It had published big figures in the '50s: Larkin; a hardback of Thom Gunn's *Fighting Terms*. It was all done by Oscar Mellor, a painter and photographer and, possibly, a pornographer. I think I might have gone to see him, knowing this connection with poetry publishing, to ask him about design or something. Anyway, we became friends. I lodged in his house for a bit. He was last heard of in Exeter. He was an odd figure.

He was mentioned in your Festschrift.

That would have been in Peter Dale's essay. Oscar published a pamphlet of Peter's. I never worked out how interested he really was in poetry. Donald Hall says that he was more interested in drinking beer than in poets. How old would he have been then? Must have been in his thirties. I never thought Oscar had opinions; he would just stroke his beard and smile.

I came to know of The Review *in the early 1960s. Who decided on the minimalist layout for the minimalist poems in it?*

They were set in Gill Sans typeface, as a tribute to Geoffrey Grigson's *New Verse*. I think it was John Fuller's idea. And it looked rather horrid. For some reason the first three issues were trimmed down in size, too; but issue number 4 we printed in ordinary Times Roman and also went back to a more traditional format, eight inches and a bit by five and a bit, it was. I'd got an appallingly bad degree from Oxford and had no prospects. I'd been expected to do much better than that; the idea had been I would do postgraduate research. Much to the irritation of the people who'd fixed all this up for me, I proceeded to get a third.

How did you manage that?

By not doing the work, particularly the Anglo-Saxon.

I'd have thought you'd have winged it, given the general standard of undergraduates.

I think I was overrated by these people. I just put on a show for them in writing essays. But really I was ignorant.

Who were your tutors?

John Carey was one, in the last two terms. I wish he'd been my tutor all through, then maybe none of this would have happened. He was a breath of fresh air after the chap I'd had before who died, an old-time Oxford don.

Did you kill him?

What – with boredom? No, no, he was sort of steadily dying; he did quite a lot of semi-dying during tutorials. He had a wonderful gift of falling asleep as soon as you started reading an essay and, when you'd finished, of waking up and saying: very good, next week you will do Byron.

Are we allowed to know his name?

No, no. He wrote one book about Oxford and that was about it. But he was a thoroughly sweet, nice chap; he was very old. And he had the gift of being able to fall asleep and to wake up on the dot just as you finished. You could probably have read the same essay over and over every week – well, probably not. He probably had some subconscious way of knowing. I didn't try it out. But I liked him. Then came Carey, a young Fellow full of life, vigour and ideas, clever as hell, and made it all very interesting. Everything became more interesting. Anyway, Carey thought that I would do well and suggested I write some thesis or other. I can't remember what about. I'd have had to stay on. I thought why not?

They would have paid you.

There were grants in those days. But there I was, with my academic career in ruins – which didn't entirely distress me: I wasn't cut out for academia. There was, though, the question of how to survive. So I started a magazine.

Was it then that you came down to London?

No, that came several years later. Most issues of *The Review* were from Oxford. 1965-66, I came to London. I'd been married since 1963. I got a job with the *TLS* and was directing the Cheltenham Festival. I commuted from a cottage in Didcot, not far from Oxford, where we were living ; but that all fell to pieces and then I moved to London.

It was through meeting Arthur Crook at the Cheltenham Festival that you got the job with the TLS?

Not entirely. That meeting firmed it up. Alexander Cockburn, who'd been at Keble and whom I'd known at Oxford, was working at the *TLS* and we'd carried on seeing each other. I'd done a few reviews for him. Anyway, Alex had talked me up a bit and then I met Arthur. And there was a job vacant because Derwent May had gone to *The Listener.*

It was about this time that we met.

That's right. I can't remember when, in somebody's kitchen.

Oliver Caldecott's. He was a publisher, also an ex-South African. You were half-asleep on a sofa. You nearly fell off it when I said I knew and liked The Review.

Well, one didn't often bump into a reader. It was fairly, you know, hand to mouth.

By this time you were writing the poems which you later collected?

I was writing poems and I'd got the Job at the *TLS.* Once I'd moved to London I ran *The Review* from the flat in Paddington.

How did the connection with Al Alvarez and Donald Davie come about?

They were older by some eight years, well-known metropolitan figures; Al was *The Observer* poetry editor. And he'd printed some of my poems and some of Michael Fried's, and he'd come to talk to the Oxford Poetry Society. He was a hero figure – of a sort. He'd brought out, in 1962, the Penguin *New Poetry* anthology. It's hard to imagine it now, but being on *The Observer* he was in a very influential position. Whereas now there's no regular poetry reviewer in *The Observer* now, is there?

Don't they review poetry?

Oh, they do, but there's certainly no central figure there who could wield Alvarez's sort of authority. Anyway, he was known to us. On the whole, out of all the metropolitan figures, he was the one that we had time for. He wrote well and wasn't tempted to like everything put in front of him and he got tough on some people we thought he should be tough on. When we decided to start *The Review* we had the idea of featuring Alvarez. It so happened that Donald Davie had just written an article in *The Guardian* called 'Towards a New Aestheticism' which was all about the imaginary museum and implied a rejection of emotional content in verse. Al took exception to this line. So we organised a dialogue between them. When you read the conversation that ensued you find that they end up agreeing over a Robert Lowell poem 'For the Union Dead'. It was agreed by both to have emotional content but also to have a sort of marmoreal shapeliness.

Well, it is one of Lowell's best poems. Was the dialogue edited much?

No, I don't think it was. We let them be as they were. And I think that's the way it came across. So there was this huge printed discussion and it got a lot of coverage and that really launched the magazine. It was taken up in a *TLS* editorial; there was also a big *Guardian* piece about it, by Bernard Bergonzi, I think. I've lots of cuttings; at that time I used to keep cuttings. In the next issue there was a long essay by Colin, 'Dreams and Responsibilities', about Al's *New Poetry* anthology which, probably, was as near to a manifesto as the magazine ever had, and a very good piece.

You published your own poems in the magazine? To begin with?

We published pamphlets. One issue, 13, consisted of three pamphlets, one by me, one by Michael, and some translations by Colin. And they came packaged in an envelope. So that was my first appearance in book, well, pamphlet, form ... But I'm not sure if I published my own poems in the magazine. Maybe I did, once, I can't remember.

I remember those pamphlets. Subsequently other people became stalwarts of a kind, didn't they? Hugo Williams?

Oh, they came in. David Harsent was another.

Peter Dale?

I think we published some of his poems. He never became quite, you know, one of the gang. There was a certain amount of indecision about him then. David Harsent appeared from nowhere. I think via the *TLS*. I was quite well placed by then, with my job at the *TLS*. I was doing the two editorial jobs simultaneously.

You were the poetry editor at the TLS?

Yes, and later I took over from Al at *The Observer.* There were lots of protests about my –

Omnipresence. Ubiquity.

– Yes. And quite right too. Except of course it seemed to me that this was completely all right; the more of me the better for the good of the cause, so to hell with these sniping charlatans and so forth. That was my position then, you understand.

Can we talk now about the poems you yourself were writing, in the midst of all this activity? There's also The New Review *to deal with, and your biographical work, so we'll have to go back and forth. But let's get on to your poetry now.*

Well, we're now in the period up to the early '70s. *The Review* ended in 1972, *The New Review* began in 1974. I had published a book of verse with Fabers, *The Visit,* in 1970 and had come to see myself as a writer of poems which I hadn't really done up till then. So that's the period which ends around 1972, when I began to dry up. The poems weren't coming, or nothing good was coming, and it was all much more intermittent, whereas before it had been something I did a bit of every day and felt confident of. I lost that in the '70s. Does one write poems or not? – it became a question. Whereas before they had been central to everything I did; indeed, you could almost say that the magazine and some of my reviewing was a way of clearing the ground for my own work, as criticism so often is.

Can you say something about your poems being so preoccupied with grief and loss, and the suffering brought to you by the suffering of another person? I'm thinking especially now of your first wife's illnesses.

Well, obviously, that was a fact, her plight.

Yes, I understand that. But it wasn't exclusively hers. It had become yours too. What do you see as the connection, if indeed you do see a connection, between the brevity and concentration of the poems and their preoccupation with pain?

The brevity of the poems? Oh, well, that was just the way it worked out. I mean some of those poems are longer poems broken into two because they weren't well glued together; there was nothing to join them properly together. It wasn't a strategy, brevity, if you like, just a technical –

A technical device?

– How much you could get into a short space. Once you'd decided to concentrate on the dramatic ingredient you had to narrow the backcloth. And also the whole idea of the power of compression. I didn't go in for a sort of Empsonian compression, making one thing stand for several at once. It was more a sense of emotional pressure, a claustrophobia, that I wanted to convey. I suppose I could only – in life – sustain that for a short time. And I turned it to my advantage in my verse or tried to. I did try longer pieces but they didn't seem to work.

You are saying then that the fact that the poems were so preoccupied with pain, with suffering, meant that they had to be compressed? That the feelings demanding poetic expression demanded brevity too?

That's certainly true. I think it does go back to my father when he was dying: the sense of being involved in someone else's suffering while being helpless to do anything about it. And from that came what amounted to a belief: that what a virtuous life would be about would be caring for somebody else. I think my mother made all of us feel very responsible for her welfare after he died. Perhaps ahead of our years we were made to feel that we had a 'job' to do in terms of looking after somebody and making sure they were okay and surrendering some our own juvenile wishes for the sake of this person. She'd been left on her own with this terribly hard life. We had to contribute in some way – not financially – she was making an extra sacrifice in keeping us at school. She could easily not have done that. That was our feeling. And then in my marriage it became clear that I had married a sick person, a person who was going to be sick repeatedly and probably forever, and so there was a continuity with what I had felt throughout my adolescence: this was what life's about. And with that maybe came the wish for a controlled structure: you had to keep your control however bad things were; you had to be in charge. And I suppose that the perfect poem became something that had to contain the maximum amount of control – and of suffering. Preferably it wouldn't be about me; rather, it would be about my inability, however intensely I felt, to do anything about the suffering, because there are certain situations in life you can't do anything about. One didn't want, on the other hand, to sound wimpishly hopeless about it.

Or Jesus-like?

No. So a certain toughness of response had to come into the vocabulary.

And into the rhythms.

But none of this was thought out at the time. It's only now I can, well, not only now, but about ten years ago, I could see that there was a pattern in my life, as one does – that possibly I exist or only feel I exist when I am called upon to serve or assist or something. Otherwise I don't really have a personality, an existence.

And what about happiness?

... Ah ... Oh, I think that's an idea you've given up on, essentially. You know it exists but you've been made to sacrifice it. You've been made to trade it in for this later thing, this feeling of conscientious service, which possibly gives you happiness; I don't know. I'm not sure. I hope it doesn't. And you must always be suspicious of making poems out of suffering which is someone else's. As that suffering person can be among the first to point this out.

I remember your saying some time ago that Gisela, your wife, brought up your poems as a kind of accusation against you.

Well: you drive me mad so as to write poems about me. It's the sort of thing a mad person might say. Anyway I don't particularly want to talk about this.

How do you explain the relationship between the need to be in control you speak of and your feeling that the poem itself is a kind of summons which you have to obey? That it doesn't arrive when you wish it to but on its own terms? The poem either comes to you or it doesn't: you've said that to me and written it on various occasions too. 'It' comes to 'you'; yet you have to be in control of it? Is there a contradiction here? How does it work?

Well, this talk is retrospective. The 'it' you imagine out there to be discovered by you, or that will visit you, with its mixture of passion and control, is a poem of perfection. So you listen out for the poem, if you like, and you imagine it. It's as if the poetry you write is what you don't seem to be able to express in your ordinary day-to-day transactions. There's a sort of platonic realm of discourse that you occasionally manage to tune into.

That is the impulse behind the poem – to be able to say in the poem what ordinarily doesn't and cannot get said or understood or listened to.

And that couldn't be said in any other way?

No, not in any other way. So it is the perfect thing to say to this person at this time. Even if the person's dead, there remains a perfect way of saying it.

So you were and still are inclined to despise poetry that doesn't have such an exclusive and demanding conception of itself. How did you manage to combine that with your job as a metropolitan man of letters? With being Mr Manager, busy running the poetry side of the TLS and The Observer. Wasn't there a problem –

Oh, then I regarded it as a cleaning of the stables. You clear the ground in which the poet comes up and might be allowed to flourish, and you wipe out the enemy. In order for the true thing to be heard, you suppressed the untrue thing, destroyed it. It was warfare. Any literary-political weapons I could summon to my cause, I summoned.

A Poundian view of the battlefield.

Yes. Well, there was. We had some fellow-feeling there. We felt that 'they' had to listen to this. But who were 'they'? I was never quite sure who they were ... Meanwhile the enemy was gaining ground in all sorts of ways. I saw myself protecting poetry against the pretenders, the charlatans, the fakers.

And the crowds that were taken in by them.

I had no interest in an audience. I mean the audience could be very few – as little as two dozen, as long as they had got it right. I didn't want an audience that got it wrong. Who would want that? You might as well become a pop singer, or Roger McGough. My feeling was that we had something to protect. I've lately come to think that there are these two types of literary intelligence; there's the protective, the kind which safeguards art against a vulgarising audience, and there's the kind that takes art to an audience and tries to civilise that audience. The protector and the teacher. I would think of Melvyn Bragg, for instance, as a teacher. He takes what there is and makes it available. I think he feels the importance of that role quite strongly. There are those who are outward-turned and those who turn inward and in truth despise the audience. They want to protect art from the audience, the only audience art usually has – i.e. people who do not know what it is. I used to feel much more affinity for artists and poets of the past than for any living ones, apart from two or three friends, my own contemporaries. I felt I was looking after their interests to some extent. You can imagine what Arnold would have said if he had read Roger McGough.

And what might he have said about Melvyn Bragg's sort of thing? There's a famous bit in one of Henry James's essays where he says that the trouble with periodical publication is that it's like a train that has to leave the station every hour, according to the timetable, and if there are no genuine passengers then you have to put in dummies, so that the train will look full.

Like the dummies that get put in the magazines? Well, with *The Review* I wouldn't think –

No, but we're also talking about yourself as a general poetry manager at journals like the TLS *and* Observer. *As Henry James's station master, in effect. The Review* was different: it was your own private, jealously guarded place.

Well, the pages of the *TLS* I was in charge of there also bear witness to much of was I up to. Remember that the *TLS* was all anonymous in those days. I think my record will stand up. At that time my feelings were so vehement . . . I was in my twenties. That sort of fervour began to dissipate a bit later.

It's interesting that the kind of vehemence you·speak of, which started with your encounter with your English teacher·in Darlington, never led you towards the Leavis camp?

A lot of people, particularly at Oxford, have said that that's what my tendency really was. I never thought so because there were so many things Leavis said that I thought were rubbish, particularly on modern poetry.

You mean his admiration for Ronald Bottrall.

Yes, I'm no Ronald Bottrall fan. I remember turning down his works at the *TLS.* According to a recollection of David Harsent's, which I have no memory of, on one particular evening I came to blows with Bottrall.

You were pretty cool about Empson too in your Poetry Chronicle.

Yes, I remain cool about Empson, apart from three or four poems which are uncharacteristic. I think he's just a clever clogs. A show-off. Most of it doesn't give me any pleasure at all, or if it does it's a crossword puzzle kind of pleasure.

Even in the crossword puzzles, though, he has some compelling lines. Rhythmically compelling, among other things.

He's very good at starting poems off and then not knowing what to do with them. Even in good poems like 'Missing Dates' there are whole stretches like 'bled an old dog dry till the exchange rills ...' What is he talking about? But then there is: 'The waste remains, the waste remains and kills.' You know what that means... As for Leavis, he was always a problem, that degree of vehemence, and seriousness and yet he got so petty, Cambridge and all that stuff. Yet there was something in him that stirred one.

When he wrote about verse that he admired –

I think in the end he just chickened out of modern poetry. I don't think he was interested in it. Apart from Bottrall who's the mystery of mysteries. Post-Auden I don't think he passed judgement on any poet. We don't really know what Leavis thought of Empson.

He did write about Empson initially. With much approval. In New Bearings *he speaks of the metaphysical mode he finds in the Empson poem 'Legal Fiction': 'Law makes long spokes of the short stakes of men ...'*

All right, but we don't know what he thinks of Dylan Thomas.

No, but one could guess. In spite of yourself and your own vehemence, it would seem, your circle of reviewers and contributors widened, didn't it?.

It became a problem when I moved to London, and started meeting people. It's probably why I stopped reviewing poetry in *The Observer.* I started meeting people, some of whom I liked, who hadn't written very good poems, and I said so. So I lost friends that way as one would. I was short of friends. Very few friendships can survive your saying, 'I like you but I don't like your poems.' Much better to say: 'I don't like you but I like your poems.' Yes, that would have been okay.

Douglas Dunn was one of the new contributors to The Review?

Yes.

And Clive James.

Clive gave the whole thing a bit of a lift. I picked him up from a piece he wrote in the *New Statesman*, which was about Ezra Pound. It was very lively so he was recruited.

He wrote on Elizabeth Bishop and Richard Wilbur for The Review. *And on Lowell?*

No, I don't think on Lowell, but he wrote well on those two and others. He wrote various things in the later issues. I'd certainly moved to London by then. We'd published about, I don't know, ten or twelve issues by the time Clive appeared. But he was a mainstay of what I think of as the second wind of the magazine. The magazine continued on and off for ten years. Originally it was supposed to be bimonthly but there were gaps, well, money-induced gaps, but it produced thirty issues in ten years.

Almost a quarterly. Did you get a subvention from the Arts Council?

Latterly, I think, but it was a pretty modest sum and still left me with a lot to do. It ran almost entirely on subscriptions.

What was the largest number of subscribers it ever had?

I can't remember. Not much more than a thousand, I would think.

That seems to me quite a lot, really.

Well, there were a lot of libraries. Once libraries start to subscribe they don't stop. But it was all done domestically, you know, addressing, licking of stamps, tying up parcels, trudging to the post office, keeping the subscriptions going. Sometimes just getting the money for the postage was a problem. You'd finally have the issue together, you'd conned some printer into printing it, and you couldn't shift it to your loyal subscribers because you didn't have the money for the stamps. Money was always very short. It left, all these things do, it left a trail –

Of disorder, strained printers, strained relationships?

No, well, my technique, as I've said, was to start another magazine when things got hopeless.

What bearing do you think your sense of obligation towards poetry that you've spoken of, your defence of the kind of poetry you most admired, the sacrifices which you felt you were ready to make for it – what bearing does all that have on the feeling of obligation which you've also alluded to, which was borne in on you during your childhood: the conviction, I mean, that a virtuous life would essentially consist of being of service to others?

I think you define what you are by what you do. But yes, if you are going to do anything at all you do it for the benefit of what it is, and if 'it' happens to be poetry, which it happened to become for me, then there's only one way to do it. There didn't seem to me to be any choice in the matter. There's no way to be quite a good poet. You either have to do it totally or not at all. Choosing not to do it at all I can understand. It's not as if I wanted everyone else to be doing this. It's just that that was what I happened to find myself doing. So either I must stop altogether, pull out of the whole deal, or do it in the way I did.

Now for a different kind of question. What about power?

Oh, power comes into it.

I'm thinking of social power. Look at the Festschrift *for your 60th birthday. Again and again the contributors write of you as a sort of capo, the gaffer, the boss.*

They're all poetry people.

No, they're not. They're all writers, true, but there are non-poets among them. You must know what I mean. That is the role they all ascribe to you; the role they saw you taking up.

Well, it happened that way; but then it had to be like that if I was going to take the line I took. And then it turned into a manner I suppose. I don't know. You mean there was a sort of demagogic streak in what I was doing? There was certainly a wish to run things.

Exactly.

You know the way things were bloody well going to be. Oh, that was certainly there from the beginning and continued. It's all because they wouldn't let me play football.

Oh dear. You sound like that poem by Stephen Spender, telling the world how scared he was of the rough boys who threw stones.

Please don't. I'd better shut up.

You could have been a contender. My point is you did become a contender.

In a way, yes. I'm still pretty good at football, except I'm a bit knackered these days. But you should see me watch football. I watch it really hard, give myself a very hard time.

There've been no further repercussions of that childhood heart murmur you mentioned?

It went away as soon as I started drinking.

You said a few minutes ago that there's no point in trying to be quite a good poet: you either have to mean it totally, or not at all. And now the same thing goes for how you wanted to run things. It had to be in your own way. But you found it a problem to do so – living in London and working on the TLS and reviewing people you met, people you liked, who had written poor poems.

It isn't true that that happened when I moved to London. It was really much later that I started losing my edge as a reviewer. I'd been in London for some years. I don't think I ever really stopped. I carried on in the *TLS*, doing that and *The Review*, wielding the axe on all sides. A bit later, some time in my thirties, I began to cool down.

Did you cool down because you had lost some of your literary conviction, the belief that the difference between good and poor poetry is a vital one; or because you had just lost energy?

Well, I certainly hadn't lost that conviction. I might have lost the feeling that one could win. And somehow it had all become an uphill and hopeless task. It kept on coming, this bad stuff. And also the whole pop poetry phenomenon by the end of the '60s and in the '70s was gaining ground, so that one felt one was being pushed into this rather marginal, rather 'academic' sort of pigeonhole.

54

Except that so many academics were rushing after the other kind of stuff.

Oh, pale-faces and redskins, all of that. Yes, one was very much out to be a pale-face but the redskins were winning. One became less interested in destroying the opposition and more in nurturing the things that one had faith in. You just got on with believing the real thing still to be important, but not that you could trounce the opposition or even that it was important to do it. And what did become more complicated, in some cases, was that there were some instances when I knew I was pulling my punches in a way that I wouldn't have done if I didn't know the people involved. As soon as that began to happen I thought it was time to stop. It had to be so, because that was the attitude *The Review* used to attack... you know, the sight of people giving their friends a leg-up and so on. It hadn't exactly come to that with me, but it was getting perilously close in some ways. And also the people who were writing for *The Review* were now all writing in the Sunday papers, and *The Guardian* and all the rest of it. They were running the show, in a way, but it didn't seem to make any difference. It seemed to me that there were now two areas: the one was that of what you might call highbrow poetry – the poetry reviewed in *The Guardian* – and one could go on belabouring people writing in that field. But outside it was another area where poetry had formed an alliance with pop music and the whole business of the 1960s scene, which had nothing whatever to do with poetry. However some spark at Penguin Books filled an anthology with these people and pretended that they were poets Then I would get annoyed again; but after a bit there was nothing I could do to stop it. It wasn't poetry. It was self-evidently not poetry. But it was something, and it was something that in its way did work, and it was only when people tried to pass it off as poetry that I felt it was my business to have anything much to say about it. And that eventually became my position.

What you said about meeting people a moment ago reminds me of a letter Orwell wrote to Stephen Spender saying that when he didn't know him it was easy to use him as an example of the kind of people he disapproved of – the 'Pansy Left' etc. But now that he'd met him and had found him agreeable he just couldn't do it any more. So here was Orwell, famous for being a flinty man of integrity, in effect just throwing in the towel.

Well, quite. It's a kind of fatigue also. Battle fatigue. It made no difference and you spent far too much time on it. And also you lose interest. The new bad poet is twenty one and you're thirty-three, this seniorish sort of figure, working on the *TLS* and so on. Why would I go out of my way to...? So things altered and I lost interest really in the fray, the day-to-day fray. In a way, early on, it was always a bit of a laugh to turn these people into grotesque caricatures – which, again, is easier to do if you don't know them. Edward Pygge could write about Adrian Mitchell's Semen for Vietnam Appeal in *The Review* but when you met Adrian Mitchell, he was a perfectly nice chap and all that. Not that I knew him very well or know him now. I can well imagine that if I did it would be difficult to portray him as a grotesque. And there were people who made it their business to get known around the place and be agreeable and liked and so on.

The Review itself never really nurtured any of the people who became big names: say, Ted Hughes?

He predated it. They all did. Ted Hughes had a reputation by the end of the '50s. So too did Thom Gunn, Philip Larkin. There was nobody new worth nurturing apart from the people we published in the early sixties.

Was Plath already out?

Plath died in 1963, a year after the first issue of the Review; and we devoted a whole issue to her final poems and would certainly have printed poems by her. She'd already had a book of poems out and a novel. I would have regarded her, Hughes, Larkin and so on as being from an earlier generation. Larkin was even earlier.

They were in fact the established figures.

Very much so. I'd read them at school.

What about people who came later on: Seamus Heaney, say?

I reviewed Seamus Heaney's first book, somewhat unfavourably *in The Observer*. Not unfavourably, I could see he was quite good but he wasn't that special and I said so. There's a mocking piece about him somewhere in *The Review*. He was around; you know, this Irishman people were talking about. There was an Irish thing developing under the auspices of Philip Hobsbaum who'd been a prominent member of another outfit called The Group, whom we were committed to attacking. Hobsbaum had taught in Belfast and then went on to Glasgow. But prior to that he was in London and he was a prime mover in The Group, he and Edward Lucie-Smith. We attacked them all the time. They were enemies. A lot was going on that we were in opposition to: there was The Group; there was pop poetry; there was the Liverpool Scene. And when Lucie-Smith, arch-organiser of The Group, went off and edited a book called *The Liverpool Scene*, praising those people to the skies we thought: 'Treasonable clerk. This is the sort of thing you'd expect from these corrupt, opportunistic, careerist-type figures.' So we went at them. As for nurturing talent, the talent that was around we ... nurtured. It was far more substantial than anything else that was there. Including Belfast. Heaney's first book didn't come out until 1968. *The Review* started in '62. By 1968 *The Review* was almost over. Heaney had published a pamphlet in a series called, I think, Festival Pamphlets, which Philip Hobsbaum used to organise. I seem to remember seeing that pamphlet and thinking they were okay, these agricultural musings, they were not bad, but nothing particularly special.

Do still feel like that about Heaney?

I admire him from a distance but I still don't get greatly excited by his work and I'm still somewhat puzzled by his phenomenal success. On the other hand I can see he's gifted and interesting. I find it very hard to quote a half a dozen lines from him in the way I would from any favourite poet of mine.

Well, it's always said that one of the tests of a poet is memorability.

It's certainly one of my tests. Seamus has kind of failed it. That may not mean anything.

What about someone like Geoffrey Hill? I've mentioned that Edward Pygge made mock of him. Was that as much as you were bothered to do for him?

I never had any time for Geoffrey Hill and still don't. The only things of his I liked were in prose, the *Mercian Hymns*. Some of those are rather good. But I think he is so pretentious and portentous, obscure and grand-mannered. I don't go with that. I never did, right from the start. 'Against the burly air I strode'. That was line one. Pretty much downhill since then, in terms of my taste for his work. No, no time for him at all.

And who else did you put forward in The Review?

We also had one eye on America, largely because of Michael Fried, and also because the impulse behind *The Review* came from this discovery that much more interesting things were going on in America than here. Poets like Roethke, Berryman, Lowell and Plath all seemed to me to be much more exciting than anything being done in this country. These were, if you like, our exemplars.

Very much the Al Alvarez line.

Yes. Well, Al was a big influence. He shaped a lot of that terrain, at least for me, and possibly too for Michael. Michael knew Al so there might have been things to-ing and fro-ing there I don't know about.

Did you publish Berryman or Roethke?

Articles about them. Roethke I preferred to Berryman. I was never a great Berryman fan. By that stage he had not published any of his *Dream Songs*. Some of those got me interested but the poems subsequent to the *Dream Songs* weren't very good. He was then rather safe, tedious. He'd written one rather weird poem called 'Homage to Mistress Bradstreet' which came out in 1959. One knew about that, it was odd and interesting, but I didn't really understand it, know what it was about. But he was there. And he was also a terrific, mad, drunk person – as was Roethke. As was, so we heard, Lowell. As was Plath. All this had this air of being intense and exciting – intensely personal experience bearing in on these highly disciplined poems. The tension between formality and discipline on the one hand and powerful emotional content on the other was what we looked for in poems. And that we looked for in poems that came in to the magazine. Some of which were by people like Hugo Williams or David Harsent and so on. It could be said that we didn't find one single voice that then went on to assume a commanding position as, say, Seamus Heaney did. I don't think we did. But I don't know whether that really matters.

I wasn't remarking on whether or not the fact is important; just that it is a fact.

Yes. If you looked at the period and tried to think of people we didn't print who were contemporaries and at the same age, in each case I would have known about them, probably, and made the decision not to. And there were literary-political elements, too, that mattered more, I think, than they should have, looking back. Like with The Group and the Belfast thing.

The Review itself was a peculiarly masculine affair. Why was that? Were there just no women poets, no women critics?

There hardly ever are any women poets. It's only recently that post-feminism has introduced the need to publish women poets, however good or bad. I don't remember anybody then appearing who was strikingly good. If someone like that had appeared we would never have turned her down on the grounds that she was a woman. On the contrary, we would have had her in at once, if she was half decent. So that was just the way it was. There wasn't a misogynistic vein in the journal. No, no. Not at all. There were bad women poets around. I could think of many women who were around but they weren't any good, in the same way that so many of the guys who were around weren't any good.

And among the Americans, apart from Plath, was there no one?

We didn't at the start really think very much of Plath. She'd only published one book of poems, *The Colossus*, which was a studied and derivative book we were not very impressed with and, in so far as she was influenced by anybody, we thought she was influenced by Ted Hughes. That influence was foisted on to these rather academic structures of hers; or so it seemed. But then, sure enough, when her last book came out, the work was greatly different from anything she had done before. They were extraordinary, some of them. So we thought yes. But where do you go from there? She was a one-off poet. She doesn't seem to me to lead in any direction. One couldn't see where one could go from there. It did fit with the things we were already looking for or which we already had found in Lowell, who was also in touch with the magazine. We didn't like Anne Sexton; we thought she was a fraud, trying it on, trying to be Sylvia Plath. There were some miniature mad talents in America, you know, Plath-derived, but there wasn't much of that here. And none of it was any good. – There was one poet whom I thought very good called Thomas Clark, an American who was living in Colchester who was writing the sort of thing we wanted. We printed two or three of his poems. But then, blow me down if he didn't suddenly become Tom Clark, objectivist, and start writing like William Carlos Williams. He went back to America and began writing objectivist poems dribbling down the page. I thought, this is awful, a talent lost. Things were cropping up all over the place that one didn't seem to able to do anything to prevent.

You had a special issue devoted to the Black Mountain school.

It was part of an issue, number 10, edited by Charles Tomlinson. It was done, as I think we said at the time, for historical reasons, but it didn't seem to fit. It was the issue we printed the least of, as a feeble protest against doing it at all. But it became the most popular issue; it's now the rarest issue of *The Review*.

How humiliating.

Yes. I was ashamed of that because it wasn't what the magazine was about. We weren't supposed to be telling people about fads. I shouldn't have done it. I don't think you'll find any other traces of that neo-Poundian stuff in the magazine.

But Pound was somebody who interested you – he affected your own work. I mean the influence he had on you as an imagist. Did you read his longer poems as containing little moments of imagism, so to speak?

Far too few.

Did you read the longer poems?

Yes, I laboured through *The Cantos* at one point, with a heavy head. I just thought they were a big, big mistake, academic, a waste. So it's the early Pound, while he was in London, who was of interest. It was his theorising, the organising ability, some of the combativeness, one or two of the poems, that we valued. The shorter poems, like 'The Return'. And I did think that he had a wonderful ear, and still think so. Which again went to waste; so much went to waste in his career. But on the other hand you can't easily see what else he might have turned into. It's almost as if there were two quite separate writers, as if the young Pound stopped and then this cranky person cropped up in his place.

I asked some moments ago what connection you see between the conciseness of your poems and their preoccupation with pain. You initially seemed to dismiss the query, saying, in effect, oh that's just the way it worked out; some were longer poems broken into two because they weren't well glued together. But you didn't leave it at that, which was just as well, in view of what you went on to say. Now I have a related question. In the poems you don't disguise or fictionalise the people you are speaking about, but you do speak of them very cryptically. Your poems are intensely private and confessional, if that's the word, and yet at the same time they are written as if to deny readers access to direct knowledge of the donnée *or actual 'situation' giving rise to the poem.*

Yes, I wouldn't want readers to have that kind of access to it. There is a reticence at work in the poems. I am expressing very private emotions as if to another person, but I have no right to make that person's real-life suffering public, as it would be if the factual background to the poem were to be published. I am creating the dramatic illusion of speaking as if to that one person alone. That's very different, say, from printing one's letters to that person. There is a difference between giving voice to moments of intensity which have a sort of general interest or application and airing in public things which are essentially confidences. So the individual becomes blurred, as in most love poetry. The addressee is non-specific, the reader doesn't need to know much about the person, even though the poem is framed as if addressed to her. You might know she is called Julia or something, but you don't know a lot more than that. You probably know less about the relationship in most love poems than you would in a poem by me – a poem that tells you something about the basis of the relationship, the most intense point of the relationship. But my poems are also about something else. They are poems about loss, about transience, disappointed hopes, if you like, about protectiveness, the wish to alter something that cannot be altered, they're about the conditions of an entire life experienced in this local and precise way. So yes, a lot disappears of the confidential detail. I don't think it would be right to have such detail in a poem anyway. You might in a prose narrative give the person a different name, use lots of details about them, and that might not seem improper. But that doesn't seem to me to be what poems ought to be doing. They ought to deal with the intense, climactic point of a drama, to the essence of the feeling it evokes. They should invite the reader to eavesdrop, you might say.

So this kind of poetry you were writing could only take the form of a direct address by the poet to another person?

Virtually all of them do. Either somebody is dead, or somebody is mad, and can't make sense of what you are saying.

But, after all, if you think of John Donne, or Shakespeare in the sonnets for that matter, there's plenty of direct address; but you don't get a sense of the reader as eavesdropper.

I think you do.

You do? I think of them more as staged affairs. Which doesn't necessarily diminish their intensity.

Well, they were writing in the literary conventions of their time. I wanted to create the illusion of privacy, of an overheard thing. What one likes, or what I like in poems, is the feeling that I am overhearing, even though I know that I am not.

Donne is often stagey, in a contrived sense; Shakespeare much less so – certainly in the most compelling of the Sonnets.

Yes, Donne is tricky and ingenious and he's enjoying his ingenuity. But in Shakespeare you get a sense of a much more troubled spirit.

And so of a much greater degree both of inward communion with himself and at the same time of engagement with the other person.

Absolutely. Something is at stake there. And has to be spoken of.

In order to maintain such a combination of intensity and privateness – and at the same time to produce a public utterance – do you perhaps not need a recognised form, a given form, which you recreate on the page? You didn't have such a form. I don't know of anybody who writes quite as you do. Some people began to write as you did afterwards, but there was, so to speak, no ready-made form or garment for you to adopt. It may be that for the mode of private-public communion you were seeking you needed the sonnet, say, you needed strict Donne-like stanzas. Do you see where I'm –

I don't think you need that for the poem to work, whatever 'work' means. Poems are always parts of other people's poems to some extent. There will be echoes, even if they may be suppressed, if they may have been almost eliminated. In my work there may be bits of Frost, bits of Hardy, bits of eavesdropped-on intensity from other poets. But to produce anything worthwhile you have to have your own voice, which does things which only you can do to whatever bits and pieces are floating around in your head – until there the poem is, there it sits. The question of printing it or pushing it as a finished artefact which you are proud to be the maker of is problematical, and I've always been nervous about that. For example, reading poems aloud has always been a problem for me because I find my poems quite upsetting to read. And I don't want people to see me upset. Except I did write the poems and I then printed them.

You are responsible for them.

Exactly. I find reading them aloud unseemly and embarrassing. I try to avoid it, have tried to avoid it. I still do; if anything it gets harder and harder.

I've heard you read just once. In the Poetry Society. It was very effective but I could see quite plainly you were not enjoying it.

No, it was hellish. I remember the occasion.

One of the reasons why you wrote the poems is that these situations mattered to you so much you couldn't bear to leave them unexpressed. Which means passing them on to others.

I sometimes wish I'd have been a different sort of poet. I wish it hadn't worked out in the way that it has: that the poems I've produced happened to be the only things I could do. I've certainly tried other things, many exercises, and I've tried to write sonnets and tried to write quatrains. I could do all of that quite fluently but I never thought it was poetry. I thought of it as verse. It had no power of the kind that made me respond to poetry in the first place.

You mentioned Hardy a moment ago. If it is true that poets can use public forms, ready-made garments, without necessarily diminishing the individuality or 'personality' of the poems they write, it occurs to me that even as you read some of Hardy's most elaborate and tormented poems you constantly get the feeling that they could be sung.

Well, I would make that claim for some of my own work. There are a lot of internal rhymings I am very keen on; and I can hear them as a kind of song sometimes, at least the early ones. Yes, that is something that holds the poems together or makes them different, makes them permissible: you've written a song. And I've always liked the idea of writing a song, though I have no musical gift. But having a musical gift *in language* is essential to any poetic performance. And that's quite true of Hardy and some at least of the poems I've written. Or so I would contend.

Shall we move on at this point to the books that followed? From The Visit *to* Fifty Poems, *which reprinted much of your early work and carried quite a few new poems – and which in turn was followed, a decade later, by the prodigal* Sixty Poems, *with an addition of just a further ten new poems? In your preface to* Fifty Poems *you said that you would have liked to bring more satire, more common life, more reportage almost, into your poetry; but it wouldn't happen, it didn't come.*

I think to sustain a poetry writer's life you have to write a lot more than I do. And write in different forms or in different modes and across a wider range of subjects. I'd attempted to do that and produced really forlorn material which was unpublishable. So I came to the conclusion that there wasn't enough in me to sustain a full poetry-writing life. There doesn't seem to be a lot of point in pretending that something is a poem when you know it isn't. I decided early on to be very careful not to pretend that something I'd written was a poem if it wasn't a poem. So it seemed that, for me, anyway, poems were going to happen rarely if they were going to match up to what I would wish them to be. It would be fairly ridiculous to go around making out that writing poems was what I was doing with my life all the time. I know most poets don't do that either, but they do feel that they have to publish a book of poems every couple of years. Well, a book of poems to me, well that's thirty or forty poems, a lot of poems. I had to recognise that I had this sort of limited thing to do from time to time, was compelled to do from time to time. So I put it to one side, kept it to myself, publishing whatever I thought was worth publishing and otherwise not fretting too much about it.

Not a career.

No, not a career and not fabricating poems in order to have a career, which I felt was going on in a lot of cases. So many people's work either got thinner, or more casual, or more artificial – they seemed to be thinking up subjects for poems. So you got these slim volumes, twenty-eight poems, say. Often I find it hard to believe that the poet himself would have thought them all poems. Three or four at the most.

You can often see poets working themselves up into their own special 'poetry mode'.

Or one can look back on books by Larkin. There might be one or two slighter pieces in each, but on the whole Larkin got out a book every ten years; and that was it. He wrote a lot more than I do; but there they are and every one is pretty much worth its place in the book. That seemed to me extraordinary. Eliot similarly hardly ever published a piece that was time-serving, space-filling. And these, as far as I had models, were my models.

To return yet again to the combination of intimacy and reserve in your work – the two impulses from which the poem seems to emerge – I wrote once that the effect can be that of the speaker actually silencing the other party, the one spoken to, in the poem. I used the word 'dictatorial' about the impression this gives. It reminded me of Donne's way of carrying on in some of his poems. The girl or woman he was addressing seemed to be expected to sit in silence, marvelling at the brilliance of the person orating at her.

That's a sort of social way to think about the poems. Who cares? It's him who's doing the talking: that's the poem. He's not actually talking to her. It's an illusion. In my poems the people are either dead or unable to make sense, in any case, which was part of what was upsetting me. And so I was speaking to someone who couldn't answer back. Although the poem created the illusion of an address, it's the sort of address you might make over someone's grave if you wanted to say something to this person who has gone. The people I addressed were gone; they were people in life one was not able to speak to but to whom one had lots to say ... Its a kind of dream-situation, not a social situation. The poems are ideal speech, what one would like to say the addressees – if they were alive or were capable of attending. Which is probably the case in a lot of Donne's work too.

Is that why the persons to whom your poems are addressed are hardly individualised? You evoke clothing, hands and hair, which are by their nature unindividualised – and that's it, more or less. By way of contrast, look at the moment in Hardy when the absent, voiceless ghost he is addressing is suddenly 'Facing round about me everywhere, / With your nut-coloured hair, / And gray eyes, and rose-flush coming and going.'

Oh, his details are wonderful, yes. 'Even to the original air-blue gown!'

Exactly.

Well, I think I've got a very limited descriptive stock. Maybe I felt that too much description might seem like a poetic *relishing* of the situation. I said earlier on that for me there was always this issue: should I be writing about this at all? I had a fear of any exploitation of the situation for the sake of writing a poem, the getting of a reputation as a poet on the back of somebody else's suffering. It may sound strange to say now, but these things did bother me. It's also the case that I'm not very good at description. I spot little things but I haven't got a stock of –

Well, if they were drawn from ' stock' they wouldn't be effective. You do manage to get a descriptive charge from your verbs. A train engine 'simmering', for instance. So domestic, that engine. Curtains 'lilting' in a breeze. 'Lilting' is the image itself. A moment ago I accused you, in effect, of clapping your hand over the mouth of the persons your poems are ostensibly addressed to; it now occurs to me that the impulse to clap your hand over your own mouth is equally strong. In the most recent poems there isn't so much of this: there you do speak out, but you do it as silently as possible. If that isn't a mad oxymoron.

No, no. That's right. That's an interesting concept, silent speech. There's more expansiveness in the later poems. Of course we do a lot of that kind of speech and maybe every so often it turns into a poem.

And we speak silently to ourselves.

Not so silently sometimes. Why me? Never, never, never, never, never.

Which reminds me. Many years ago I asked you if you had ever thought of writing fiction.

Yes, so you did.

You said, no, I can never get the other voice, the answering voice. You actually used that phrase. So that does have a bearing on what we're talking about.

It might a bit. But, in another way, it doesn't at all, which is why I've written what I've written, and not fiction. Because I think I'd be guessing a lot of it, trying to remember, or make somebody sound plausible, anyway as a —

Self.

The thing that is wrong with most novels is that you never feel that any of these people is a self — you feel that the *novelist* is dictatorial, that his characters are extensions of parts of him; they are given other names, male or female, but they're not actually independent created beings.

When you decided that poetry was going to be an occasional thing with you – well, not decided exactly – when you discovered that that's what it was going to be – a change seemed to take place in the verse itself.

Would you agree?

The middle stretch of poems do have slightly more narrative content or something. They are slightly longer and also had other things going on in them. I'd written them about things that were interesting or sad, rather than intensely usurping. So there's more neutrality, objectivity, in some of those poems and they're the best of – well, the only publishable ones, of a whole batch of things I was trying to do at the time, in an attempt to escape from the very tight, almost imprisoning subjectivity, that marked the poems I'd written before. They're the best, believe me, of that later period. And I was doing quite a lot; I haven't always, but at that time I did, I remember, write a lot. But most of it was no good. Then, of course, I was writing more and more journalism, so a lot of jokes and suchlike that might have gone into lighter poems went into reviewing. And I became interested in book reviewing, in writing the entertaining or amusing review, in the construction of reviews and essays. I became more interested in writing prose, in what prose sounded like.

John Gross once said to me, 'It's amazing how much power Ian can generate with just a slight nuance of the voice.' He was speaking of your reviewing then. I'm not buttering you up but I knew what he meant, and – to invert something that Pound once said in greatly different circumstances about Hardy – it occurs to me now that the power John was speaking of was your 'reward' for having written the poetry first. You may think of it as a poor recompense, though: that reviewing is an unsatisfactory way of using such hard-acquired skills.

I don't know that I do. Obviously I would like to have written lots of wonderful poems, but I also have a high regard for the responsibility of the reviewer. I like reading book reviews, if they are any good. And I know they are very hard to write. Mostly they are written by people who think they are easy to do. In fact, they are not. They ought to be constructed, and listened to, and they shouldn't contain a word out of place. And there should be some rhythm in their sentences and some wit. They should be entertaining and evince some justice and fair play to the thing reviewed. There's a lot that goes into a good book review, and it does irritate me when I see kids just out of university working away in the book pages as if the review is just an extension of some dinner party throwaway thing, a bit of idle opinionating. The idea of the well-made review and of the essay form itself interests me as something between fiction and non-fiction – a form you can do all sorts of things in. An underrated form. There's a joy in finding the right word in a book review that's comparable to finding it for a poem. It doesn't have the same prestige and status, even in one's own mind; nonetheless I don't take it lightly.

That's apparent from the reviews themselves. But to go back to your poems, the latest ones this time, those in the slimmest and most recent of your volumes, Steps. *They seem to me to be different again from what has gone before; also possibly the best you've done. You said about the earlier poems that they were 'perfect' or 'ideal' speech – perfected speech, perhaps would be the way to put it – which gave voice to what couldn't be said to this 'gone person' in any other fashion. But the batch of ten poems in* Steps *don't take the form of retrospective or restitutive monologues addressed to another person. They are outright soliloquies. And that gives them a freedom to be reflective and generalised that wasn't possible in the earlier mode.*

Even somebody as sparse as myself does develop, I suppose. I think there is more in these poems.

They're dreamier, too.

They're strange. They have a different atmosphere and are more other-worldly, in a curious way. As one has perhaps become. They are poems of later life. I could not have written them earlier. They maybe don't have the urgency and tightness of the earlier work.

They are bemused. I mean that as a compliment. They suggest that things have turned out not only painfully or tragically, as revealed in the earlier poems, but more bewilderingly too than you could ever have imagined.

Well, that's what we all feel when we get to a certain age. Life isn't the way we thought it was going to be, and also it has changed in ways we don't and can't fully understand. It's as if we're living in a world that's not meant for us; it's meant for the next lot; yet we are still here.

There's an approach to religious sentiment in these poems. I said they were 'soliloquies', but some of them do suggest that you are speaking to God, a God who probably doesn't exist and who wouldn't answer anyway, about the mysteriousness of the place you've found yourself in; of what the place has shown itself to be.

Well, I think there was a certainty of personal survival in the earlier poems, and so you worried about somebody else's precariousness or extinction. But as life goes on you get to the point where you know just how precarious you are too. You cannot be, you cannot represent yourself to yourself, as a source of strength; you're more in touch with your own weakness, your own vulnerability, your own ... well, precariousness is the feeling those poems seem to turn on. And yes, the feeling that it's all coming to an end. What next? It's as if you are experiencing the future in advance. There's a feeling of disaster in the air, which I now know I have felt for a long time.

This, I hope won't sound mawkish, but the poems strike me as gentler too. The title poem, the one about the stairs, for example.

I know what you mean. It starts off with a line from Emerson.

I didn't know that.

Yes. I should have said it. Actually, I did say it, somewhere when it appeared in the press. In the *LRB*, I think.

You use the word diligence *in the poem about the speaker's ascent of the endless staircase on which he finds himself. It's a beautifully unexpected noun in that context.*

Well, it's first of all a poem of personal disappointment, of late-acknowledged bewilderment. But it can also be read as a kind of cultural lament. If you devote your life to literature and reach this set point you are bound to feel, particularly with the culture as it is now, that we have lost whatever it was we set out to achieve. I do have that feeling; but even so – and it's a big even so – there wasn't any other way for me to take and there isn't going to be one. I mean, I'm not going to join the other side and I'm not going to give up. The whole culture these days, I can't seem to fit with it, find any place in it, as if it's got very little to do with me. So much of what I think is important has been forgotten or isn't read anymore. People don't know about it. So I do have a feeling of being left over. One has to keep back from old bufferdom, but ...

It is astonishing to go back to the things that were said decades ago, the cultural speculations and expectations that people took seriously, none of them knowing what was actually ahead.

All that solemnity in the 1950s, it just seems so remote. It's very close too because it determined so much of one's own thought and action; and yet it is a million miles away. They said: Look out, people are doing these demoralising things, we are going to enter a society dominated by mass-communications and consumerism, a society that isn't going to care about the things you care about. You do realise that's the way we're going, don't you? That was the Leavisite cry. And we said, Yes and we must prevent that. And we devoted whole lifetimes to trying to prevent it – and look what's happened. Yet the vehemence remains.

We seem to have got well ahead of ourselves. Perhaps the best way of getting back to a biographical sequence of some kind would be for me to ask you about Robert Lowell – as an influence on your work, that is, and only then as what he later became: a 'life', the subject of your first full-length biography. You did and do admire him greatly as a poet, yet in his poetic practice didn't he trample all over the distinctions, the reticences and borderlines, you set so much store by in your own verse?

Yes. I suppose that is where the whole idea of confessional poetry came from. There are two factors with Lowell: one is that his family is a famous one, he had a famous name. So to have a Lowell write derisively about his father as Lowell the poet did ...

I suspect that some of the grandness of the Lowell name was almost a kind of Lowell invention. Or ploy, at least. I know that the Lowells spoke only to the Cabots and the Cabots spoke only to God; but he did get maximum literary mileage out of the connection, nevertheless.

I think that it was in other people's minds that he was an American aristo-crat, a famous name; certainly when he became a conscientious objec-tor, a huge fuss was made in the press of the fact that he was a Lowell, not merely a poet. There was a certain amount of that too with the publica-tion of his *Life Studies*, because it's a very Boston-based book. I think the real lapses of taste, the indiscretions, came with his letters later and when he versified Lizzie Hardwick's letters. That seemed to me too much.

Those unstoppable sonnets.

I'm thinking more of the letters Lizzie wrote to him which he then turned into more sonnets and then said I'm sorry about this at the end ...

Do you see any kind of road not taken for you in the way Lowell went about things? In all those indiscretions and abandonment of any consid-

eration for others?

Not at all. I don't like that side of Lowell. Indeed, by the time of the Hardwick thing I'd gone off his work in a big way, largely because of his sonnets which I thought were atrocious and boring, somewhat catch-penny. He could still come out with the odd line but something about him appalled me: his messiness, his willingness to sprawl and sprawl. If you met him he'd show you things and you'd say I'm not sure about that so he'd throw it in the bin and yank another out of his pocket. All of which went against my sculptural instincts, I suppose. And it was just a shambles on the page. He didn't seem to care what he published, the act of publication was no longer invested for him with any momentousness; there was just this sprawling out. Whereas before, with *Life Studies*, what I liked about him was the spareness, or what seemed spareness to me then. In fact *Life Studies* was the first book of his I read; I hadn't read the earlier rhetorical stuff. I went on to that and didn't like it. So I ended up loving passionately about six poems in *Life Studies*. I didn't particularly like the family poems; I thought they were too near to prose. They were okay but having read his prose essay on the family, it was as if he was just versifying bits of it. 'Home after Three Months Away' and 'Man and Wife', though, really hit me as what poems should be. There are about half a dozen poems that had that kind of impact on me: the passionate speaking voice and intimate subject-matter. The internal rhymes and basic iambic line broken up into free verse sounded like somebody really talking; but it was highly disciplined as verse too. That was my response. Those po-ems hit me hard. A lot of other things being done at the time were imita-tions of Lowell. I at once wrote to him saying I was starting a magazine. He condescended to send something which had already appeared some-where else. But we printed it with a feeling of reverence; I think he was the only living poet I really revered. When I was a student at Oxford I knew almost nothing about American poetry. And then came Lowell, you know, a hero, and one who continues to be a hero, at any rate on the strength of those poems. I regret a great deal however of what he did in his life and what he was. I didn't particularly warm to him personally later on when I eventually met him and got involved with him. Nor did writing his biography make me feel any more warmly disposed. I thought he was deranged by ambition in a way that American poets often are. There was this competitiveness, this obsession with how he rated compared to Ber-ryman. All that shit I couldn't stand – and there was so much of it. Also I hated all the mania, because I'd been all through that for many many years, albeit at second hand.

You didn't need to go looking for yet more of it.

Absolutely not. All in all he was a disappointment to me, because my tendency was to treat him as a kind of uncle figure, a wise man, someone from whom I could learn things. To see him being manic was ghastly. I was fond of him, felt protective towards him, but the things he did with his vanity and ambition were appalling. There was a sort of giganticism about everything ...

As you say, it's a very American thing.

Hugely so.

You have written amusingly about what a small-time English contender Larkin seemed to be, by comparison. Some of the same kind of ambition, but so discreetly felt and so discreetly concealed.

You remember Lowell trying to cultivate Larkin, sending him a copy of *The Dolphin* or something ? Larkin retaliated with *High Windows* and inscribed it: 'From a drought to a flood.'

What a put-down.

Lowell took it as a compliment.

I'm sure he would. From this costive Englishman.

Yes, a tribute to his fertility.

You carried your preoccupation with Lowell from The Review *to* The New Review, *didn't you? How did the latter magazine come into existence?*

The Review sort of petered out in 1972. It had come to an end effectively around '68, '69, but for various reasons I wanted to get to number thirty so we did this ploy of a double issue, 29-30, 'The State of Poetry', into which we roped every known versifier.

You did one on Fiction too, didn't you?

That was in *The New Review*. A similar ploy, the last issue, a double. With *The Review* I just had this superstition: I wanted to get to number thirty. But by then the magazine was on its knees financially, and – in terms of the poetry – everybody was imitating everybody else. A sort of self-parodying was going on, and it had become a bit ridiculous. And the combative side of thing had become marooned; by then our little war had been lost, the encroaching barbarians and popsters were now getting mainstream attention, publicised all over the place, and they were a lot better than we were at drawing attention to themselves. I was in London and working on the *TLS* so a lot of my vitriol was being siphoned off. There was the problem with money too. The printers were saying they wouldn't print another issue and I didn't mind too much because I didn't have anything to put in the magazine. We'd also started doing things like printing opinion columns. Some person we'd long thought of as an enemy would be asked to give his views on this and that. Thus we would have a 'Letter from America' by Louis Simpson or some such. So *The Review* had become more magazine-y than polemical. Something had gone, some genuineness, some verve. Some energy and commitment. It was time to jack it in. That would have been 1971 or '72. Then I went to America for a year. No. It felt like a year. I went to make some money and spent all of it while I was there.

Was that when you met James Dickey?

He played blue-grass music and he had this lake on his property and was forever showing off his muscles and thighs. At one point he said: 'Yes, I'm so big, I'm so goddamn big! And no cocksucking English critic's gonna tell me any different!' There he was. 'Come into the house; I'm gonna play you some music, some real music.' And you passed this table where all his publications were set out on display. 'Yeah, my pamphlet, preddy good, ha.' He was riding high on the film of his novel, *Deliverance,* which had just come out and in which he played the sheriff, so he was a movie star to boot. Preposterous figure. He's the only man I've ever seen who could take off his hat and throw it and land it precisely on the peg.

I had a falling-out with him in Syracuse N.Y. Late one night I found myself stuck with him in a bar, while he got drunk boasting to a little claque of students. It was somewhere out on a highway, miles out of town, and I was the only one in the party who had a car –

I'd have thought he'd have had a horse or an aeroplane –

And I said, well I'm going now, and he couldn't believe it. He said, how am I going get back to town? and I said, phone for a cab. I was fed up with him so off I went. I really thought he was going to brain me with his mighty fist.

He was a strange man. I'd gone to his house on the way to the airport and a cab was coming to get me. When I left he gave me a rib-crushing bear-hug and there were tears running down his face. 'Oh, it's been so *good*,' he said. And when I looked back he was leaning against his doorpost, his head in his hands, as if he'd just lost his nearest and dearest. And I'd been there only two hours. But that poet had big emotions.

So you came back to England?

I'd left the *TLS* by then and was pretty much at a loose end and didn't know what I was going to do. I didn't have a job, so ended up reviewing and was generally in financial trouble. I didn't care too much; but then, shortly after *Encounter* stopped publication because of the revelations about the CIA involvement in its finances, another idea came up. Some of those figures like Stephen Spender, Frank Kermode, Stuart Hampshire, and Auden wanted to start a counter-magazine.

I don't think Encounter *had folded by then.*

No, it hadn't but Spender had left. Spender was a big figure in the CIA controversy. So the projected magazine would be a counter-*Encounter* in the sense that it would counter what remained of *Encounter*. There were endless meetings about which duke or millionaire would provide the money.

I went to one of them.

Did you? Anyway, by that stage, I had been dragged in as a possible editor of this thing.

I know they wanted to get Karl Miller at one point.

But Karl had recommended me and for Karl's sake I agreed to talk. It was thought I knew how to start magazines.

Irony.

Anyway by then I'd been at the *TLS*, so I did know more about it than they did. I drew up endless documents about how this magazine would go, with the help of a marketing, advertising chap at the *TLS* who really did know about such things. Anyway, that was done and it had an air of professionalism. Then of course nothing happened. Nobody got any money together; meetings at the Garrick Club stopped happening; people went out to lunch with some wealthy person and came back with nothing; just gossip. So the whole thing became half-hearted and you could see it wasn't getting anywhere. Then it petered out completely. I was left with these blueprints. It was going to be a monthly and I had got genuinely interested in how it could be done. Also I'd perhaps begun to have mild delusions of grandeur, after having worked on a periodical like the *TLS*. In some way I really wanted something larger than a little magazine. As it happened the Arts Council had kept aside some money for this counter-*Encounter*, not a great deal, but anyway, it was just lying there. Charles Osborne who was literature director of the Council at that point saw no reason why, if I reinvented *The Review* as a new monthly magazine, that money – I think about £20,000 – couldn't go to launch one issue of it. And that's how *The New Review* began. A year later, April 1974, it appeared, coinciding happily with nationwide labour troubles and Edward's Heath's 3-day working-week; and of course it was large and plush – and expensive to buy. I wanted something that looked good. I think now it stands up pretty well in terms of its appearance.

People objected precisely on the grounds that it looked too good for a minority literary magazine.

We didn't know it was going to be such a minority magazine when we started it. No, I'd looked at a lot of magazines in America. They have a thriving magazine culture there. We don't. But I didn't see why we shouldn't. I made the mistake of getting a proper professional designer who had lots of expressive ideas and I was too keen on using pictures. Looking back, I think I should probably have done it differently, but I didn't, so there it was. And it still looks pretty okay to me and has some really quite good stuff in it. Anyway it did come under a lot of fire on all the waste-of-public-money issues – which was bollocks, because public money paid only for about half of any single issue. The Arts Council never did pay for *The New Review*. In fact, the whole connection with the Council was a bit of a burden, because of the way they doled it out. You were always having to go and see them to ask for some public money to pay for the last issue, so that you could do the next one. The grant for issue three had to go on issue two. But the money problem was extreme; it was *The Review* times ten. I was the manager of this magazine and discovered I didn't know how to run a business. I thought I did. Looking back, that side of it was a complete shambles.

It certainly was.

A shambles in business terms. In real life terms it required a hell of a lot of astuteness to keep the thing alive, even shambolically.

A lot of dodging and diving.

Oh, a lot of fiddling – nothing illegal, nothing like that – and a lot of holding one's nerve.

And you managed to keep it going for fifty issues.

Yes, over five years. It ended in '79. Fifty issues, some of which were extremely good in my opinion.

Well, I published in it, after all...

Glad to have had you aboard.

Did you have any sort of programme for it?

There wasn't an ideological one but as a business man I thought there was a gap in the market. The new colour magazines in the Sundays were coming through at that time. They weren't what they are now. Then they carried a good deal of popular high-brow journalism: long profiles and long articles, any number of which could possibly have found their way into a literary magazine, ten years earlier. I got interested in the long essay and the short story: things for which there was no market place.

I was going to say that something striking about The New Review *– and I haven't been back through the fifty issues –*

They're here if you like.

– was that your initiatives as editor were focused on prose-writers rather than poets.

I'd already decided that there weren't all that many poets around, possibly three, and I'd lost any wish to make any great impact on the poetry scene except in a marginal, policing sort of way. So the interest in prose and the idea of a magazine that made a difference to something did, I think, appeal to me.

It made a difference to some individuals' careers.

I was actually getting in work that struck me as much more sophisticated and literate than the poetry manuscripts I'd been struggling through before. A bad poem tends to be much worse than a bad short story, I found. I was reviewing a lot of novels at the time and was fed up with the poetry scene. And irritated by it. And then one or two things happened: a very good story came in from a guy called Jim Crace. He was just an unknown chap who came from Birmingham or somewhere. Another story came in unsolicited from someone called Ian McEwan. There did seem to be these gifted people out there, so we were up and running. People I knew about, like you and Edna O'Brien, were also in the first issue and there were a couple of new things. What was coming in was nothing like as bad, on the whole, as a comparable pile of poems would have been. Certainly not as pretentious. Often there was a bit of humour to it. I was keen to have some amusing writing, just as I'd always wanted it in *The Review*. And stylish writing. Also I wanted an effective reviewing department, again to try to make a bit of a difference. There were people I'd come across in the *TLS* whom I hadn't been able to use in quite the right way or had been anonymous. There were people like Clive James who had appeared in the later issues *of The Review*. He was terrific and I wanted to use him. I felt I had enough younger people whom I admired, and still had my old chums from *The Review*, Colin, Hugo, David Harsent; they just carried over and became part of this larger thing.

Did you get any help from the eminenti *who'd tried to float a magazine?*

None at all. I didn't really know them. And didn't admire them, particularly. There was a whole social aspect to that group which I didn't belong to at all. And it was clear to them that I didn't belong. No, I had no contact with them later on.

Another surprising thing about the magazine was that it wasn't greatly interested in politics. I don't mean party politics but the politics of culture. Which isn't the same thing as the politics of the literary world either, though it would include that, obviously. When I think of magazines like Eliot's Criterion *or* Scrutiny *or* Partisan Review *and* The Nation *in the States, or the old* New Statesman *here, not to speak of* Encounter *– all of them had a strong political-cultural thrust, which your journal just didn't have.*

The magazine was not there to promote a position. But that isn't to say we didn't cover topics I was interested in, like psychoanalysis and South Africa. There was a lot about America. Watergate stuff. And on Lord Lucan.

On hostage taking, that Dutch train hijack ... We had huge pieces on these, as well as on the IRA and their bombings.

But you yourself didn't have a line at all?

No. We printed reports. I was very keen on this documentary idea, descriptions from people who were there when things happened.

Looking back, do you not feel now that the magazine might have been stronger if it had had a position?

No, no. We had as much of a position as anybody else probably, in terms of British politics.

Wordsworth once said that he'd spent more of his life thinking about politics than about poetry. Has that ever been true for you?

I used to do a certain amount at Oxford: go on marches, and sit down, anti-this and anti-that. I fell in with a crowd of New Left people who seemed knowledgeable and I had some regard for their intelligence. But there's a certain shiftiness about 'political' people. I was much more interested in what I knew to be the case. In most political situations I didn't know what the case was. I was reading a lot about the 1930s then – and what seemed to me the worst sort of position was this: to be stuck with a line. I was also reading a lot of Orwell too – with admiration.

Orwell was associated with an attempt to start a magazine at one point. It never came to anything much. It lasted about four issues.

Well, if it had lasted it would no doubt have had a political position, but it would have been concerned with the truth; it would have been pragmatic and independent. And I think that was the atmosphere of *The New Review* – or should have been. A fear of big resounding lies.

Your reference to your immersion in the 30's reminds me that a name that hasn't come up here is Auden's. What did you make of him? Were you already aware of him in Darlington?

I'd come across odd things in anthologies then. He's wonderfully memorable and skilful of course and I have a high regard for him but no real fondness, if you see what I mean. He's one of the greatest technicians of the last century, if not the greatest. He could do anything.

Did he write for The New Review *at all?*

He died in '73 and the magazine started in '74. We had pieces about him. John Fuller was a great admirer. I'm not sure if he wrote of him in the magazine but there were things about Auden. We also had a lot of literary reminiscences in which he figured.

Speaking earlier about the business-side of the magazine, you made light of it – after a fashion. But the sums of money involved in must have been frightening ...

They became enormous. It was partly my megalomania at the outset. Although *The New Review* was famous for not paying its contributors, that only became the case in the end.

But you had to pay the people who supplied that high-quality paper.

Yes, and as a result we had to give up paying contributors. I overextended the office and took on people to do things, mostly part-time, but they still needed to be paid ...

The debts just went on piling up?

Yes. The way they do. And of course I was not employed; I didn't get a salary for doing any of this. It was all down to me: I was the sole owner, and, indeed, for years afterwards I was paying the bills, paying the rates, empty rates on this office we'd been thrown out of virtually. And mysterious bills would arrive from way back. It wasn't a proper company; it couldn't go bust. It was a company limited by guarantee like a society. And the guarantors had 'limited liability'.

Who were the guarantors?

Me – so the liability was not in effect 'limited'.

You?

Yes, all I had to do – or so they said – was guarantee ten pounds; but this turned out to be no fence against creditors. So there was this pretence of *The New Review* being a big magazine when it had, in fact, reverted to the little magazine spirit, as it were. So we stopped it. Well, it stopped itself rather. It was out of control and I was hating it at the end because all

I ever thought about was money and not the magazine and what to put in it.

There was never any interest from anybody to take it and make it – ?

It was debt-ridden. I couldn't see anybody buying debts.

The goodwill?

It had goodwill in the quarters that mattered to me.

I meant goodwill in the business sense.

I know. I was speaking in the literary sense.

What happened to you after The New Review *closed down? Presumably you were doing very little writing while all that was going on.*

I did a lot of journalism, because that was what I lived on. I was reviewing television for *The New Statesman* on a weekly basis and that was basically my income. And fending off creditors and generally not doing much myself. And I was forty, this was in '78. I had no idea what I was going to do, less idea than I had had earlier. I knew I didn't want to do another magazine. But that's about all I knew how to do.

You didn't want to go back into employment, like with the TLS?

It had been so long I don't think I would have lasted five minutes. There was also a certain amount of a 'who cares?' in my feelings. And then came the suggestion that I write the Lowell biography. And that became the next thing.

The magazine was finished by then?

Yes, finished in '79. Well, it finished effectively in '78 but it was closed down in '79. And Lowell had died in '77. By '79 I was in a 'position to consider my options'. And the only one that came up was the proposal that I write the Lowell biography.

The suggestion came from the States?

It came from various quarters. Which it had to, because there were two warring camps: the English side and the American. I was looked upon favourably by both for some reason and I knew people on both sides. Jason Epstein at Random House was very keen that I should do it. But I had to get a letter from Lowell's last wife, Caroline Blackwood, and then get a letter from Lizzie Hardwick to whom he'd been married previously. She knew I had a letter from Caroline. There was a 'which-side-is-he-on?' anxiety right from the start.

You'd never thought of yourself as a biographer before?

Not a biographer. I'd written studies, including a biographical thing about the poet Alun Lewis years earlier.

I remember that – it was the preface to the collection of his stories and poems you edited.

Yes, it's quite a long piece. It took ages and involved the conventional sort of research, going to see his widow and so on. So I'd done that many years earlier. But I remembered quite enjoying doing it and also I'm a bit of a squirrel and browser. I had done a fair amount of what could be described as literary history and of course I was attracted by the Lowell project because he'd always intrigued me.

You'd known him for some time by then.

Oh yes. I knew him quite well.

I remember you once showed me a cheque for £20,000 he'd written out in one of his manic states – this was in settlement of a boozy lunch for the two of you.

Yes. There was a good bit of stuff like that. Well, I was very involved with various phases of his illnesses. Lowell was around a lot. He saw *The New Review* office as a sort of literary centre and also we were very hospitable to his works. I hated most of what he was writing at this time and said so in print. It didn't seem to make any difference to him.

Where did you review it?

In the *TLS*. He used to sit in the pub in Greek Street, next to our office, you know, surrounded by admirers, and he was in his element. It was somewhere for him to go; he was lonely in London because he was used to being a big shot socially in New York.

And in Boston.

He was a figure, particularly in the late Sixties. He went on marches with Norman Mailer, he helped to start up the *New York Review of Books*. In fact it was some of his money that started it up. But in London he knew hardly anyone. Anyway, he was around our office a lot. Then he died, very suddenly, aged sixty. As he had said he would. His mother and father both died at the age of sixty and he always said sixty would be the end for him. The people who proposed the biography came up with enough money to keep me for a couple of years – and I needed it. In fact I did finish the book within a couple of years, which now seems to me very speedy. But one moved fast in those days. I had access to almost everything, once various barriers were broken down and trust established, particularly in America, where everybody at first was very suspicious and where most of the research had to be done. There wasn't much material here. Anyway, I did it.

I am sure your being English actually helped you in the States.

Except for the taint of Caroline. But in the end, yes, it worked out. I got to like Lizzie and she got to like me and began to sort of trust me. I didn't like Caroline anyway so that was okay. I was rather on Lizzie's side, really. I thought Caroline was awful. I couldn't understand why he'd wanted to be with her. Lizzie, on the other hand, according to everything I found out about her, was a much more noble individual. Anyway, I felt sorry for her about those letters he turned into verse.

It makes sense that you should have moved into biography, but only retrospectively, if you know what I mean. You would hardly have predicted such a move.

I would never have predicted it but it didn't seem that odd to me at the time. It didn't at all. In fact it seemed exciting – I mean the politics of it and the morality of it, which I had also encountered with Alun Lewis. With him the question was whether or not he had killed himself. All the evidence suggested he had. But there was a living widow and a living mother who were completely committed to the idea that he didn't. So I had to proceed very obliquely there. In the Lowell case there were all sorts of issues. For instance, he'd had affairs with people who didn't want it known. So what did you do? Tell the truth or bear in mind their feelings? Also there were children of the last two marriages. Did I need to say this; did I have to say that?

Did you have any problem with the libel laws?

No, none at all. Nothing like that. There was just this delicate human stuff. And Lowell was so indiscreet. One was used to the idea of the biographical quarry having to be hunted down. In his case, he flung it all in your face; and much of it was untrue because of his mania. A lot of sorting out was needed. You had to brood on these matters.

It was later you had a brush with the law?

Civil law. So I did, with Salinger. After the Lowell book came out and was successful in its way people started wondering who I should do next.

I remember your telling me that Sylvia Plath came up.

Yes, I had the idea of doing her without the last months, you know, of drawing a decent veil over the last months. They weren't too keen on that.

What other suggestions were there?

The most serious one was Pound. The idea of going from Lowell to Pound ... !

Who suggested it?

Jason Epstein.

Before or after the Salinger?

Before. There was a brief period of talking about Eliot, lunches and so on. But I didn't want to become a jobbing biographer. There had to be some point to it.

There had to be a personal attachment. Not that you didn't have that with Eliot's work.

It was hardly as personal as ... Salinger had always been a passion of mine. You know, from adolescence onwards, as with so many people. Eliot was different, although I had a huge admiration for him.

So you wrote the Salinger book.

Yes I did the Salinger and that of course raised all sorts of questions, so then I wrote a book about history and biography, *The Keepers of the Flame*, which I think is the book I'm really most fond of.

It's an outstanding book. It's so funny about the people it deals with and at the same time so thoughtful in its consideration of the whole biographical enterprise. The theme – all those literary widows and heirs – gave you so many stories to be sardonic about. And sometimes to be charitable about too. Such a heap of material.

Oh, I could have done it all over again on quite other people.

Keepers of the Flame II. *When did you become an admirer of Salinger?*

At school. I was a pretty sad schoolboy ... I think every book I've written has some strong autobiographical element in it. That seems to me okay. It saves me from being a jobbing biographer, I think.

That's what I meant by the need for a personal attachment or engagement. You have to deal with something of your own story in the life you are writing.

Yes, something about oneself. I also have the feeling that the people I am closest to are dead writers of the past. Those are the people who are watching over you, keeping you up to the mark.

People you are answerable to.

Yes. Answerable to them if you make any sort of claim at all. You are up before the highest court. Do you feel that?

Yes I do, though not in those terms. There's a phrase of Edmund Wilson's which has always stuck in my mind. When he started to write, he says, his ambition was to earn 'the freedom of the company' of the writers he most admired. He wasn't speaking only of his contemporaries – far from it. And I thought: yes, that's it.

Certain writers, although you revere them as writers, don't have this overshadowing or overbearing presence. I wouldn't be that interested in Yeats's opinion of my work, whereas I would be interested in Matthew Arnold's.

Is there anyone alive that you feel about in some way as you do about such writers from the past?

I don't really know. The whole idea of the companionship of past writers is enacted in the head and on the page, so there are people I still think of as alive, as it were, in certain poems and pieces of writing. But literally alive? No, not ... well, you and Karl.

I'm flattered that you say so.

Oh, I think it's probably true.

The words 'overshadowing' and 'overbearing' which you used a moment ago make the writers of the past sound so forbidding. Like inspectors at school. Isn't it more a matter of trying to be in contact with them, to communicate with them, or of hoping that you can do so?

Yes, you want to live up to their standard, rather than the standards of any current critic.

And you no longer feel like that – because you evidently did feel so at one time – about Michael Fried?

Well, one is avid for heroes when one's young; especially among one's contemporaries. Everybody has memories of that. Somebody like Francis Hope, for example, who died young in an air crash, used to dazzle me with his cleverness. He'd been to a better school, probably. He seemed hugely clever in ways I wanted to be clever in.

I remember watching and listening to Francis, when he was working under Karl at the New Statesman, *acquire some of Karl's speech mannerisms, his rhythms, his delivery, the lingering stress on particular syllables.*

Karl was a bit of a hero to all of us, and particularly so in the editing; I was mightily intrigued by him and I learned from him.

If we could hark back to magazines for a moment, I'd like to know what you made of Encounter's *coming to an end – supposedly in disgrace, because of that CIA-rap. Wasn't the fight was going out of it anyway, because of the ending of the Cold War?*

I thought *Encounter* a very good magazine. At one time everybody wanted to be in it. It had a range of such good writing. You could read it.

Its Anglo-American sponsorship – CIA or otherwise – gave it a large a pool of talent to draw on. And the editors knew pretty well who was worthwhile carrying and who wasn't.

I used to look forward to *Encounter*. I can't remember before or since a magazine that I looked forward to more.

You've spoken of the Lowell biography, and of your great dislike for Caroline, and the difficulties you'd had with her and others in writing the book. But your schoolboy worship of Salinger, which led you into your next biography, resulted in worse trouble still – what with his rage against you and the involvement of the civil courts in the whole affair. I wonder whether you have anything to say about all that now and how you felt then about finding yourself becoming briefly famous or notorious as a result.

Well, I didn't like it very much. It was embarrassing. The bottom line was that someone I had hero-worshipped was turned into my worst enemy. Well, not worst enemy. But publicly that's how I was seen.

He saw you as his worst enemy.

Yes. Hamilton v. Salinger. Those were not words I'd ever imagined seeing. Not in my wildest dreams.

That was how the proceedings were styled?

Yes. Or the other way round. It became a sort of law-journal case. In some respects the law was changed as a result. Every so often I get congratulated on the outcome.

This blow you struck for freedom ...

Freedom of snoopery, yes.

In the biography itself you incorporated some of the embarrassment you felt at finding yourself in this situation.

Well, the first version of the book got as far as page proofs. That's how Salinger came across it. It was just a straightforward biography, making generous use of his unpublished letters, all passed by the Random House lawyers – somewhat to my surprise. But I thought they knew what they were doing. I was of course glad to have all this stuff which I'd discovered at Texas University. Next came the bound proof copies, incorporating quite long extracts from these letters. Then came the lawyers and various court cases which resulted in Salinger ultimately getting an injunction to stop the book being published. So I wrote another book about the whole thing, quoting as much as I could from the letters in the form of para-phrase, but mainly turning it into a story of a biographical investigation. I'd gone from a writer like Lowell who was voluminous in his personal testimony to a writer about whom nothing at all was known. My theory at the outset had been that Salinger was a fairly whimsical person who would enter into the spirit of this; over the years he'd gone in for a certain amount of games-playing with his image, a certain manipulation of it, you know, in the sense that he printed falsehoods about himself on dust-jackets, teased people's curiosity to some extent. So I thought that he would think: what fun – and would start a cat-and-mouse game with me. Of course it didn't work out like that.

It was a genuinely paranoid response that met you?

Well, he was genuinely indignant and outraged. And, of course, the more I know about him the less whimsical he appears to actually be.

Considering what's been published about him since by others...

That's what I mean, his daughter –

And his girlfriend. Compared with them your enquiries could hardly have been more considerate.

I couldn't have been more mistaken about him. So then the book came out in this heavily revised form. And that was that.

As a matter of publishing-scoundrel curiosity, did the legal carry-on do anything for the book's sales?

It must have done something. It wasn't a big seller, twenty-five thousand copies, something like that in the States. The case had lots of publicity on this side of the Atlantic too but over here the book still fell like the usual stone. It was such a familiar story by the time it appeared I don't think anybody felt like reading any more about it.

Did you make an appearance in court?

No, I had to give a day-long deposition, as he did too. So he was lured out of his hiding-place. I didn't come face to face with him.

And you weren't in the court room at any time?

No. Nor was he. I don't know who appeared in the court. It went to the Supreme Court, I think, whatever that means. It was all unpleasant. One makes the best out of it, saying, oh well, I've got this amusing book, this sometimes amusing book. On the whole, I'd sooner not have done it. Looking back.

So you've said. You wrote that you felt mortified because it was so remote from what –

Yes. It was not what I meant at all.

Apart from the odd reference to the case nothing has followed from it? You're not being asked for help by other would-be Salinger sleuths?

Oh, there's a certain amount of that. I back away from it.

Can I ask you about another biography, the most recent in fact, the one on Matthew Arnold? You said that for you there had to be an autobiographical element in any such book, an engagement of a personal kind with the writer and his career. You couldn't do it otherwise. I'm not the only person who's wondered whether – with all the differences allowed for – you didn't feel there to be a parallel of some kind between the course of Arnold's career and yours.

I think there is a thread running through all the biographical books I've done – one which goes back to the Lowell. What's at issue is the idea of a life given over to creativity; and the belief that because a person believes himself to be possessed of some profound and special gift, he has certain rights to live his life in a certain way. I suppose the real question is: what price do such persons pay and what price does the world pay for this gift which they think they have, which they claim to have, and perhaps do have? Lowell seemed alarmingly and repugnantly, overweeningly, to believe that he was a great poet; so he thought he could pretty well do what he liked. And everybody else around him seemed to agree.

At times I felt that some people around him insisted on his greatness almost as much as he did, because if he wasn't a great poet then they were just stuck, landed, with this pathological case. They had to believe that it was worth paying what you've just called the price.

For some of his friends it was almost a privilege to be allowed to pay that price. Lowell's own preoccupation was only with great people. And he knew that there had to be the necessary, less-than-great people to help the great ones to break through. That's how he saw life, and a lot of damage, a lot of suffering, was the result. He was oblivious to most of it and, so far as he did know about it, well, it was okay because that's what geniuses do, that's the price the world must pay for having them. I could see that there are elements of this which make sense. Writers I have known and, indeed I myself, have traces of it; but one tries to suppress them. Also I have a revulsion against, I am repelled by, that sort of manic, tyrannical self – partly through my own personal experience of it with other people in private life.

How do you see what you've just said in relation to Salinger?

Well, with Salinger there was also a sense of specialness, a sense of *I Am*. He, Salinger, just adopts a different method of distancing himself from the mob. His method is tantalising, almost mischievous, but it also has a certain regal aspect. His relation to the world is almost as odd in its way as Lowell's, although not as actively destructive.

And is also vindicated in his case, as with Lowell's, by his being an artist?

Yes. And it is up to us to puzzle out this wondrous personage, just as it was his right to disdain the rough and tumble of the daily market-place and to bully book editors and repel biographers. If biographers did penetrate his defences it was also his right to get up on his high horse. The two personalities – Lowell and Salinger – seemed very different but they had similarities too, which interested me. These touched on the question of the price that has to be paid by themselves and others. Neither of the two struck me as fulfilled people. They had paid the price for the belief they had in their own genius. 'Genius' gave them certain rights but it also had its penalties. In there lies the question of how you are to live if you decide that you are special. If you decide that you want to devote your life to the pursuit of that specialness, how do you live? You know: how do you do it non-fraudulently? And this I think led me towards *Writers in Hollywood*, the book about writers who had sold out in some way. That's a book about those who are unable to cleave to the high road. How do you stick to it? Should you stick to it? Can you do it and yet not do it too? I got interested in people who started off as serious poets and playwrights and ended up churning out shit in Hollywood for money. I couldn't, in my heart of hearts, deplore them since I'd done a certain amount of that kind of stuff myself. Not least, I should say, with the Salinger – one of the reasons I didn't abandon the assignment early on was because I'd have had to pay back all the money they'd given me. It just wasn't on. I wouldn't have been able to function. I'd have had to do even more book reviews, and even more crappy things, if I didn't do this crappy thing, if you see what I mean. I'm trying to think of the way in which all this leads forward to *Keepers of the Flame*. That is the book about literary estates and posterity. Certainly in the Lowell case, and in the Salinger too, there is an idea that greatness involves immortality, no less. Immortality, the idea of it, would be the excuse or reason why you'd be prepared to make certain sacrifices. The quest for 'after-fame' is tyrannical in itself, or can become so when you try to organise your immortality in advance, or when somebody tries to organise it for you. Writers surround themselves with flunkeys and acolytes who will always be ready to assist. Often these are widows.

They too are then entitled to be tyrannical, to use your word, and in so doing seize their own portion of immortality.

Yes, the hem of the garment. In Arnold, one finds an idea of two lives, the workaday life you have to lead and the quest for literary immortality. Arnold would have had to pay prices of various kinds if he had carried on being a full-time poet. All his background, and his father's as an esteemed educationalist, was dead against it. The question for Arnold was: how much do you give to the world in a real, effective way, day to day, and how much do you say: 'I haven't got time for the day-to-day world because I have this bigger thing to give to it. So leave me alone.' The question for him was how to lead a poetic life without turning into a monster, or without making terrible compromises that might sap whatever creativity he had in the first place. And let's not forget the debilitating stress for such a person of wondering whether he is any good at it anyway. The one thing you have got to be is sure of yourself, or pretty sure. What if the truth dawns on you half-way through your creative life, as it does in the quotation I put at the beginning of the Arnold biography, which moves me a lot. Do you remember it? It's just a few lines, here it is:

> 'It is a sad thing to see a man who has been frittered away piecemeal by petty distractions, and who has never done his best. But it is still sadder to see a man who has done his best, who has reached his utmost limits – and finds his work a failure, and himself far less than he had imagined himself.'

> (Notes for Arnold's unwritten 'Lucretius')

A very painful quotation, I find. To have that perception visit you perhaps a half or a third of the way through what you imagined your life was going to be ... I think in some ways Arnold had that self-doubt. Paradoxically it also helped in several ways to make him a good poet.

A couple of minutes ago you put a sentiment in the mouth of an unpleasant imaginary person, a writer of a particular kind: 'I've got this gift and therefore the world must yield itself to me on my terms.' Something like that. It's an attitude you perceive strongly – though it showed itself in a different mode in each case – in both Lowell and Salinger. What you've just said amounts to saying that you were attracted to writing about writers you admired and yet who in important respects actually repelled you.

To some extent, yes. The kind of lives to be afraid of. To be afraid of falling into. But I suspect other biographers write about lives they consider to be exemplary or admonitory. Would I have liked to be like this, would I have done that? And so on. One wants to give something to the world and if what you give to the world is, say, some or a lot of poetry then a) it may not be any good and b) the world doesn't want it anyway. Is that enough for you to go around putting on airs? Aren't there other things you could give to the world? I think Arnold felt that powerfully because the world needed a lot of what he could do for it.

And there was a lot that needed to be done.

He was there at that time. And the idea of a society in need of education was of great significance to him. I think all this comes back to something I mentioned earlier on, that there are two ways, as it were, of dealing with culture: one either protects the culture from the mob or takes culture to the mob. The kingly or lordly attitude is one way: I make these wonderful objects and don't you come and mess about with them or misunderstand them. Or, on the other hand, you say: I can make you a better person if only you had the wit to take a look at this. And there are more humble and unsung ways of contributing to the common welfare. Which would one rather have – a good school or a good poem?

The personal engagement which you have with all your biographical subjects arises then – in part anyway – from a deep ambivalence about the activity of writing as such, let alone about the nature of the persons who actually do it.

The airs and postures that attach to the activity and the sky-high hopes that are attached to it – about all that I certainly do feel ambivalent. Think of whole life-times devoted to an objective that may be worthless because of a lack of talent anyway. And because it doesn't do anything ... I think my new book, *Against Oblivion,* goes into all this too. It's a 20th century *Lives of the Poets.* The idea captured my interest when I looked at Johnson's *Lives of the Poets.* I saw how few of the poets he deals with I had ever heard of. But in their day they were all famous enough to be included in his book.

And no doubt took themselves and their work with immense seriousness.

Yes – although perhaps a good deal less seriously than a full-time poet nowadays would. They were all vicars and that sort of thing. Poetry was just something one did. Presumably they didn't go around making quite such a fuss about it, or constructing their entire lives on the premise that they were special, set apart.

From which another question arises: one which has a direct bearing on the claims of ordinary life against the claims of art, and the higher forms of life supposedly manifested in it and through it. I remember your saying to me once that your biography of Arnold was not going to be one of those in which a chapter opens: 'June passed uneventfully ...' In saying that, weren't you yourself selling the claims of ordinary life short?

I imagine I meant that if there were no documents I wouldn't know that June passed uneventfully, not for certain. Also I would want to avoid writing, 'Arnold sweltered in the June heat' – that sort of thing. You may know for a fact that temperatures in London were higher than they'd been for twenty-five years. But if we don't know for certain that Arnold was in London and we don't know for certain that he sweltered, then we shouldn't say it. And, anyway, who cares? If he didn't write anything or do anything that is relevant to our purposes, do we need that sort of stuff? By ordinary life, I don't mean, you know, whether one put the cat out in June or forgot to. There is an ordinary life, an ordinary world, which we all have to engage with. And the truth is that the more creative the person the less successful their practical relations with that world are likely to turn out to be.

Well, I don't know if you should generalise in that way. After all, Larkin the librarian –

No, I don't think one can.

Or Eliot the publisher. William Shakespeare engaged very successfully with the workaday world.

Of course.

As for your Lives of the Poets, *which you've just finished, can you tell me which of the poets are in it?*

Well, they're pretty much the ones you'd expect. They are all dead and they were all of sizeable reputation in the 20th century. Even though I hadn't heard of perhaps two thirds of Johnson's poets – and there were fifty-two of them – when I came to compile a list of people who absolutely had to be in the book of dead 20th century poets I was up to fifty-two in no time. Yet history seemed to be suggesting that of those fifty-two essential inclusions only a half a dozen would be left in a couple of hundred years' time.

Winnowed down pretty severely.

So who's going to do the winnowing and how will it be done? Some will be unjustly winnowed and some will be justly winnowed. We could get down to winnowing right away. There's an essay by Donald Justice on 'Oblivion', about how reputations disappear. And the subject has a lot of pathos, in that he talks about lives spent devoted to creative objectives with all that that involves; and yet some of those so devoted are doomed to, at best, of middle rank, doomed to be respectable minor figures from a particular, not very long, period of history. I think the underlying question arises: is it worth it? Of course that depends what 'it' is. In the case of Lowell some people would say it wasn't worth it because they don't value his poems highly enough. It so happens that I do value some of them very highly but I value them for the discipline that he managed to bring to the work which was largely absent from the life.

Let's go a-winnowing. You are doing some of it in the very book you've just described. And then somebody else will come along and winnow your winnowing. Of course that somebody else can be as prone to misjudgement as you might be.

Oh, I do concede that. One can't know one is right. Probably the only way to know you are right is to be around in two hundred years to find out who people are interested in.

Can you see a parallel between your interest in inquiries of this kind and Matthew Arnold's turn towards writing criticism and carrying out his inspectorial duties – because he felt, I suspect rightly, that his lyric gift had deserted him?

It either deserted him or he felt it wasn't substantial enough to maintain a fully engaged 'poetic' life. Therefore he had to do other things he believed in. And he had to earn a living. The question of how to live and to survive and at the same time to hold to the idea of a 'poetic' life has always interested me, as I think it interests all writers. How do you do it? How do you pull it off?

In moving towards biography you must have felt that journalism was insufficiently rewarded to provide a living and also that its bittiness was in itself too limiting? That it just wasn't serious enough?

I've always taken journalism pretty seriously and thought a healthy literary journalism to be very important. I think I would have been happy to live by just writing literary essays. I'd have been happy to pen the odd lyric when I felt I had something to write and otherwise to write essays of one sort or another, not necessarily literary essays, prose essays, non-fiction. And if I'd had a private income that's probably what I would have been happy to do. I wouldn't have taken on great things that involved legging around libraries, but biography was well paid – and I didn't have a private income.

For a time in the '80s didn't you present the BBC TV programme, Book-mark? *Sucessfully too, as I remember?*

That was a dispiriting period for me, though it got me interested in Hollywood figures who were also beguiled by the screen, as I suppose I was to an extent. Whatever people say about TV being all to do with money there was always a bit of stardust in it. I could see people around me wanting that stardust and could also see that maybe I wanted some of it too. Not enough, however, to hang about for hours in some field waiting to interview a third-rate novelist.

Do you think the notion that it's beneath the dignity of a serious writer to cater for something like television – do you think that notion has simply vanished? That people with literary ambitions nowadays believe it to one of the perks of the job – there they are, or there they feel they should be, on the screen, well sprinkled with stardust?

I'm sure there is a commercial appetite to appear on television in order to sell books. And the appetite to be a 'celebrity' too, if you can manage it. But in a way it comes back to your view of what you are up to. Somebody like Melvyn Bragg, as I've said, is an educationist. He sees his role as bringing culture to the masses via television. Those who find this appalling would say this isn't culture you're bringing to the masses, it's some cheapened version of culture. The real thing, they would say, needs to be protected from the masses. About that kind of purism, there is also something slightly repugnant.

I've already quoted you earlier on the subject of Larkin's worldly ambitions. He had them all right, you said in effect; the trouble is that compared with those of the Americans they appeared to be so small.

Small-scale, yes.

Do you feel that your own output of poems ... ? Well, I'll put that another way: have you ever dried up completely?

No, never, no.

Your exiguous oeuvre notwithstanding?

There's a difference between what you write and what you publish. That's as it should be. So I do a lot of 'penning' in odd moments but most of it is just unpublishable. One wants to keep this area, as it were, as free of taint as far as one can.

You're deeply exclusivist, then, as well as being so interested in those who are not?

Yes. But the one might follow from the other in the sense that you can believe that none of what you do is going to make a difference. So you might as well do your best to ensure that whatever you produce makes a difference to yourself.

What do you mean by 'making a difference'?

Well, it won't alter the world or make the world a better place because, as Auden said, poetry doesn't make anything happen.

So you're not thinking of the 'poetry world', the poetry lit-business, when you say it won't make a difference?

I'm not thinking of the poetry world. I'm thinking of the general life of human beings.

The community –

I don't know about the community. It's just the sense that what you are doing matters, and is felt to matter. Which I think it probably should and, in an ideal world, would. It connects with the feeling that one's poems aren't as good as they could be and will inevitably fall short in some way; and that even if they don't nobody will notice, because people don't read poetry. So one might as well cherish some platonic idea of the perfect poem and not go around publishing in magazines some version of a poem that you already know is inferior; that you already know is not as good as you could make it. Only publish what you know is as good as it can ever be, allowing always for a sort of private footnote that it's still not good enough. Then you might be getting somewhere toward the correct view of how to live as a poet.

You were never attracted to going into academic life?

I think I might have been. I just fouled up my degree.

That was when you were a lad. I'm thinking of later on. I know there was a move at one point to get you to come and do some teaching at University College London. And you wouldn't hear of it.

Really?

I remember on one occasion I simply asked you to come and give a single graduate seminar at UCL, and you wouldn't even do that. The possibility was also raised the that you might come for a more extensive visit. And you were pretty shirty about that too.

Oh, really? I'm sorry about that. I don't remember. When *The New Review* started, was just about to start, I was offered some job at Princeton, but I went for the magazine. I felt then that I had made a decision between these two worlds. The academic one didn't suit me. I hadn't got a taste for it.

What about your time at Hull University?

That was a sort of fellowship in poetry.

When Douglas Dunn was there?

Yes, Douglas was there. And Larkin. In fact it was Larkin who fixed it all, I think. I was supposed to sit in an office in his library, waiting for these young poets to bring me their work so I could appraise it. I think about two people came in the course of the year, with what looked to me like the lyrics of pop songs. And once you pronounced that these weren't quite up to what they could be, you never saw them again. So there was that side to it. On the other side there was the English Department, which couldn't understand why money was being spent on somebody sitting around in the library doing next to nothing. So the next thing I knew I was having to give a series of lectures on Yeats, or somebody – proper lectures, which I had to mug up the night before. I came out with all this off-the-cuff rubbish about Yeats, and students were sitting there taking notes. I thought, Is this all true? Have I had time to work this out properly? The place seemed to be full of time-servers and charlatans of one sort and another, and I just didn't get on with it, and retreated to my office and waited for the next non-poet to arrive – who never did. In the end I went back to the *TLS*, and wrote an article about it, and made myself even more ...

Eminent.

Even more eminent – certainly in Hull. 'Enemies' was the word I had in mind.

What were your relations with Larkin while you were there?

Friendly, very friendly. He was rather avuncular. I'd met him many years before. In 1964, I'd gone up to Hull to do an interview with him for the *London Magazine*. I think it was the first interview I did with anybody, and we had a quite good time. He was funny and relaxed. Then he visited me once or twice in Oxford, when he was off on one of his miserable summer holidays and was passing through. So we always got on quite well. He liked calling in on ... set-ups ... He liked set-ups. I'd just got married, and had this domestic set-up, and he liked dropping in, and being treated as the visiting uncle, who'd sit miserably by the fireside ... He seemed rather cosy. I noticed it again when he often used to go round to Douglas Dunn's house in Hull. For all his thing about solitude, he was quite – on that level – gregarious. He wouldn't want to go to parties, or anything like that, but he liked dropping round solo to a domestic set-up where he was valued and an honoured guest.

That's rather touching.

Yes, it was.

I remember being struck, the few times I met him, by how courteous his manner was.

Extremely. And he was always most kind to my first wife, Gisela, and to Lesley, Douglas's first wife, who was very fond of him. Those two had a really good friendship. He was strange – you know, the old-style visiting bachelor-uncle, much valued in the family, who just wanted a bit of re-spect and attention ...

Worthy of high regard, and yet somewhat forlorn.

Yes, then going off to his lonely bedsit, while they tucked themselves up in bed. 'Oh well, never mind.' There was something touching about him. The other thing I remember about him was that he was immensely tall and very deaf. I don't speak loudly, so I could never be sure he heard anything I said. We used to go and have a beer in the bar, and I've really no idea how much he heard.

I remember being surprised when I first met him not just by how tall he was, but how big generally ... He had such big hands.

Everything about him was big – big head too. He had a slight clown's face. He could look very clownish sometimes. He had a strange, boyish smile.

Did you ever talk about poetry with him?

No, never. That would be absolutely out of the question. I really don't know what we did talk about – not very much – him probably, or some magazine, or money. He was always very supportive of the magazine-type things I did, and occasionally gave me things to print, but he was just generally kindly. We lost touch a bit later on, after my Hull experience. I think he had an institutional loyalty to the place, and I don't think he thought I'd ...

Played the game.

Which I hadn't. I'm not sure there were many more Fellows in Poetry after me.

You made a thorough job of it, didn't you?

Not deliberately. The betrayal was to go back to London and write about it in a jokey kind of way. As I thought in an affectionately jokey way. But of course, I don't know if there's any such thing, if you happen to be on the receiving end of it.

No, other people are always much, much more sensitive to what you say of them than you feel they ever have any right to be ...

So that didn't endear me to Hull. Had I had any ambitions in that direction I suppose I would have made a better fist of it, or tried to, during that year.

Can we talk about another part of your writing-life I'm curious about, and which I imagine others might be too? ... Don't look so apprehensive.

No, I'm just trying to think what other part there could be.

Your writing about sport. Do you feel – this is such a banal, plodding question, but you'll have to be forbearing – do you feel there is a common factor between your obsession with poetic excellence and your obsession with sporting excellence?

Well, I suppose, just that.

Just what?

Would one really rather score a wonderful goal than write a wonderful poem? Or do they have a lot in common? My admiration for certain footballers does have a lot in common with my admiration for certain poets, just on the *How did he do that?* level. Just something that simply takes your breath away, and yet is a combination of high discipline and spontaneous instinct, in a highly competitive situation.

So there is competitiveness in it?

Well, yes, there's an element of that, of writing a better poem than some-one else, or scoring better goals – yes, sure. Or as good as.

But do you really see the writing of poetry as an inherently competitive activity? I'm thinking of the act of writing, not of the reputation you might gain by doing so. You kick a goal because you want to win, that's the whole point of the activity. But when you write a poem ... ?

Hm. Spectator sports, with rather larger crowds attending the one than the other. No, I think once one stopped being able to play soccer oneself ... I mean that some of the players I most admire – like Jimmy Greaves, my all-time hero – was exactly the same age as myself, so while Greaves was doing it, I theoretically could do it too, I wasn't too old to do that ...

In your dreams, as they say.

But then it became clear to me, when I was thirty-eight, that this wasn't going to happen. The players I admired were in fact twenty-three, and I was never going to be twenty-three. But by then I'd acquired enough knowledge and expertise to make soccer another thing I could write about. It wasn't until Paul Gascoigne came along that I found another player whom I had those Greaves-like feelings about. Here was somebody who took your breath away. How did he do that? Wouldn't it be wonderful to be able to do that? Where did it come from? The football was so highly sophisticated and intelligent, and yet the player, in Gascoigne's case, was such a fool in many ways.

Like some good poets, are you suggesting?

There's a mystery about the origins of the gift, and the application of the gift involves a kind of level of intelligence or discipline that you don't always discern in the personality. And the same is true of poets I've known. But I wouldn't push the analogy too hard. Soccer for me is just a hobby. I think that so far as there is a parallel, in poetry real competitiveness wouldn't be with contemporaries; it would be with figures from the past. It's not about wanting to be more famous than Seamus Heaney. No, it's more that there is a level of excellence to which you should aspire. Are you up to it? Some figures have this gift, and some don't. In sports, yes, it's quite clear who are the geniuses and who are the ones who are just quite good, who've been well-trained ... That's probably true in any sport, and probably true in literature too.

You spoke previously about feeling yourself answerable to certain figures of the past, and about being answerable to them. Now you seem to be saying that that 'answerability' is a kind of competitiveness, too.

Well, aspiration involves competition to some extent. Am I anywhere as good as that? Could I be, if I gave it my best? But no, I don't seriously suppose that feeling answerable to standards set in the past need involve competitiveness, not in the way that might apply to wanting to win some sort of cup. The prize-business I find silly and irritating, and genuinely don't have any stake in. I don't do any of that sort of 'being around' as a poet, giving readings, and so on. In fact, I don't greatly like the company of poets, because the poetry business is all they're inclined to talk about – readings, reviews, and stuff like that. I can't stand it. It's all on such a low level, and none of the poets – or very few of them – are any good anyway, so it hardly matters. The best tend not to be bothered with all that crap. No, there are standards that were set in the past, and if you don't aspire to them then you may as well not write poetry at all. If you take this role on yourself then you take on certain responsibilities too, of emulation or aspiration. If competition comes into that, as I think it must, then so be it.

Are there particular poets whose voices you hear in what you write?

Yes, I can certainly hear the odd trace of Larkin, the odd trace of Lowell, the odd trace of Snodgrass. Poets I've been enthusiastic about – Arnold, certainly. And there might be others, who would be obvious to others but not to me.

Can you think who they might be?

Poets?

Yes. Or indeed, prose writers, to whom you might owe some of your cadences?

No, but I'd always be ready to have an influence pointed out to me, if it were there. There's no sort of imitation that I'm aware of. I would try to get rid of it if I were.

It's not imitation: I'm talking about a manner of speech that has somehow infiltrated one's own voice.

I'm sure there are, but then it could be from some teacher at school or someone I read in the school magazine.

You never went in for poetry in other languages, at all. Or did you?

Reading poetry in other languages, you mean? I've ploughed through the odd Penguins, but ...

No, I mean reading them in the original ...

I don't know any foreign languages well enough to be able to read poems.

You never had the impulse to acquire a foreign language?

Oh, very much so, but I think I would have to acquire it a lot better than I'm likely to if I'm to respond to poetry in such a language in the way I do to poetry in English.

Still, there might be things there for you that are worth responding to.

Well, there might, but I can't think what these would be, because poetry has so much to do with language, with music, with the way the language is actually spoken. I like the spoken voice, and I don't really know enough about the spoken word in any other tongue.

And reading prose in translation – have you done much of that?

Yes, I read a fair amount early on – Thomas Mann, for example, and I've had flirtations with the likes of Camus, and so on. But I'm not a great reader of foreign literature. These days, alas, I mostly read what I get sent to review. I'm all too aware of missing out on vast areas of verbal activity, of course.

Have you had spells when you read novels with anything like the intensity that you read poetry?

No, not that I can think of.

Since you were talking about emulation and aspiration, I'm wondering especially about the capacity that reading has to fire ambition. Reading

novels can be particularly provocative in that way. You read about ambi-
tious people and the work they do and the cities they live in and the
love-affairs they have, and you think: I'd like to do that or be that ... or at
the very least to write about that as if you have.

I envy novelists that sort of content. I think that content is the problem.
One wearies sometimes of the contentlessness of one's own poems, in
terms of their quotidian detail, detail which you'd feel obliged to deal
with as a novelist. I'm not sure I could do it. I'm not very good at describ-
ing things, anyway.

You spoke rather dismissively earlier of your visual sense.

I have a rather melodramatic or pinpoint visual sense. One thing strikes
me. You can ask 'And what did the rest of the street look like?' and I
wouldn't have a clue. I've no sense of direction, for example. I am always
getting lost.

Have you got any further thoughts on the combination in your poems of
the impulse to confess and the impulse to conceal?

I think we all have a quarrel in ourselves between divulgence and con-
cealment. You want to say what happened, but not necessarily who it
happened to. The mysteriousness can itself contribute to the effect of the
poem. Sometimes four different people may think it's about them, when
it hasn't really been about any of them. There's a Lowell poem, 'Home
After Three Months Away' I think it is, that is actually addressed to two
people, but neither of the two know it was also addressed to the other.
He fixed it pretty well, so that it could apply to either. And he got away
with it. No, I don't think I've got anything more to say about that. Well,
there are probably a lot of scandalous things I could say ...

About your own life or other people's?

The intersection of the two. *Between The Lines* is one thing, but ...

▽

INTERVIEWING IAN

DAN JACOBSON

The idea of interviewing Ian Hamilton suddenly occurred to me when he and I were having lunch at the Greek restaurant in Soho which was our regular meeting place. He had spoken to me previously about the book-length interviews with poets which Between the Lines was publishing, and had mentioned his own connection with the firm. Now, out of the blue, I suggested that he should let me interview him for the series.

Why would I want to do such a thing? he asked. It would be interesting, I answered. Fun too, perhaps. At this he simply stared. Nothing more was said by either of us at the time. However, when we next met at the same restaurant, I asked if he had given the idea any further thought. Slightly to my surprise, it turned out that he had been thinking about it, and had duly come up with a reason why it shouldn't be done. Since he was a founder-member of the editorial board of Between The Lines, he said, anything we produced would look like a piece of 'vanity publishing'. By this time I had read two or three of the books the firm had published and had enjoyed doing so. As a result I had become more serious about the sug-gestion than before, and I did my best to make this plain, insisting that the 'vanity publishing' plea was a red herring and that he should at least ask his colleagues on the board if they were agreeable to our going ahead. Why shouldn't he feel as free as anyone else to speak of whatever aspects of his life and work he chose? I would certainly find it worthwhile, he might do so too, and I was sure the same would be true for whatever readers the interview might eventually find.

The upshot was that he agreed to put the proposal to his colleagues. They raised no objection and we set up a date, late in January or early February 2001, for the first taping . 'If it's no good we'll stop,' Ian said, by way of encouragement. Then everything changed. Early one morning, a day or two before we had arranged to meet, he phoned to say that the sudden appearance of some 'spectacular' symptoms – which he went on to describe with a mixture of astonishment, alarm and the grim mirth he was capable of even at such a moment – had made it imperative for him to go into hospital without delay. Eleven months later, soon after we had finished correcting the last draft of the completed interview, he died of the cancer that had been diagnosed during the weeks immediately after his call.

Hence the publishers' request that I should now write an Afterword to this volume. Because of his illness the process of getting the interview together turned out to be much more arduous and took far longer than we had ever imagined it would. Ian had to cope not only with his illness and the consequences of the 'aggressive' course of chemotherapy he was being put through, but also with his determination to finish the last of his books, *Against Oblivion*. For my part, I had to go abroad on three occasions, twice because of previous undertakings and once because of the wholly unexpected death in Australia of my older brother. Still, intermittent though our meetings were, and always accomplished only after last-minute rearrangements by phone or letter, we did manage to get into something like a routine. My pocket-diary shows that in all we made six appointments for taping – only one of which, so far as I can remember, failed entirely.

Every three or four weeks, roughly speaking, I would get on a morning train at Gospel Oak, Kentish Town, and make the brief journey on the old British Rail North London line (now called 'Silverlink', but as shabby as ever) to Ian's flat, which was just a few yards across the road from Kensal Rise station. He occupied the upper floor of the last house in a terrace of low buildings that ran parallel to the railway line. Perhaps because it was a cul-de-sac, the street had a strangely tranquil, private, tucked-away air, that was accentuated, if anything, by the comings and goings of the little trains that ran along the line. The flat itself, up a narrow flight of stairs, was both austere and comfortable. It overlooked the railway on one side and an even quieter street wheeling downhill on the other. Almost all the taping was done in Ian's study: a large room furnished with two heavy desks, many bookshelves, some comfortable chairs, a small table, a dictionary-stand, his old typewriter (he had never acquired a word processor), no pictures, windows facing in both directions.

First, a cup of tea. Then I would ask a few questions I had prepared beforehand, none of which had been sent to Ian, and he would answer – or not. That was enough to get us going. When the phone rang he almost invariably left it to the answer-machine to respond. Sometimes he would get up to hunt for a book or a magazine he had referred to. He smoked incessantly, as he always had; if anything, even more than before his illness had been diagnosed. We generally began at about 10:30. Our first session went on until lunchtime, and we then took a taxi to a restaurant in the West End – not our usual one, which we found to be closed for some reason, but the very next Greek affair down the road – and carried on talking and taping to the background clatter of cutlery and other people's conversations. That strenuous performance was not repeated, however.

All the other sessions lasted for about two hours, at most; after which we would have a neat, light, cold lunch prepared and laid out before she left for work by Ian's partner, Patricia Wheatley, who lived with their children in a house nearby. We ate the meal in a smaller room, also book-lined, at the other end of the flat. Ian would have two or three glasses of white wine; I would have one, and usually left immediately afterwards.

Not once did I feel my presence, and what we were doing together, to be unwelcome to him. On the contrary, I had to take care not to let either of us go on for too long, given the sudden fatigues he was subject to. ('Waves of weakness,' he called them.) How poorly he felt generally can be judged from the fact that he looked at none of the transcripts of the tapes as they were returned to him: he read them through for the first time only after I had edited them all into a more or less coherent 'narrative'. Then he did go through them with his customary editorial scrupulousness. Subsequently, when he was enjoying a kind of respite from both the disease and its treatment, we did twice get together in town, chiefly for the pleasure of seeing each other, but also to clear up a few, final troublesome points in the completed print-out.

It is impossible to guess how things might have gone if our meetings had taken place in other circumstances. Perhaps I would have pressed him harder on certain issues; on the other hand I suspect that he might have been less willing to speak frankly on some of the topics that did come up. The interview itself reveals his distaste at the idea of 'making poems out of suffering which is someone else's', so I am reluctant to write here of what I saw (little enough, relatively) of the physical and mental hardships he went through during the last months of his life. He greatly wanted to live yet had few illusions about his chances of being restored to health, and guessed that a briefer or longer postponement of the end was all he could expect. However, he clung to what hope there was, and put up as stoically as he could with the dire effects of the chemotherapy and the steroids he was compelled to take. ('We're talking World Cup here,' he said at one point, after an unexpectedly good report from his oncologist. That is to say: the summer of 2002.) The physical traits that made his presence so vivid – the mobility and intensity of his wide, blue-green gaze, the Bogart-like turn of his mouth as he spoke, the unstudied combination of smoothness and urgency in his voice, the carriage of his shoulders and his 'noble head', as his brother Ronald was unforgettably to describe it at the funeral – all these were grievously undermined by what was happening within him; but they were never wholly lost. Again and again they would re-emerge, almost as before, either because of a conscious effort on his part or through the sheer force of his engagement with whatever he wished to say.

His mind remained throughout what it always had been. Not one of the observations and reflections that appear in the interview – some of which, readers have since told me, made them wince or laugh out loud as they read them – was subsequently written into the transcript: not one is an *esprit de l'escalier*. They appear in print as he said them, gravely, sardonically or simply off the cuff. Of his illness he did not speak at all into the tape-recorder, but a few of the remarks he made when the machine was switched off bear repeating. A friend who (in Ian's view) wished too anxiously to visit him in his infirmity provoked the writer of *Robert Lowell, The Search for J.D. Salinger,* and *The Poetic Life of Matthew Arnold* to say severely, 'Anybody would think he was a *biographer!*' An incomprehensible print-out from the oncology department of the hospital, which he took from his shirt-pocket and unfolded to show me, he referred to as his 'diploma'. And, half-expecting to be offered yet another bout of chemotherapy, but doubting his capacity to endure it: 'I've been nine parts dead already; so this time I might as well go the distance.'

Well, he did go the distance, sooner than he and the people around him had hoped. To have been allowed to accompany him for a small part of it was a more sorrowful experience than I can easily say. But I always knew it to be a privilege too.

FAMILY ALBUM

In this one you look miles away
And I'm wearing a tolerant half-smile
That seems to say I've fixed things rather well.
What things?

The turreted edifice behind us
I don't recognize at all. Nor can I place
These avenues of trees, abundant
But municipal, well-kept.

It's evidently summertime, and getting late,
A little before supper-bell, I'd guess,
Or prayers.
Another grainy, used-up afternoon.

But what about that speck
There, to the right, a figure on a bench
Perhaps, not looking and yet looking?
And who does that dark, motionless dog-shape belong to?
There, beside that tree.
And look at how those shadows,
So uneven, seem to corrugate the lawn.
We're out at sea,
So you would say, or would have said.

Not all that many years ago,
I might have asked you to explain
Where, when and who,
And maybe why,
And you'd have wanted to. You'd have been
Able to. Not now, though,
Not today. Don't even try.

Almost Nothing

It is an almost-nothing thing, I know
But it won't let me go. It's not a scent
Exactly, but on hot days or at night I do remember it
As slightly burnt, or over-ripe:
Black wheatfields, sulphur, skin.
It's noiseless too
Although from time to time I think I've heard it
Murmuring: a prayer
Presumably, a promise or a plea. And no,
It's not at all substantial; that's to say
It's substanceless, it's not a thing
That you could touch or see.

It doesn't hurt but it belongs to me.
What do we call it then,
This something in the air, this atmosphere,
This imminence?
Today, because you've turned away,
I'll call it nothing much,
I'll call it, since you're frightened, here to stay.

Robert Tough Hamilton
1936

Robert Tough Hamilton
with, from left to right, Ronald, Ian and Stuart,
King's Lynn, 1943

Daisy (McKay) Hamilton
with, from left to right, Stuart, Jeanette, Ian and Ronald,
Scarborough, 1955

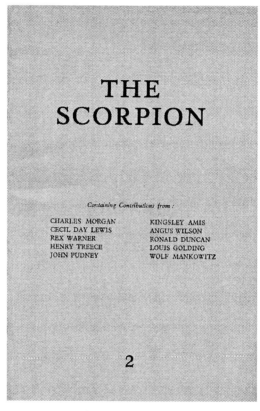

THE SCORPION

Containing Contributions from :

CHARLES MORGAN
CECIL DAY LEWIS
REX WARNER
HENRY TREECE
JOHN PUDNEY

KINGSLEY AMIS
ANGUS WILSON
RONALD DUNCAN
LOUIS GOLDING
WOLF MANKOWITZ

2

The Scorpion, No. 2
Hamilton's first magazine, issued while
he was still a pupil at Darlington Grammar School, 1955

National Service, Germany, 1958

Oxford Undergraduate, 1959

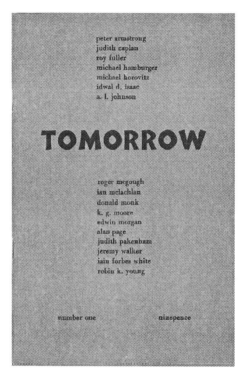

peter armstrong
judith caplan
roy fuller
michael hamburger
michael horovitz
idwal d. isaac
a. l. johnson

TOMORROW

roger mcgough
ian mclachlan
donald monk
k. g. moore
edwin morgan
alan page
judith pakenham
jeremy walker
iain forbes white
robin k. young

number one   ninepence

Tomorrow, No. 1, 1959, the literary magazine founded and edited by
Hamilton while he was an undergraduate

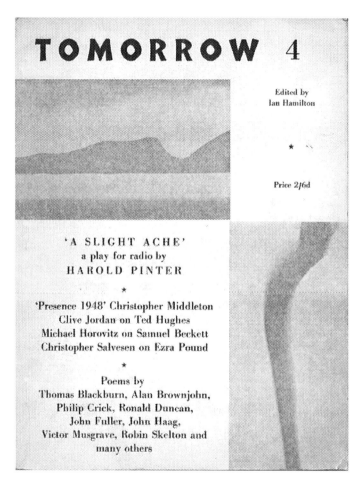

TOMORROW 4

Edited by
Ian Hamilton

★

Price 2/6d

'A SLIGHT ACHE'
a play for radio by
HAROLD PINTER

★

'Presence 1948' Christopher Middleton
Clive Jordan on Ted Hughes
Michael Horovitz on Samuel Beckett
Christopher Salvesen on Ezra Pound

★

Poems by
Thomas Blackburn, Alan Brownjohn,
Philip Crick, Ronald Duncan,
John Fuller, John Haag,
Victor Musgrave, Robin Skelton and
many others

Tomorrow, No. 4, 1960, featuring Harold Pinter's 'A Slight Ache',
and with cover illustrations by Oscar Mellor

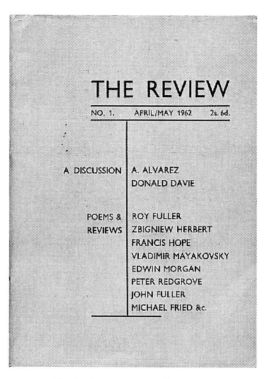

The Review, No. 1, April/May 1962

With Gisela Dietzel, on their wedding day, 1963

South Cornwall, 1963

With John Fuller, Cheadle Hume, 1964

With Colin Falck,   Isle of Wight, 1964
Isle of Wight, 1964

Kensington Gardens, 1967

Karl Miller, off the Berwickshire coast, 1970

the Review

Nos 29 - 30   10th Anniversary Issue   75p.

THE STATE OF POETRY—A SYMPOSIUM

With contributions from: Danzio Abse, A. Alvarez, Kingsley Amis, John Bayley, Patricia Beer, Alan Brownjohn, John Carey, Martin Dodsworth, Alan Dugan, Douglas Dunn, Richard Eberhart, Gavin Ewart, Colin Falck, John Fuller, Roy Fuller, Donald Hall, David Harsent, Adrian Henri, Clive James, Elizabeth Jennings, Philip Larkin, Michael Longley, George MacBeth, Edwin Morgan, Jeff Nuttall, Peter Porter, Jonathan Raban, Peter Redgrove, Vernon Scannell, Jon Silkin, Julian Symons, Anthony Thwaite, Charles Tomlinson, Richard Wilbur, Hugo Williams.

The Review, Nos. 29-30, Spring-Summer 1972
[The last issue]

THE TIMES
LITERARY SUPPLEMENT
TIMES NEWSPAPERS LIMITED, PRINTING HOUSE SQUARE, LONDON, E.C.4
Telephone: 01-236 2000 Telex: 26 2622/3

A letter from Hamilton to his brother Stuart, announcing Faber & Faber's
acceptance of his first book of poems – provisionally entitled *Father and*

Son – and also announcing his intention to limit commitment to the *TLS* to one day a week, because he was 'trying to set up the new mag.' (1969)

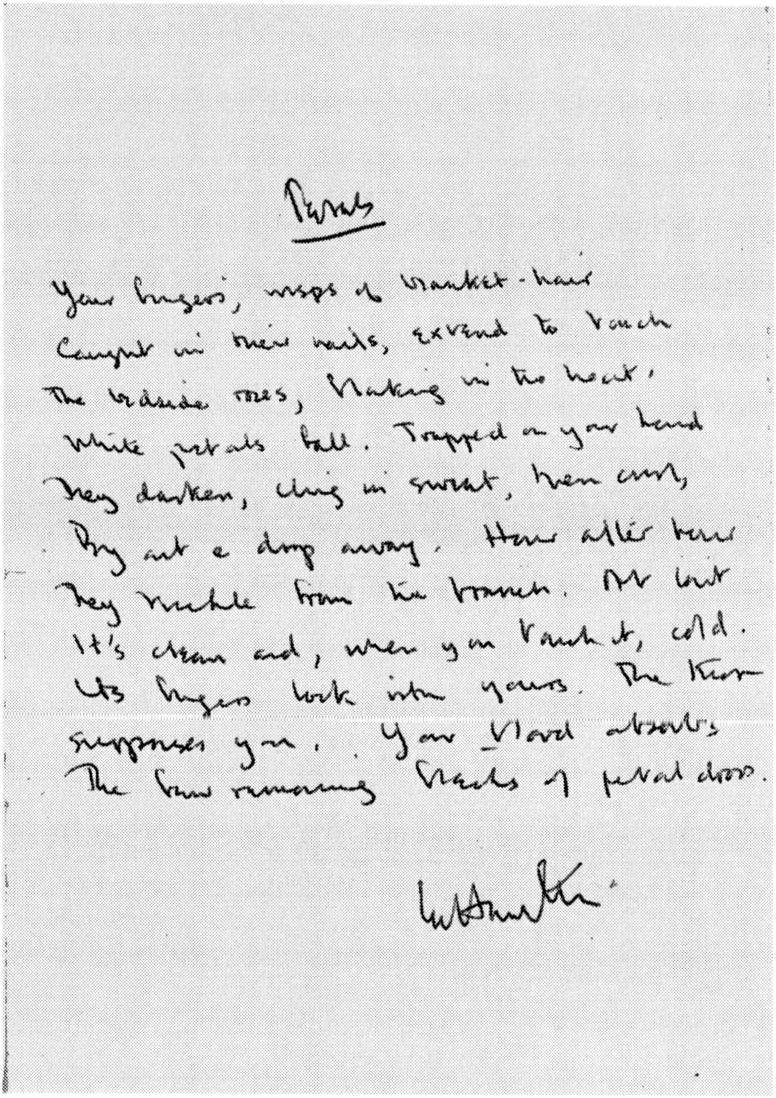

Poem

Your fingers, wisps of blanket-hair
Caught in their nails, extend to touch
The bedside roses, flaking in the heat.
White petals fall. Trapped on your hand
They darken, cling in sweat, then curl,
Dry out & drop away. Hour after hour
They trickle from the branch. At last
It's clean and, when you touch it, cold.
Its fingers lock into yours. The thorn
surprises you. Your blood absorbs
The few remaining traces of petal dross.

An early draft of the poem, 'Father, Dying'

With his mother, on her 60th birthday, outside 4 Kettlewell Lane,
King's Lynn, where the family lived until 1951, 1970

The Visit,
published by Faber & Faber in 1970,
and a Poetry Book Society Choice

The New Review, Vol. 1, No. 1, April 1974

Edward Pygge at The ICA, London, June 25th 1973
A satirical cabaret devised by Hamilton and Clive James,
with, from left to right, Russell Davies, Hamilton, James and Amanda Radice
[The poems read included Hadrian Enri's 'I want to Write Poems', Ted Huge's 'Crow
Resting', R.S. Themes's 'Ngh' and Aeon Hamilton's 'Plea']

With Stuart Hamilton, in Greek Street, Soho,
where *The Review* and then *The New Review*
had their offices, 1976

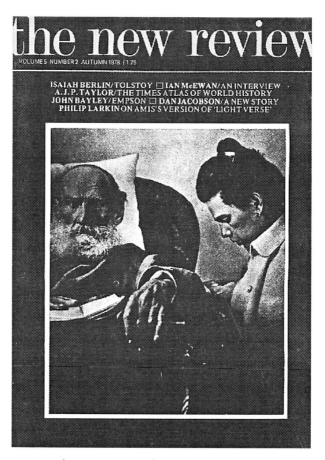

The New Review, Vol. 5, No. 2, Autumn 1978
[The last issue]

With Michael Fried, Baltimore, Maryland, 1981

With Karl Miller and Liz Calder, London, 1981

130

Dorset Square, London, 1985

Gezira Club, Cairo, 1985

With Peter Taylor, Charlottesville, Virginia, 1986

With Simon Gray, Highgate, c.1987

Century Wilshire Hotel, Los Angeles, 1988

133

Wimbledon, c. 1989

Herefordshire, 1990

With Margaret and Dan Jacobson, Hampstead Heath, 1998

Dover Beach, 1998

BIBLIOGRAPHY

Compiled by Philip Hoy and Ryan Roberts

While everything has been done to ensure the completeness and accuracy of this bibliography, the compilers can be sure that their efforts have not been entirely successful. The editors would therefore be pleased to hear from anyone who can identify omissions or errors, which it would be their hope to repair in future editions.

PRIMARY WORKS

POETRY

BOOKS

The Visit (Faber, London, 1970).
Fifty Poems (Faber, London, 1988).
Sixty Poems (Faber, London, 1998).

PAMPHLETS

Pretending Not to Sleep (*The Review*, 13, Pamphlet Series No. 3, London, 1964).
Returning (Privately Printed, London, 1976) [An edition of 150 copies].
Steps (Cargo Press, Cornwall, 1997) [A limited edition of 250 signed copies].

BROADSIDES

Anniversary and Vigil (Poem of the Month Club Ltd., London, 1971).

PROSE

BOOKS

AUTHOR

A Poetry Chronicle: Essays and Reviews (Faber, London, 1973/Barnes and Noble, New York, 1973).
The Little Magazines: A Study of Six Editors (Weidenfeld and Nicolson, London, 1976).
Robert Lowell: A Biography (Random House, New York, 1982/Faber, London, 1983).
In Search of J.D. Salinger (Heinemann, London, 1988/Random House, New York, 1988).
Writers in Hollywood, 1915-1951 (Heinemann, London, 1990/Harper & Row, New York, 1990).
Keepers of the Flame: Literary Estates and the Rise of Biography (Hutchinson, London, 1992/ Faber, Boston and London,1994).
Gazza Italia (Granta, London, 1993); reissued as *Gazza Agonistes* (Granta/Penguin, London, 1994; Bloomsbury, 1998).
Walking Possession: Essays and Reviews 1968-1993 (Bloomsbury, London, 1994/Addison-Wesley, Reading, Massachussetts, 1996).

A Gift Imprisoned: The Poetic Life of Matthew Arnold (Bloomsbury, London, 1998/Basic Books, New York, 1999).
The Trouble with Money and Other Essays (Bloomsbury, London, 1998).
Anthony Thwaite in Conversation with Peter Dale and Ian Hamilton (BTL, London, 1999).
Donald Hall in Conversation with Ian Hamilton (BTL, London, 2000).
Against Oblivion: Some Lives of the Twentieth-Century Poets (Viking Penguin, London, New York, 2002).

EDITOR

The Poetry of War, 1939-45 (Alan Ross, London, 1965).
Alun Lewis: Selected Poetry and Prose, with a biographical introduction by IH (Allen and Unwin, London, 1966).
The Modern Poet: Essays from 'The Review' (Macdonald and Jayne's, London, 1968/Horizon, New York, 1969).
Eight Poets (Poetry Book Society, London, 1968).
Robert Frost: Selected Poems, with a critical introduction by IH (Penguin, London, 1973); the introduction is reprinted as 'Robert Frost' in Walking Possession, 1994: 81-93.
Poems Since 1900: an Anthology of British and American Verse in the Twentieth Century [with Colin Falck] (Macdonald and Jane's, London, 1975).
Yorkshire in Verse (Secker and Warburg, London, 1984).
The New Review Anthology (Heinemann, London, 1985).
Soho Square (2) (Bloomsbury, London, 1989).
Emily Dickinson: Selected Poems (Bloomsbury, London, 1992/St Martin's Press, New York, 1995).
Thomas Hardy: Selected Poems (Bloomsbury, London, 1992).
Gerard Manley Hopkins: Selected Poems (Bloomsbury, London, 1992).
D.H. Lawrence: Selected Poems (Bloomsbury, London, 1992).
W.B. Yeats: Selected Poems (Bloomsbury, London, 1992).
The Faber Book of Soccer (Faber, London and Boston, 1992).
Christina Georgina Rossetti: Selected Poems (Bloomsbury, London, 1992/St Martin's Press, New York, 1995).
Matthew Arnold: Selected Poems (Bloomsbury, London, 1993).
Elizabeth Barrett-Browning: Selected Poems (Bloomsbury, London, 1993/St Martin's Press, New York, 1993).
Samuel Taylor Coleridge: Selected Poems (Bloomsbury, London, 1993/St Martin's Press, New York, 1994).
John Donne: Selected Poems (Bloomsbury, London, 1993/St Martin's Press, New York, 1994).
John Keats: Selected Poems (Bloomsbury, London, 1993/St Martin's Press, New York, 1993).
Walt Whitman: Selected Poems (Bloomsbury, London, 1993/St Martin's Press, New York, 1993).
William Blake: Selected Poems (Bloomsbury, London, 1994/St Martin's Press, New York, 1995).
Emily Brontë: Selected Poems (Bloomsbury, London, 1994/St Martin's Press, New York, 1994).
Robert Browning: Selected Poems (Bloomsbury, London, 1994).
Robert Burns: Selected Poems (Bloomsbury, London, 1994).
Lord Byron: Selected Poems (Bloomsbury, London, 1994).
John Dryden: Selected Poems (Bloomsbury, London, 1994).
Rudyard Kipling: Selected Poems (Bloomsbury, London, 1994).
Alexander Pope: Selected Poems (Bloomsbury, London, 1994).
William Shakespeare: Selected Poems (Bloomsbury, London, 1994/St Martin's Press, New York, 1995).
Percy Bysshe Shelley: Selected Poems (Bloomsbury, London, 1994).
Alfred Tennyson: Selected Poems (Bloomsbury, London, 1994).
William Wordsworth: Selected Poems (Bloomsbury, London, 1994).
Rupert Brooke: Selected Poems (Bloomsbury, London, 1995).

Andrew Marvell: Selected Poems (Bloomsbury, London, 1995).
Wilfred Owen: Selected Poem (Bloomsbury, London, 1995).
Walter Scott: Selected Poems (Bloomsbury, London, 1995).
Edward Thomas: Selected Poems (Bloomsbury, London, 1995).
Oscar Wilde: Selected Poems (Bloomsbury, London, 1995).
John Clare: Selected Poems (Bloomsbury, London, 1996).
Robert Herrick: Selected Poems (Bloomsbury, London, 1996).
John Milton: Selected Poems (Bloomsbury, London, 1996).
The Oxford Companion to 20th-Century Poetry (OUP, Oxford and New York, 1996).
Thomas Gray: Selected Poems (Bloomsbury, London, 1997).
George Herbert: Selected Poems (Bloomsbury, London, 1997).
Edward Lear: Selected Poems (Bloomsbury, London, 1997).
Elegies (Bloomsbury, London, 1997).
Love Sonnets (Bloomsbury, London, 1997).
Odes (Bloomsbury, London, 1997).
W.D. Snodgrass in Conversation with Philip Hoy [with Peter Dale and Philip Hoy] (BTL, London, 1998).
Michael Hamburger in Conversation with Peter Dale [with Peter Dale and Philip Hoy] (BTL, London 1998).
The Penguin Book of Twentieth-Century Essays (Penguin, London, 1999; published as *The Book of Twentieth-Century Essays*, Fromm, New York, 2000).
Anthony Hecht in Conversation with Philip Hoy [with Peter Dale and Philip Hoy] (BTL, London, 1999).
Geoffrey Chaucer: Selected Poems (Bloomsbury, London, 1999).
Henry Wadsworth Longfellow: Selected Poems (Bloomsbury, London, 1999).
Charlotte Mew: Selected Poems (Bloomsbury, London, 1999).
Edgar Allan Poe: Selected Poems (Bloomsbury, London, 1999).
Algernon Charles Swinburne: Selected Poems (Bloomsbury, London, 1999).
Edmund Spenser: Selected Poems (Bloomsbury, London, 1999).
Thom Gunn in Conversation with James Campbell [with Peter Dale, Philip Hoy and J.D. McClatchy] (BTL, London, 2000).
Richard Wilbur in Conversation with Peter Dale [with Peter Dale, Philip Hoy and J.D. McClatchy] (BTL, London, 2000).
Seamus Heaney in Conversation with Karl Miller [with Peter Dale, Philip Hoy and J.D. McClatchy] (BTL, London, 2000).
Donald Justice in Conversation with Philip Hoy [with Peter Dale, Philip Hoy and J.D. McClatchy] (BTL, London, 2001).

CONTRIBUTOR

AGENDA

'Theodore Roethke', 3:4, April 1964: 5-10 [Theodore Roethke, *The Open House* and *The Lost Son*].

THE DAILY TELEGRAPH

'In Wartime, Everyone Gets to Be a Writer', 28 March 1992: 112.
'Athletes With Minds, Not Just Muscles', 6 December 1992: 10.
'Most Alcoholic of All Authors? Ian Hamilton on an Informative Account of Malcolm Lowry's Sozzled Life', 11 October 1993: 10.
'Ghostwriters Playing the Game', 12 December 1993: 11.

ENCOUNTER

'Strange Bedfellows', 24:3, March 1965: 81-83 [David Holbrook, *The Quest for Love*].

EVENING STANDARD

'Confessions of a Secret Censor', 20 January 1977.
'Why a Poet Isn't Averse to Going Pop', 5 May 1977.

FINANCIAL TIMES

'Socialist Out of His Depth', 5 November 1995 [Fred Inglis, *Raymond Williams, A Biography*].
'Symbolic Search for El Dorado', 10 June 1995 [Charles Nicholl, *The Creature in the Map*].

GRANTA

'J. D. Salinger Versus Random House Inc.', 23, 1988: 197-218.
'A Colossal Hoard' (The descendants of James Boswell), 41, 1992: 203-218.
'Gazza Agonistes', 45, 1993: 9-125.
'The Trouble with Money', 49, Winter 1994: 59-66; reprinted in *The Trouble with Money and Other Essays*, 1998: 3-8.
'Sohoitis', London Issue, 65, Spring 1999: 291-303.

GQ

'Heavy Duty', May 1993: 107-111, 180; reprinted as 'Lennox Lewis: A Profile' in *Walking Possession*, 1994: 291-302 [Profile of the boxer].

THE GUARDIAN

'Lowell's God', 1966 [Jarome Mazzaro, *The Poetic Themes of Robert Lowell*].
'Grigson's Position Papers', 18 October 1984.
'Genial Learning Offered With Shy Generosity', 23 January 1992 [John Updike, *Odd Jobs: Essays and Criticism*].
'Mexico, Where Love Is a Bowl of Chillies', 20 February 1992: 25.
'The Likely Lad', 6 November 1993: 6.
'The Italian Job; Gazza: A Fan's Portrait', 13 November 1993: 40.
'A Victory of Sorts', 3 June 1994: T6.
'Confessions of Soccer's Neglected Clown Prince', 9 July 1994: 25.
'Past the Studio Gate', 5 May 1995: T9.
'Letter: Hugo's Dance on Harold's Coffin', 26 May 1995: 18.
'Letter: Unionists Take the Stand', 17 February 1996: 24.
'Letter: Been There', 2 April 1996: 8.
'Letter: Cutting That Redwood Down to Size', 8 June 1996: 28.
'Biographer as a Bad Neighbour', 14 June 1996: T11 [Jeffrey Meyers, *Robert Frost: A Biography*].
'Last Gasp of the Dinosaurs', 9 October 1997: 18.
'Your Welfare at Heart', 27 December 1997: 18.
'Haunted by Fame', 9 May 1998: 1.
'The Garden', 16 May 1998: 10.
'The Guardian Profile: Peter Porter; Triumph of the Downside', 20 February 1999: Saturday Page,

6.

'Bohemian Rhapsodist', 10 July 1999: Saturday Page, 6 [Shena Mackay].
'With Friends Like These. . .', 6 July 2000: 21.
'Education: A True Vocation', 14 July 2000: 23.
'Against Oblivion', 16 March 2002: Saturday Review, 1-2 [Extract from IH's *Against Oblivion*].
'It Was All Greek to HD', 23 March 2002: Saturday Review, 2 [Extract from IH's *Against Oblivion*, discussing Hilda Doolittle].
'Well, Here's to You, Mr Robinson', 30 March 2002: Saturday Review, 3 [Extract from IH's *Against Oblivion*, discussing Weldon Kees].
'Enigma with an Identity Crisis', 6 April 2002: Saturday Review, 3 [Extract from IH's *Against Oblivion*, discussing Stephen Spender].

HARPER'S

'Say More – An Introduction', 276:1657, June 1988: 27.
'A Biographer's Second Thoughts', August 1994: 25.

HARPER'S & QUEEN

'In Search of J.D. Salinger', September 1988.

HUDSON REVIEW

'Letter from England', 17, Autumn 1964: 447-450.

THE INDEPENDENT

'The Beat Goes On - and On and On', 25 February 1990: 20 [Barry Miles, *Ginsberg: A Biography*].
'More Pricks Than Kicks in the Movies', 27 May 1990: 16.
'Pale Imitations and Other Unoriginal Sins', 2 September 1990: 24 [*Unauthorised Versions: Poems and their Parodies,* edited by Kenneth Baker].
'Letter: The Conservative Leadership Election: the Issues, the Candidates and the Implications', November 1990: 18.
'Letter', October 1992: 23.
'Letter: Briefly', February 1993: 18.
'The Daily Poem', August 1994: 4.
'Scots Have a Surprise for You. England Has Taken Union with Scotland for Granted, but Soon It Is in for a Shock, Says Ian Hamilton', July 1996: 13.
'Why Is Black Rod the Only Black Here? Let Me As a Scot, a Foreigner Who Always Wishes England Well, Try to Describe Your State Opening Ceremonial to You', October 1996: 17.

THE INDEPENDENT ON SUNDAY

'A Plain Man's Guide to Writer Chappies', 20 May 1990: 22 [Anthony Powell, *Miscellaneous Verdicts: Writings on Writers 1946-89*].
'More Kicks than Pricks in the Movies', 27 May 1990: 16.
'Diary of an Average Moron', 13 September 1992: 29 [Nick Hornby, *Fever Pitch: A Fan's Life*].
'Blind Side of a One-Eyed Prophet',10 January 1993: 26 [H.G. Wells, *The Invisible Man*].
'Vanishing Point', 21 February 1993: 23 [Christopher Benfey, *The Double Life of Stephen Crane*].

'A Showdown in Spain', 5 May 1966: 656 [Peter Stansky and William Abrahams, *Journey to the Frontier*].

'Bugging Hemingway', 29 September 1966: 464 [A.E. Hotchner, *Papa Hemingway*; Nelson Algren, *Notes from a Sea Diary: Hemingway All the Way*].

'Nothing Or Me', 24 November 1966: 779 [*Selected Letters of Dylan Thomas*, edited by Constantine Fitzgibbon; *A Garland for Dylan Thomas*, edited by George J. Firmage; William T. Moynihan, *The Craft and Art of Dylan Thomas*].

'Miss Onlymind', 1 December 1966: 815 [Brigid Brophy, *Don't Never Forget: Collected Views and Reviews*; Malcolm Muggeridge, *Tread Softly for You Tread on My Jokes*].

'Invulnerable Poet', 16 February 1967: 235; reprinted in *A Poetry Chronicle*, 1973: 145-147 [*Letters of Wallace Stevens*, selected and edited by Holly Stevens].

'P.M.'s Poetry', 16 March 1967: 362 [Robert H. Ross, *The Georgian Revolt: Rise and Fall of a Poetic Ideal, 1910-22*].

'The New American Dictatorship', 23 March 1967: 403 [*The New Writing in the USA*, edited by Donald Allen and Robert Creeley; *Modern Occasions*, edited by Philip Rahv].

'Possum Posthumous', 25 May 1967: 690 [*T.S. Eliot: The Man and His Work*, edited by Allen Tate; T.S. Eliot, *Poems Written in Early Youth*].

'Fiction: Comfortably Surreal', 13 July 1967 [Angela Carter, *The Magic Toyshop*; J.G. Farrell, *A Girl in the Head*; Francis Clifford, *All Men are Lonely Now*].

'Fiction: Dreamscapes', 27 July 1967 [John Gooding, *People of Providence Street*; David Benedictus, *Hump or, Bone by Bone Alive*; Jack Cope, *The Man Who Doubted, and Other Stories*].

'Unearned Wisdom', 17 August 1967 [Alejo Carpentier, *The Kingdom of This World*; Paula Fox, *Poor George*; Cecilia Holland, *Rakossy*; Gore Vidal, *Washington DC*; Alberto Ongaro, *Excelsior*].

'Savage Squealer', 21 September 1967 [Mario Vargas Llosa, *The Time of the Hero*; Nicholas Wollaston, *Jupiter Laughs*; Leslie Thomas, *Orange Wednesday*; Robin Brown, *A Forest is a Long Time Growing*; Alan Sharp, *The Wind Shifts*; Tony Gray, *Gone the Time*; August Strindberg, *The Scapegoat*].

'Growing Girls', 26 October 1967 [A.L. Barker, *The Middling*; Diana Athill, *Don't Look at Me Like That*; Marvin Cohen, *The Self-Devoted Friend*].

'Revenger', 30 November 1967 [Mikhail Bulgakov, *The Master and Margarita*].

'Of Cars and Men', 11 January 1968 [Simone de Beauvoir, *Les Belles Images*; Uwe Johnson, *The Third Book About Achim*].

'Scenes from Prison Life', 8 February 1968 [Malcolm Braly, *On the Yard*; Pier Paolo Pasolini, *A Violent Life*; Paolo Volponi, *The Memorandum*].

'Crofter's Carpet', 7 March 1968 [Iain Crichton Smith, *Consider the Lilies*; *The Stories of James Stern*; Mervyn Jones, *A Survivor*].

'Lacerations', 4 April 1968: 448 [John Williams, *The Man Who Cried I Am*; John Wyndham, *Chocky*].

'Growing Pains', 6 June 1968; reprinted in *A Poetry Chronicle*, 1973: 148-151 [*The Letters of Rupert Brooke*, edited by Geoffrey Keynes].

'Cutting Candy Dead', 12 September 1968; reprinted as 'Terry Southern's *Candy*' in *Walking Possession*, 1994: 186-189 [Terry Southern, *Candy*].

'Drowning Aesthete', 28 November 1968: 726-727 [Richard Aldington, *Life for Life's Sake*].

'Professor of Poetry – Ian Hamilton Writes About Roy Fuller', 5 December 1968: 761-762; reprinted as 'Roy Fuller' in *Walking Possession*, 1994: 108-112.

'Somebody Down There Bugs Me', 16 January 1969: 87 [Jeff Nuttall, *Bomb Culture*].

'Music-Hall Terrors', 20 February 1969: 244 [J. P. Donleavy, *The Beastly Beatitudes of Balthazar B*].

'Disciplinarian', 20 March 1969: 395 [Geoffrey Grigson, *Poems and Poets*].

'Manual for Beginners', 17 April 1969; reprinted as 'Philip Roth's *Portnoy's Complaint*' in *Walking Possession*, 1994: 182-185 [Philip Roth, *Portnoy's Complaint*].

'Television: Speeches in Palestine – Ian Hamilton on "Son of Man"', 24 April 1969.

'Flight From America', 8 May 1969: 655-656 [Thomas Rogers, *The Pursuit of Happiness*].
'Bountiful Hotels', 15 May 1969: 695 [*The Complete Poems of C. P. Cavafy*, translated by Rae Dalven].
'Television: Swinging Paris by Ian Hamilton', 22 May 1969.
'Merry Widows', 19 June 1969: 871-872.
'Errant Apostles', 3 July 1969: 24 [John Fowles, *The French Lieutenant's Woman*].
'Twittering Transistorised Infallibility', 17 July 1969: 90-91.
'A Healthy Death', 31 July 1969: 158 [Edward Upward, *In the Thirties; The Railway Accident and Other Stories; The Rotten Elements*].
'The Aspiring Survivor', 14 August 1969: 225-226.
'Never Let Everton Get on Top', 11 September 1969: 355-356.
'A Generation Ago: What Happened When the Vim Ran Out — Ian Hamilton on the Writers of the Early Fifties and the Magazines They Wrote For', 25 September 1969: 406-407.
'Rupert and Robert', 9 October 1969: 495-496.
'Brother Booker', 16 October 1969: 527 [Christopher Booker, *The Neophiliacs*].
'Lord Snowdon's Outlandish Pet-Lovers', 6 November 1969: 646-647.
'Television: Essays and Cowboys by Ian Hamilton', 11 December 1969.
'A Man at Arm's Length', 1 January 1970; reprinted as 'Aldous Huxley's Letters' in *Walking Possession*, 1994: 27-30 [*The Letters of Aldous Huxley*, edited by Grover Smith].
'This Year's Christmas Box', 1 January 1970: 27-28.
'Who's Afraid of Programmes about Virginia Woolf', 29 January 1970.
'All Play and No Work', 26 February 1970: 291.
'The Song That Made Dublin Happy', 26 March 1970: 427-428.
'Oh, What an Interesting Detective', 23 April 1970: 562-563.
'Requiem for a Novelist', 21 May 1970: 695-696.
'Ian Hamilton Considers British Coverage of the World Cup', 18 June 1970: 838-839.
'Investigations', 16 July 1970: 94-95.
'Accusations', 6 August 1970: 189-190.
'A National Cynicism', 3 September 1970: 319-320.
'Art Therapy', 1 October 1970: 462-463.
'Back to School', 29 October 1970: 606-607.
'Trouble at the Cattle-Market', 26 November 1970: 759.

LONDON MAGAZINE

2:4, July 1962: 73-77 [Ned O'Gorman, *The Night of the Hammer*; Robert Conquest, *Between Mars and Venus*; John Heath Stubbs, *The Blue Fly in His Hand*; Robin Skelton, *The Dark Window*].
2:8, November 1962: 83-85 [Alan Ross, *African Negatives*; Dannie Abse, *Poems, Golders Green*; Vernon Scannell, *A Sense of Danger*; Earle Birney, *Ice Cod Bell or Stone*].
3:2, May 1963: 81-83 [*Anthology of Modern Poetry*, edited by John Wain; *Contemporary American Poetry*, edited by Donald Hall].
'Poetry', 3:3, June 1963: 63-66 [Ted Hughes].
'Poetry', 3:4, July 1963: 54-57 [Sylvia Plath].
'Poetry', 3:5, August 1963: 58-61 [American Poetry].
'Poetry', 3:6, September 1963: 78-81 [Walter de la Mare].
'Poetry', 3:8, November 1963: 62-66 [Louis MacNeice]; reprinted as 'Louis MacNeice' in *A Poetry Chronicle*, 1973: 30-36.
'Poetry', 3:9, December 1963: 59-62 [American Sixties Press]; reprinted as 'The Sixties Press' in *A Poetry Chronicle*, 1973: 122-133.
'Recent Verse', 3:10, January 1964: 101-104 [Ted Hughes, *The Earth-Owl and Other Moon-People*].
'Poetry', 3:12, March 1964: 67-70 [Poetry Book Society].
'Poetry: The Forties, 1', 4:1, April 1964: 81-89; reprinted as 'The Forties: 1' in *A Poetry Chronicle*,

1973: 55-66.

'Poetry', 4:2, May 1964: 70-74 [Philip Larkin, *The Whitsun Weddings*]; reprinted as 'Philip Larkin' in *A Poetry Chronicle*, 1973: 134-138.

'Poetry: The Forties, 2', 4:3, June 1964: 67-72; reprinted as 'The Forties: 2' in *A Poetry Chronicle*, 1973: 66-74.

'Poetry', 4:4, July 1964: 65-69 [William Carlos Williams]; reprinted as 'All American' in *A Poetry Chronicle*, 1973: 45-54.

'Poetry: The Forties, 3', 4:5, August 1964: 75-79; reprinted as 'The Forties: 3' in *A Poetry Chronicle*, 1973: 74-80.

'Selected Books', 4:6, September 1964: 91-94; reprinted as 'Donald Davie' in *A Poetry Chronicle*, 1973: 139-144 [Donald Davie, *Events and Wisdoms*].

'Four Conversations: Thom Gunn, Philip Larkin, Christopher Middleton and Charles Tomlinson', 4:8, 4 November 1964: 64-85.

'Poetry', 4:9, December 1964: 80-83 [Edward Lucie-Smith].

'Poetry: The Forties, 4', 4:10, January 1965: 83-87; reprinted as 'The Forties: 4' in *A Poetry Chronicle*, 1973: 80-86.

'Poetry', 4:11, February 1965: 93-100 [John Berryman]; reprinted as 'John Berryman' in *A Poetry Chronicle*, 1973: 111-121.

'Poetry', 4:12, March 1965 [Anne Sexton, *Selected Poems*].

'Poetry', 5:2, May 1965: 56-59 [Robert Lowell]; reprinted as 'Robert Lowell: 2. *For the Union Dead*' in *A Poetry Chronicle*, 1973: 102-107.

'Poetry', 5:3, June 1965: 67-70 [Roy Fuller, *Buff*]; reprinted as 'Roy Fuller' in *A Poetry Chronicle*, 1973: 87-91.

'Poetry', 5:4, July 1965: 78-80 [John Wain, *Wildtrack*].

'Poetry', 5:11, February 1966: 81-83 [Christopher Middleton].

'Selected Books', 5:12, March 1966: 95-97 [Hugo Williams, *Symptoms of Loss*].

'Poetry', 6:3, June 1966: 85-87 [George Barker, *Summer Night*; Kathleen Raine, *The Hollow Hill*].

'Poetry', 6:4, July 1966: 103-104 [Charles Tomlinson, *American Scenes*].

'Poetry', 6:8, November 1966: 97-99 [Norman MacCaig, *Surroundings*; David Wevill, *A Christ of the Ice Floes*].

'Poetry', 6.10, January 1967: 88-89 [Brian Jones, *Poems*].

'Poetry', 7:3, June 1967: 88-90 [*The Liverpool Scene*, edited by Edward Lucie-Smith].

LONDON REVIEW OF BOOKS

'Letter to the Editor', 1:1, 25 October 1979: 2 [Comments on the first issue of the magazine].

'Snowdunnit', 1:2, 8 November 1979: 13 [C. P. Snow, *A Cost of Varnish*].

'Blowing It', 2:4, 6 March 1980: 11 [Norman Podhoretz, *Breaking Ranks*].

'Smileyfication', 2:5, 20 March 1980: 15-16 [John le Carré, *Smiley's People*].

'Hard Man', 2:20, 16 October-5 November 1980: 15 [Gordon Williams, *Walk Don't Walk*; *The Camp*; *From Scenes Like These*].

'Fame', 3:12, 2-15 July 1981: 14-15 [Clive James, *Charles Charming's Challenges on the Pathway to the Throne*].

'The Comic Strip', 3:16, 3-16 September 1981: 20; reprinted in *London Review of Books: Anthology Two* (Junction Books, London, 1982): 83-87; reprinted again in *Walking Possession*, 1994: 259-264; reprinted again in *The Trouble With Money and Other Essays*, 1998: 351-356.

'Ugly Stuff', 3:19, 15 October-4 November 1981: 17 [William Trevor, *Beyond the Pale*; Patricia Highsmith, *The Black House*; Adam Mars-Jones, *Lantern Lecture*].

'Diary', 4:12, 1-14 July 1982: 21.

'Diary', 4:13, 15 July-4 August 1982: 21; reprinted as 'TV's World Cup '82' in *Walking Possession*, 1994: 272-276.

'Diary', 4:14, 5-18 August 1982: 21.

'Diary', 4:16, 2-15 September 1982: 21.

'Cinders', 4:19, 21 October-3 November 1982: 12; reprinted as 'Just the Job: Cynthia Payne's Comforts' in *Walking Possession*, 1994: 265-271 [Eileen McLeod, *Women Working: Prostitution Now*; Paul Bailey, *An English Madam: The Life and Work of Cynthia Payne*; Martin O'Brien, *All the Girls*].

'Diary', 5:2, 3-16 February 1983: 21.

'Mummies', 5:11, 16 June-6 July 1983: 6; reprinted as 'Norman Mailer's *Ancient Evenings*' in *Walking Possession*, 1994: 174-181 [Norman Mailer, *Ancient Evenings*].

'Diary', 5:17, 15 September-5 October 1983: 21.

'Diary', 5:18, 6-19 October 1983: 18; reprinted as 'Litfest in Oz' in *Walking Possession*, 1994: 223-227.

'Diary', 6:5, 15 March-4 April 1984: 21.

'Martin and Martina', 6:17, 20 September-3 October 1984: 3-4; reprinted as 'Martin Amis's *Money*' in *Walking Possession*, 1994: 190-197 [Martin Amis, *Money: A Suicide Note*].

'Diary', 6:23, 15 November-6 December 1984: 21.

'Diary', 7:16, 19 September 1985: 21.

'The Waugh Between the Diaries', 7:21, 5 December 1985: 10 [*The Diaries of Auberon Waugh: A Turbulent Decade 1976-1985*, edited by Anna Galli-Pahlavi].

'Diary', 8:1, 23 January 1986: 25.

'Real Questions', 8:19, 6 November 1986: 7; reprinted as 'Julian Barnes's *Staring at the Sun*' in *Walking Possession*, 1994: 198-204 [Julian Barnes, *Staring at the Sun*].

'Diary', 9:13, 9 July 1987: 21 [Literary Journals].

'Excusez-Moi', 9:17, 1 October 1987: 10-11; reprinted as 'Seamus Heaney' in *Walking Possession*, 1994: 154-161; and reprinted as 'Seamus Heaney's Anonymity' in *The Trouble with Money*: 330-337 [Seamus Heaney, *The Haw Lantern*].

'Phil the Lark', 10:18, 13 October 1988: 3, 5; reprinted in *Walking Possession*, 1994: 123-129; and reprinted again in *The Trouble with Money*, 1998: 307-313 [Philip Larkin, *Collected Poems*, edited by Anthony Thwaite].

'Dogface', 11:18, 28 September 1989: 6-7 [Paul Fussell, *Wartime: Understanding and Behaviour in the Second World War*; Andrew Sinclair, *War like a Wasp: The Lost Decade of the Forties*].

'They Never Married', 12:9, 10 May 1990: 5-6; reprinted as 'The *DNB*' in *Walking Possession*, 1994: 72-78 [*The Dictionary of National Biography: 1981-1985*, edited by Lord Blake and C. S. Nichols].

'What's Wrong With Desmond?', 12:16, 30 August 1990: 6; reprinted as 'What's Wrong with Desmond' in *Walking Possession*, 1994: 250-256 [Hugh and Mirabel Cecil, *Clever Hearts: Desmond and Molly MacCarthy*].

'One for the Road', 13:6, 21 March 1991: 3; reprinted as 'Kingsley Amis's Memoirs' in *Walking Possession*, 1994: 59-64; and reprinted as 'Kingsley Amis's Self-Love' in *The Trouble with Money*: 345-350 [Kingley Amis, *Memoirs*].

'Cold Shoulders, Short Trousers', 14:5, 12 March 1992: 22; partially as 'Evelyn and Auberon' in *Walking Possession*, 1994: 65-71 [Auberon Waugh, *Will This Do?*; *Mr Wu and Mrs Stitch: The Letters of Evelyn Waugh and Diana Cooper*, edited by Artemis Cooper].

'Whangity-Whang-Whang', 14:10, 28 May 1992: 19; reprinted as 'Damon Runyon' in *Walking Possession*, 1994: 52-58; and reprinted as 'Innocent Bystander – The Forgetfulness of Damon Runyon in *The Trouble with Money*, 1998: 338-344 [Jimmy Breslin, *Damon Runyon: A Life*].

'Evil Days', 14:14, 23 July 1992: 9; reprinted as 'John Carey and the Intellectuals' in *Walking Possession*, 1994: 207-213 [John Carey, *The Intellectuals and the Masses: Pride and Prejudice among the Literary Intelligentsia*].

'Bugger Me Blue', 14:20, 22 October 1992: 3-4; reprinted in *Walking Possession*, 1994: 130-136; and reprinted again in *The Trouble with Money*, 1998: 314-320 [*The Selected Letters of Philip Larkin*, edited by Anthony Thwaite].

'Irving, Terry, Gary and Graham', 15:8, 22 April 1993: 12-13; reprinted as 'Irving Scholar's Spurs' in *Walking Possession*, 1994: 283-290 [Irving Scholar and Mihir Bose, *Behind Closed Doors*; Chris Horrie, *Sick as a Parrot: The Inside Story of the Spurs Fiasco*; Colin Malam, *Gary Lineker: Strikingly Different*].

'Disastered Me', 15:17, 9 September 1993: 3, 5. [Karl Miller, *Rebecca's Vest: A Memoir*].

145

'Being There', 15:19, 7 October 1993, 19-20 [Ved Mehta, *Up at Oxford*].

'Young Wystan', 16:17, 8 September 1994, 12-13; reprinted as 'Auden's Juvenilia' in *The Trouble with Money*, 1998: 87-94 [W.H. Auden, *Juvenilia: Poems 1922-28*].

'Call Me Unpretentious', 16:20, 20 October 1994, 10 [Terry Major-Ball, *Major Major: Memories of an Older Brother*].

'Tel's Tale', 16:22, 24 November 1994: 24; reprinted in *The Trouble with Money*, 1998: 203-208 [Terry Venables and Neil Hanson, *Venables: The Autobiography*].

'Neglect', 17:2, 26 January 1995: 19 [Edward Upward, *An Unmentionable Man*; *Journey to the Border*; Christopher Isherwood and Edward Upward, *The Mortmere Stories*].

'Smartened Up', 17:5, 9 March 1995: 3-4; reprinted as 'Louis MacNeice: Anxious and Aloof' in *The Trouble with Money*, 1998: 30-35 [Jon Stallworthy, *Louis MacNeice: A Biography*].

'There Shouldn't Be a Licence to Get Things Wrong', 17:11, 8 June 1995: 24-25; reprinted as 'Harold Ross of *The New Yorker*' in *The Trouble with Money*, 1998: 40-48 [Thomas Kunkel, *Genius in Disguise: Harold Ross of the 'New Yorker'*].

'Heart-Stopping', 18:2, 25 January 1996: 19-20; reprinted as 'On Being a Soccer Bore' in *The Trouble with Money*, 1998: 196-202 [David Bennie, *Not Playing for Celtic: Another Paradise Lost*; David Platt, *Achieving the Goal*; Gary McAllister with Graham Clark, *Captain's Log: The Gary McAllister Story*; John Brown with Derek Watson, *Blue Girl: The John Brown Story*; Rogan Taylor and Andrew Ward, *Kicking and Screaming: An Oral History of Football in England*; Tom Watt, *A Passion for the Game: Real Lives in Football*].

'Many-Modelled', 18:12, 20 June 1996, 10; reprinted as 'Ford Madox Ford: Who Am I?' in *The Trouble with Money*, 1998: 139-144 [Max Saunders, *Ford Madox Ford: A Dual Life*, Vol. 1: *The World Before the War*].

'Diary', 18:16, 22 August 1996: 29; reprinted as 'I Love Concordances' in *The Trouble with Money and Other Essays*, 1998: 16-21.

'Just What Are Those Teeth For?', 19:8, 24 April 1997: 27; reprinted in *The Trouble with Money*, 1998: 237-242.

'Diary', 19:16, 22 May 1997: 29; reprinted as 'Cups and cups: Chelsea, the Boro, Alan Hudson' in *The Trouble with Money*, 1998: 215-220 [Alan Hudson, *The Working Man's Ballet*].

'Frown by Frown', 19:13, 3 July 1997: 10-11; reprinted as 'R.S. Thomas – Frown by Frown' in *The Trouble with Money*, 1998: 145-166 [R.S. Thomas, *Autobiographies and Collected Poems 1945-90* and Justin Wintle, *Furious Interiors: Wales, R.S. Thomas and God*].

'The Least You Can Do Is Read It', 19:19, 2 October 1997: 30-31; reprinted as 'Poor Cyril' in *The Trouble with Money and Other Essays*, 1998: 22-28 [Jeremy Lewis, *Cyril Connolly: A Life*].

'Taste, Tact and Racism', 20:2, 22 January 1998: 16-17; reprinted in *The Trouble with Money*, 1998: 266-286 [Ahmad Ata, *Assassination of a Princess*; Ilham Sharshar, *Diana: A Princess Killed by Love*; Muhammad Ragab, *Who Killed Diana?*; Tim Dale, *Harrods: A Palace in Knightsbridge*].

'Redeemable Bad Guy', 2 April 1998: 21-22 [John Updike, *Toward the End of Time, Golf Dreams*].

'How Much?', 20:12, 18 June 1998: 7-8 [*Guide to Literary Prizes*, edited by Huw Molseed; *The Cost of Letters: A Survey of Literary Living Standards*, edited by Andrew Holgate and Honor Wilson].

'Diary', 20:15, 30 July 1998: 33 [On the World Cup, France, 1998].

'Hobnobbing', 20:19, 1 October 1998: 29-30. [Philip Ziegler, *Osbert Sitwell*].

'Eric the Nerd', 20:21, 29 October 1998: 18-20. [*The Complete Works of George Orwell*, Vols. I to XX, edited by Peter Davison].

'Diary: Snoop Doggy Dogg for Laureate', 21:1, 7 January 1999: 37.

'A to Z', 21:5, 4 March 1999: 22-23. [Michael Schmidt, *Lives of the Poets*; David Goldie, *A Critical Difference: T. S. Eliot and John Middleton Murry in English Literary Criticism, 1919-28*].

'Diary: Whoop, Whoop, Terrain', 21:9, 29 April 1999: 33 [Malcolm MacPherson, *The Black Box: Cockpit Voice Recorder Accounts of In-Flight Accidents*].

'A Couple of Peep-Holes in the Pillowcase and off We Go a-Lynching', 21:20, 30 September 1999: 64-65 [*Inside the Klavern: The Secret History of a Ku Klux Klan of the Twenties*, edited by David Horowitz].

'Glittering Fiend', 21:24, 9 December 1999: 32-33 [*Berryman's Shakespeare*, edited by John Haffenden; Richard Kelly, *John Berryman's Personal Library: A Catalogue*].

'Ashamed of the Planet', 22:5, 2 March 2000: 16-17 [Randall Jarrell, *No Other Book: Selected Essays*, edited by Brad Leithauser; Mary von Schrader Jarrell, *Remembering Randall: A Memoir of Poet, Critic and Teacher*].

'Sorry to Go on Like This', 22:11, 1 June 2000: 3, 5 [*The Letters of Kingsley Amis*, edited by Zachary Leader].

'"OK, Holy Man, Try This"', 22:12, 22 June 2000: 36-37 [Philip Roth, *The Human Stain*].

'The Power of Des', 22:13, 6 July 2000: 27 [On the screen rights to the English Premier League].

'Going Flat Out, National Front and All', 22:24, 14 December 2000: 7-8 [Alan Clark, *Diaries: Into Politics*; *The Assassin's Cloak: An Anthology of the World's Greatest Diarists*, edited by Irene and Alan Taylor; *The Journals of Woodrow Wyatt*. Vol. III: *From Major to Blair*, edited by Sarah Curtis].

'Tough Guy', 23:3, 8 February 2001: 17-18 [*Keith Douglas: The Letters*, edited by Desmond Graham].

'"I Intend to Support White Rule"', 23:10, 24 May 2001: 30-31 [Thomas Underwood, *Allen Tate: Orphan of the South*].

THE MAIL ON SUNDAY

'History in Mistaking', 27 February 2000 [David Mamet's 'Wilson'].

NEW REPUBLIC

'The Buried Life', August 1994: 29-30, 32-34; reprinted as 'The Buried Life: Elizabeth Bishop's Letters' in *The Trouble with Money*, 1998: 49-60 [*Elizabeth Bishop, One Art: The Selected Letters*, edited by Robert Giroux].

THE NEW REVIEW

[Editorials are not listed]

'Divine Afflatus', 1:2, May 1974: 43-53; reprinted in *The Little Magazines*, 1976: 11-43 [Margaret Anderson's *The Little Review*].

'The Little Magazines – 2: The Billhook', 1:5, August 1974: 50-57; reprinted as 'The Billhook' in *The Little Magazines*, 1976: 81-98 [Geoffrey Grigson's *The New Verse*].

'The Little Magazines – 3: Poetry in Porkopolis', 1:8, November 1974: 39-47; reprinted as 'Poetry in Porkopolis' in *The Little Magazines*, 1976: 44-66 [Harriet Monroe's *Poetry*].

'The Little Magazines – 4: Styles of Despair: Cyril Connolly's *Horizon*', 1:9, December, 1974: 3-9; reprinted as 'Styles of Despair' in *The Little Magazines*, 1976: 125-146.

NEW SOCIETY

'Poetry Helplessly', 2 June 1964: 24-25.

'Facing Facts', 3 October 1968; reprinted as 'George Orwell's Essays and Reviews' in *Walking Possession*, 1994: 214-218 [*The Collected Essays, Journalism and Letters of George Orwell*, edited by Sonia Orwell and Ian Angus].

'Running for Congress', 21 November 1968; reprinted as 'John Updike's *Couples*' in *Walking Possession*, 1994: 169-173 [John Updike, *Couples*].

'Expatriate Attitudes', 23 January 1969 [D.J. Enright, *Memoirs of a Mendicant Professor*; Mordecai Richler, *Hunting Tigers Under Glass*].

'Fines and Privates', 29 May 1969 [C.H. Rolph, *Books in the Dock*].

'Weak Tea', 24 September 1965 [George Rostrevor, *Rapids of Time*; Leonard Clark, *A Fool in the Forest*; Alexander Lenard, *The Valley of the Latin Bear*].

'Fatal Fascinations', 14 January 1966 [Kathrin Perutz, *The Ghosts*; Joyce Carol Oates, *With Shuddering Fall*; Tarjei Vesaas, *The Ice Palace*; Hubert Selby Jr., *Last Exit to Brooklyn*].

'Take a Chair', 25 February 1966 [Rachel Trickett, *The Elders*; Michael Standen, *A Sane and Able Man*; Andrew Fetler, *The Travellers*; Thomas Armstrong, *Our London Office*; Phyllis Bentley, *A Man of His Time*; Winifred Holtby, *South Riding*; Mario Puzo, *The Fortunate Pilgrim*].

'Redemptions', 8 April 1966 [Evan S. Connell Jr., *At the Crossroads*; Jonathan Baumbach, *A Man to Conjure With*; Christiane Rochefort, *Cats Don't Care for Money*; Alexis Lykiard, *Zones*].

'Abu's America', 20 May 1966 [W.J. Weatherby, *Out of Hiding*; Maureen Duffy, *The Microcosm*; Stanley Crawford, *Gascoyne*].

'Sunsets', 1 July 1966 [Nadine Gordimer, *The Late Bourgeois World*; Melvyn Bragg, *The Second Inheritance*; Nigel Balchin, *In the Absence of Mrs Petersen*; Ian Norrie, *Quentin and the Bogomils*; Albert Lebowitz, *Laban's Will*].

'Frolics', 12 August 1966: 235 [Aubrey Beardsley, *Under the Hill* (completed by John Glassco); Stephen Vicinczey, *In Praise of Older Women*; Nicholas Freeling, *The Dresden Green*].

'College Boy', 23 September 1966 [John Hersey, *Too Far to Walk*; Julian Mitchell, *A Circle of Friends*; Brian Glanville, *A Roman Marriage*; Jakov Lind, *Landscape in Concrete*; Raleigh Trevelyan, *The Big Tomato*].

'Living', 4 November 1966 [Edna O'Brien, *Causalties of Peace*; Alison Smithson, *A Portrait of the Female Mind as a Young Girl*; Hugo Charteris, *The Coat*; Anthony Carson, *The Golden Kiss*; John Vaizey, *Barometer Man*; Compton Mackenzie, *Paper Lives*; Basil Davidson, *The Andrassy Affair*; Robert Homan, *On the Verge*].

'Smiling Sweeney', 16 December 1966 [Gerald Green, *The Legions of Bible Christians*; Fumio Niwa, *The Buddha Tree*; Peter Cowan, *Seed*; *Henry Lawson's Best Stories*, chosen by Cecil Mann].

'Night Noises', 27 January 1967 [Paul Bowles, *Up Above in the World*; Mohammed Mrabet, *Love with a Few Hairs*; Robert Harling, *The Hollow Sunday*; Philip Purser, *The Twentymen*; Mikhail Sholokhov, *One Man's Destiny*; Tibor Dery, *The Portuguese Princess*].

'Everybody Stopped Singing', 3 February 1967 [Siegfried Sassoon, *Memoirs of an Infantry Officer*; Michael Thorpe, *Siegfried Sassoon: A Critical Study*].

'Weekend Competition — No. 2,004' [as 'Edward Pygge'], *New Statesman* (9 August 1968): 181

'Bedtime Story', 23 October 1970: 534.

'In Dreams', 27 November 1970: 723.

'Frost at Midday', 19 February 1971: 245-246; reprinted in *A Poetry Chronicle*, 1973: 154-157 [Lawrance Thompson, *Robert Frost: The Years of Triumph 1915-1938*; Edward Connery Lathem, *The Poetry of Robert Frost*].

'Sad Heart', 19 March 1971: 389-390; reprinted in *A Poetry Chronicle*, 1973: 151-153 [John Unterecker, *Voyager: A Life of Hart Crane*].

'The Making of the Movement', 23 April 1971: 570-571; reprinted in *A Poetry Chronicle*, 1973: 128-133 [Robert Conquest, *New Lines*].

'Rational Rigour', 25 June 1971: 882-883 [Roy Fuller, *Owls and Artificers*].

'Chop-Chop', 19 January 1973: 101.

'More Flicks than Kicks', 2 February 1973: 174.

'E.P. — R.I.P', 9 February 1973: 209-210 [Poetry event celebrating Ezra Pound].

'On the Game', 9 March 1973: 355 [TV review].

'Desperate Dick', 16 March 1973: 388 [TV review].

'In Point of Fact', 13 April 1973: 564 [TV review].

'Skin Flicks', 20 April 1973: 595-596 [TV review].

'Be My Guest', 27 April 1973: 629-630 [TV review].

'Where There's Brass', 4 May 1973: 668 [TV review].

'Champion', 11 May 1973: 705 [TV review].

'Deadly Virtues', 18 May 1973: 746-747 [TV review].

'In Hazard', 25 May 1973: 785-786 [TV review].
'Falling Stars', 1 June 1973: 820 [TV review].
'Up Your Street', 8 June 1973: 857-858 [TV review].
'Mind How You Go', 15 June 1973: 903 [TV review].
'Life Studies', 22 June 1973: 937-938 [TV review].
'Open Day', 29 June 1973: 978-979 [TV review].
'Bank Account', 6 July 1973: 29 [TV review].
'DJ-Day', 13 July 1973: 59-60 [TV review].
'Portrait of a Lady', 20 July 1973: 97 [TV review].
'The Big Sleep', 27 July 1973: 130-131 [TV review].
'Tickled Pink', 3 August 1973: 166-167 [TV review].
'Pox On't', 10 August 1973: 199 [TV review].
'Rebores', 17 August 1973: 231-232 [TV review].
'The Big Parade', 24 August 1973: 262-263 [TV review].
'That's My Boy', 31 August 1973: 296 [TV review].
''Ullo, 'Ullo', 7 September 1973: 326-327 [TV review].
'Time Machine', 14 September 1973: 363 [TV review].
'Many Thanks', 21 September 1973: 398-399 [TV review].
'Birds, Beasts and Bockies', 28 September 1973: 446 [TV review].
'Eton Crop', 5 October 1973: 492-493 [TV review].
'Lumping It', 12 October 1973: 534 [TV review].
'Forty Years On', 19 October 1973: 573-574 [TV review].
'Eyestrain', 26 October 1973: 622 [TV review].
'Fun People', 2 November 1973: 661-662 [TV review].
'Ashes to Ashes', 9 November 1973: 709 [TV review].
'Bridal Paths', 16 November 1973: 749-750 [TV review].
'Smart Set', 23 November 1973: 787-788 [TV review].
'Magic Moments', 30 November 1973: 834 [TV review].
'Hard-Pressed', 7 December 1973: 880-881 [TV review].
'Goodness Me, a Poem!', 8 August 1975: 172 [Stevie Smith, *Collected Poems*].
'I'm an MA!', 18 June 1976: 823 [TV review].
'Vigilantes', 25 June 1976: 858 [TV review].
'Yankee Go Home', 9 July 1976: 58-59 [TV review].
'Fatcats', 16 July 1976: 88-89 [TV review].
'It's Supermen', 23 July 1976: 124-125 [TV review].
'The Best of British', 30 July 1976: 154 [TV review].
'Choked', 6 August 1976: 186-187 [TV review].
'Slum Pickings', 13 August 1976: 217 [TV review].
'Stir Quality', 20 August 1976: 253 [TV review].
'Adult Education', 27 August 1976: 287-288 [TV review].
'Dry Eye', 3 September 1976: 352 [TV review].
'Pork Pies', 17 September 1976: 384-385 [TV review].
'Making Up His Mind', 24 September 1976: 414 [George Orwell, *Animal Farm, Burmese Days,
    A Clergyman's Daughter, Coming Up for Air, Keep the Aspidistra Flying*, 1984].
'Dear Aunty ...', 22 October 1976: 608 [TV review].
'Do It Yourself', 5 November 1976: 648-649 [TV review].
'Watchdog', 12 November 1976: 690-691 [TV review].
'No Biz', 19 November 1976: 726 [TV review].
'Where Were You?', 26 November 1976: 767-768 [TV review].
'One-Man Plan', 3 December 1976: 817-818 [TV review].
'Sob-Editor', 10 December 1976: 851 [TV review].
'Toytowns', 17 December 1976: 880-881 [TV review].
'Christmas Box', 24 December 1976: 929 [TV review].
'Totalled', 7 January 1977: 26-27 [TV review].
'Daddy's Girl', 14 January 1977: 62-64 [TV review].

'Rogues' Gallery', 21 January 1977: 97 [TV review].
'Mod Coms', 28 January 1977: 134 [TV review].
'Myxing It', 4 February 1977: 166-167 [TV review].
'Rough Trade', 11 February 1977: 198 [TV review].
'Loaded', 18 February 1977: 230 [TV review].
'Rat-a-Tat', 25 February 1977: 265-266 [TV review].
'That's Life', 4 March 1977: 299 [TV review].
'TTFN', 11 March 1977: 330-331 [TV review].
'Dad's Army', 18 March 1977: 374 [TV review].
'The Fidgets', 25 March 1977: 409-410 [TV review].
'Ming-Pong', 1 April 1977: 440-441 [TV review].
'Make It Mine', 8 April 1977: 472 [TV review].
'A Star Is Born', 15 April 1977: 506-507 [TV review].
'Parson's Pleasure', 22 April 1977: 542 [TV review].
'Like a Trouper', 29 April 1977: 578-579 [TV review].
'Papier Macho', 6 May 1977: 615-616 [TV review].
'The Bottom of the Line', 13 May 1977: 652, 654 [TV review].
'Book Review 800' (as 'Edward Pygge'), 13 May 1977 [Tom Wolfe, *Mauve Gloves & Madmen, Clutter & Vine*]: 647-648.
'Blackheads', 20 May 1977: 690 [TV review].
'Bet Your Boots', 27 May 1977: 720-721 [TV review].
'They Spy', 3 June 1977: 758 [TV review].
'Our Fair Lady', 10 June 1977: 790 [TV review].
'Care for a Smoke', 17 June 1977: 830 [TV review].
'Yokel Colour', 24 June 1977: 864-865 [TV review].
'There'll Always Be an English', 1 July 1977: 28 [TV review].
'Tough Talk', 5 August 1977: 189-190 [TV review].
'Jarndyced', 12 August 1977: 224 [TV review].
'Face to Faith', 19 August 1977: 254-255 [TV review].
'Mummy Go Home', 26 August 1977: 281 [TV review].
'Left Eye', 2 September 1977: 314 [TV review].
'Dutch Cop', 9 September 1977: 347 [TV review].
'Shamanly', 16 September 1977: 376-377 [TV review].
'Heave Ho', 23 September 1977: 419-420 [TV review].
'Optional Extras', 7 October 1977: 484-485 [TV review].
'Psyched Out', 14 October 1977: 516-517 [TV review].
'Poetasters', 21 October 1977: 562-563 [TV review].
'Record Bids', 28 October 1977: 595 [TV review].
'Sin City', 28 October 1977: 588-589 [Dan Jacobson, *The Confessions of Jozef Baisz*].
'Symposium: F. R. Leavis, 1895-1978', 21 April 1978: 536-537.
'Trunch', (as 'Edward Pygge'), 30 June 1978 [Judy Hindley and Donald Rumbelow, *The Knowhow Book of Detection*]: 890-891.
'Blasts from the Past', 11 August 1978: 193-194 [*The Women Pirates, Anne Bonney and Mary Read; The Eclipse; The Dark Horse*].
'Those Wide Open Spaces', 18 August 1978: 220-221 [*The Woman*].
'Peek-a-Boo', 25 August 1978: 251-252 [*Vieux Carré; Ivanov*].
'The Works', 10 November 1978: 632-633.
'DT's', 17 November 1978: 674-675.
'Pink 'Uns', 24 November 1978: 714-715.
'Tripping Up', 22 December 1978: 881-882 [*The Best of John Betjeman*, selected by John Guest].
'Dank You, Man', 16 February 1979: 228 [*Just a Gigolo; Sergeant Pepper's Lonely Hearts Club band; Skip Tracer*].
'Delta Plus', 23 February 1979: 262-263 [*National Lampoon's Animal House; Too Many Chefs; In Praise of Older Women*].
'Gooks Tour', 2 March 1979: 298 [*The Deer Hunter; The Chant of Jimmie Blacksmith; The Pas-*

sage].

'Truly True', 9 March 1979: 336 [*Same Time, Next Year; The Last Supper*].

'The Prudence Farmer Award', 14 September 1979: 384 [IH judges poems for the annual competition, selecting John Fuller's 'In the Corridor' as the winner].

'Will They Survive? A Look at Literary Reputations', 29 May 2000, [On T.S. Eliot].

THE NEW YORKER

'Spender's Lives', 28 February, 1994: 72-85; reprinted as 'The Sensitivities of Stephen Spender' in *The Trouble with Money*, 1998: 61-86.

'Tennyson Anyone?', 22-29 August 1994: 116-121; reprinted as 'Tennyson: Two Lives' in *The Trouble with Money*, 1998: 169-179 [Michael Thorn, *Tennyson*; Peter Levi, *Tennyson*].

'The First Life of Salman Rushdie', 25 December-1 January 1996: 90-97; reprinted in *The Trouble with Money*, 1998: 95-138.

'An Oxford Union', 19 February 1996: 70-74 [On Iris Murdoch and John Bayley].

'Anti-Star: A Profile of Julie Christie', 1998; reprinted in *The Trouble with Money*, 1998: 250-265.

THE NEW YORK TIMES

'The Tatty Wreckage of Her Life', 25 October 1987: 12.

'Killjoy', 154: 2085, 8 June 1997: Magazine, 6, 72; reprinted as 'Us and Them' in *The Trouble with Money and Other Essays*, 1998: 9-15.

THE OBSERVER

'Laureate of Lust' (as 'Peter Marsh') 1966; partly reprinted as 'George Barker: *Dreams of a Summer Night*' in *A Poetry Chronicle*, 1973: 158-160 [Gavin Ewart, *Pleasures of the Flesh*; George Barker, *Dreams of a Summer Night*; Kenneth White, *The Cold Wind of Dawn*; Johannes Bobrowski, *Shadow Land*; Herbert Read, *Collected Poems*].

'Potions of the South' (as 'Peter Marsh'), 1966 [Lawrence Durrell, *The Ikons*; William Plomer, *Taste and Remember*; Norman MacCaig, *Surroundings*; David Wevill, *A Christ of the Ice Floes*].

'Props for a Proposition' (as 'Peter Marsh'), 1966 [Charles Tomlinson, *American Scenes*; R.S. Thomas, *Pieta*; Brian Higgins, *The Northern Fiddler*; Seamus Heaney, *Death of a Naturalist*].

'Straight from the Heart' (as 'Peter Marsh'), 1966 [Randall Jarrell, *The Lost World*; Louis Simpson, *Selected Poems*; Louis Zukofsky, *All the Collected Shorter Poems, 1923-58*].

'The Desire to Please' (as 'Peter Marsh'), 1966; partly reprinted as 'Robert Creeley: *Poems 1950-65*' in *A Poetry Chronicle*, 1973: [Robert Creeley, *Poems 1950-65*; Philip Hobsbaum, *In Retreat*; Keith Harrison, *Points in a Journey*].

'On the Rhythmic Run', 26 March 1967 [Austin Clarke, *Old Fashioned Pilgrimage*; Robert Bly, *Silence in the Snowy Fields*; Ted Walker, *The Solitaries*; Alan Brownjohn, *The Lions' Mouths*].

'Piling on the Agony', 14 May 1967 [Anne Sexton, *Live or Die*; George MacBeth, *The Colour of Blood*; Ken Smith, *The Pity*; David Holbrook, *Object Relations*].

'The Furies in Suburbia', 18 June 1967; partly reprinted as 'John Fuller: *The Tree That Walked*' in *A Poetry Chronicle*, 1973: 163-165 [John Fuller, *The Tree that Walked*; Anthony Thwaite, *The Stones of Emptiness*; Geoffrey Grigson, *A Skull in Salop*].

'Poetry in Brief', 18 June 1967 [Matthew Mead, *Identities*; Brian Patten, *Little Johnny's Confession*; Tom Pickard, *High on the Walls*].

'MacDiarmid Nicht?', 13 August 1967; reprinted as 'Hugh MacDiarmid: *Collected Poems* and *A Lap of Honour*' in *A Poetry Chronicle*, 1973: 171-173 [Hugh MacDiarmind, *Collected Poems*; Hugh MacDiarmid, *A Lap of Honour*; Poems *Addressed to Hugh MacDiarmid*, edited by Duncan Glen].

'Common Sense and Sensibility', 24 September 1967; reprinted as 'Elizabeth Jennings: Collected

Poems' in *A Poetry Chronicle*, 1973: 170-171 [Elizabeth Jennings, *Collected Poems*].

'Dead Ends and Soft Centres', 12 November 1967 [Thom Gunn, *Touch*; Kingsley Amis, *A Look Around the Estate;* Anthony Hecht, *The Hard Hours;* W.S. Merwin, *The Moving Target*].

'Women's-Eye Views', 31 December 1967; partly reprinted as 'Elizabeth Bishop: *Selected Poems*' in *A Poetry Chronicle*, 1973: 160-162 [Elizabeth Bishop, *Selected Poems*; Adrienne Rich, *Selected Poems*; Patricia Beer, *Just Like the Resurrection*; Rosemary Tonks, *Iliad of Broken Sentences*].

'Bringing Out the Worst', 11 February 1968 [Howard Nemerov, *The Winter Lightning;* Cid Corman, *Words for Each Other;* Galway Kinnell, *Poems of the Night;* Alan Ross, *Poems 1942-67;* Peter Dale, *The Storms*].

'Deaths and Entrances', 10 March 1968 [Charles Causley, *Underneath the Water;* George Barker, *The Golden Chains;* Philip O'Connor, *Selected Poems 1936-66;* Adrian Mitchell, *Out Loud*].

'Poet from Poland', 17 March 1968 [Zbigniew Herbert, *Selected Poems*].

'Love Me, Love My Poems', 12 May 1968 [Tony Connor, *Kon in Springtime;* William Wantling, *The Awakening;* W.W. Robson, *The Signs Among Us;* Edwin Morgan, *The Second Life*].

'Public Gestures, Private Poems', 30 June 1968 [Robert Bly, *The Light Around the Body;* Brian Jones, *A Family Album;* Gavin Ewart, *The Deceptive Grin of the Gravel Porters;* Stewart Conn, *Stoats in Sunlight;* Dannie Abse, *A Small Desperation;* Norman Jackson, *Beyond the Habit of Sense*].

'All in the Game', 24 November 1968 [Arthur Hopcraft, *The Football Man*].

'Confessions and Professions', 15 December 1968; partly reprinted as 'W.D. Snodgrass: *After Experience*' in *A Poetry Chronicle*, 1973: 174-175 [W.D. Snodgrass, *After Experience;* R.S. Thomas, *Not That He Brought Flowers;* Barry Cole, *Moonsearch;* Philip Oakes, *In the Affirmative*].

'In the Dust of Battle', 1968 [Richard Murphy, *The Battle of Aughrim;* Derek Mahon, *Night-Crossing;* George MacBeth, *The Night of Stones;* Edward Lucie-Smith, *Towards Silence;* Barry MacSweeney, *The Boy from the Green Cabaret Tells of His Mother*].

'Landscapes and Footlights', 1968 [Molly Holden, *To Make Me Grieve;* Allen Ginsberg, *Ankor Wat;* Adrian Henri, *Tonight at Noon;* Robert Lowell, *Life Studies*].

'Picking Over the Rubble', 1968 [Robin Skelton, *Poetry of the Forties*].

'Tremblings of Promise', 13 April 1969 [Brian Patten, *Notes to the Hurrying Man;* Philip Hobsbaum, *Coming out Fighting,* Jennifer Couroach, *On This Athenian Hill;* Edward Storey, *North Bank Night;* Alan Bold, *A Perpetual Mochine Machine;* James Simmons, *In the Wilderness;* W.S. Merwin, *The Lice*].

'Miller's Complaint', 29 June 1969: 24 [Henry Miller, *Sexus*].

'Declarations of Despair', 21 September 1969 [James Wright, *Shall We Gather at the River;* Galway Kinnell, *Body Rags;* Vernon Scannell, *Epithets of War;* George MacBeth, *A War Quartet*].

'Once More With Feeling', 7 December 1969 [Donald Davie, *Essex Poems;* Douglas Dunn, *Terry Street;* Brian Jones, *Interior;* Robert Graves, *Love Poems*].

'Down from the Mountain', 1969 [Denise Levertov, *The Sorrow Dance;* Kenneth Patchen, *Selected Poems;* Austin Clarke, *The Echo at Coole and Other Poems;* Spike Hawkins, *The Lost Fire Brigade*].

'In the Public Service', 1969 [Peter Porter, *A Porter Folio;* Alan Brownjohn, *Sandgrains on a Tray;* Iain Crichton Smith, *From Bourgeois Land;* Christopher Logue, *New Numbers*].

'It's All in the Game', 1969 [Vasko Popa, *Selected Poems;* Jon Stallworthy, *Root and Branch;* Elizabeth Jennings, *The Animals' Arrival*].

'Wrapping It Up', 1969 [Geoffrey Grigson, *Ingestion of Ice Cream;* Robert Conquest, *Arias from a Love Opera;* David Wright, *Nerve Ends;* Peter Whigham, *The Blue Winged Bee*].

'Call to Arms', 4 January 1970 [F.R. Leavis, *English Literature in Our Time and the University*].

'Loads of Heavy Thinking', 18 January 1970 [Michael Hamburger, *Travelling;* Anne Sexton, *Love Poems;* Norman MacCaig, *A Man in My Position;* Charles Tomlinson, *The Way of a World*].

'Who is Sylvia?', 1 February 1970 [Charles Newman, *The Art of Sylvia Plath*].

'A Very Private Poet', 22 February 1970 [*The Complete Poems of Emily Dickinson*, edited by Thomas H. Johnson].

'Special Pleading', 24 May 1970: 30 [Mary McCarthy, *The Writing on the Wall*].

'A Matter of Balance', 19 July 1970 [Hugo Williams, *Sugar Daddy;* Glyn Hughes, *Neighbours;*

Peter Dale, *Mortal Fire*; George MacBeth, *The Burning Cone*].

'Poetry', 6 September 1970 [Robert Mezey, *The Door Standing Open: New and Selected Poems 1954-1969*; Robert Creeley, *The Finger*; Charles Olson, *The Maximus Poems*; Adrien Stoutenberg, *A Short History of the Fur Trade*; David Wagoner, *Working Against Time*].

'Soul Expanding Potions', 4 April 1971 [Thom Gunn, *Moly*; Jon Silkin, *Amana Grass*; Richard Wilbur, *Walking to Sleep*; Martin Seymour-Smith, *Reminiscences of Norma*].

'Origins and Ancestors', 11 July 1971 [Louis Simpson, *Adventures of the Letter I*; J.V. Cunningham, *Collected Poems & Epigrams*; Tony Connor, *In the Happy Valley*; Fleur Adcock, *High Tide in the Garden*; John Cotton, *Old Movies*; James Simmons, *Energy to Burn*].

'The Bones in the Dyke', 29 August 1971 [Geoffrey Hill, *Mercian Hymns*; George Mackay Brown, *Fishermen with Ploughs and Poems New and Selected*; Adrian Mitchell, *Ride the Nightmare*].

'Watering the Waste Land', 7 November 1971 [T.S. Eliot, *The Waste Land: Facsimile and Transcripts of the Original Draft*, edited by Valerie Eliot].

'Dark Cupboard', 11 February 1973 [Leslie A. Fiedler, *The Stranger in Shakespeare*].

'Poetry and Self Control', 11 March 1973: 37 [Donald Davie, *Thomas Hardy and British Poetry*].

'Ringing the Changes', 24 June 1973 [Robert Lowell, *The Dolphin, For Lizzie and Harriet*].

'Arms and the Poet', 9 June 1974 [Desmond Graham, *Keith Douglas 1920-1944*].

10 April1977: 20 [*Writers at Work: The 'Paris Review' Interviews*, edited by George Plimpton].

'Dylan: A Bard But Not a Poet', 11 June 1978 [Terry Seago, *Montage*].

'Crime Ration', 8 April 1979: 38.

'Crime Ration', 22 April 1979.

'Crime Ration', 6 May 1979: 36.

'The Poet in His Madness', 27 March 1983: 25 [An extract from the forthcoming *Robert Lowell: A Biography*].

'Mogul of the Avant-Garde', 29 May 1988 [Humphrey Carpenter, *A Serious Character: The Life of Ezra Pound*].

'Love and Kisses', 31 July 1988 [*We Dream of Honour: John Berryman's Letters to His Mother*, edited by Richard J. Kelly].

'Whose Sylvia: the Estate's or the Biographer's?', 29 October 1989; reprinted as 'Sylvia Plath: 2' in *Walking Possession*, 1994: 47-51 [Anne Stevenson, *Bitter Flame: A Life of Sylvia Plath*].

'Why It Is Still Hard to Forgive and Forget and to Apologize for Dresden', 22 January 1995: 18.

'Haunted by Ghost Writers', 19 March 1995: 16.

'The British Regard Him As a Bit Of a Joke: A Pharoah Tale', 25 January 1998: 7 [On Mohammed Al-Fayed].

THE OTTAWA CITIZEN

'A Poet's Reply. Was Sylvia Plath Her Husband's Victim?', 15 February 1998: E5.

'Stranger on the Shore. This Week, Mohamed Fayed Lashed Out at a British Establishment That Still Won't Give Him Respect', 15 February 1998: D7.

PUNCH

'Glenn and "Glenda"', 1997; reprinted in *The Trouble with Money*, 1998: 229-236.

RADIO TIMES

'Putting on the Poetry', 1973: 66.

THE REVIEW

[Editorials are not listed]

'There is a Happy Land', 1, April-May 1962, 35-36 [David Holbrook, *Llareggub Revisited*].

'A Pretty Pair' (as 'Edward Pygge', with John Fuller), 1, April-May 1962: 38-39. [Ned O'Gorman, *The Night of the Hammer*; Patrick Creagh, *A Row of Pharoahs*].

'An Unconvincing Handful' (as 'Peter Marsh'), 2, June-July 1962: 33-36.

'Tedium' (as 'Edward Pygge'), 2, June-July 1962: 47 [Dannie Abse, *Poems, Golders Green*].
'Robert Lowell', 3, August-September 1962: 15-24; reprinted as 'Robert Lowell' in *The Modern Poet*, 1968: 32-41; reprinted again as 'Robert Lowell: I. *Lord Weary* to *Life Studies*' in *A Poetry Chronicle*, 1973: 92-102 [Robert Lowell, *Lord Weary's Castle, The Mills of the Kavanaughs, Imitations, Life Studies*].
'Edward Pygge Reports' (with John Fuller), 5, February 1963: 51.
'A Girl Can't Go On Laughing All The Time', 6-7, June 1963; reprinted as 'William Empson' in *A Poetry Chronicle*, 1973: 37-44 [William Empson].
'Edward Pygge Reports', 8, August 1963: 59-60.
'Edward Pygge Reports' (with John Fuller), 9, October 1963: 63.
'Edward Pygge Reports' (with Colin Falck), 16, October 1966: 46-50.
'Edward Pygge Reports', 18, April 1968: 69 (inside front cover).
'Edward Pygge Reports', 20, March 1969: 67.
'Edward Pygge Reports: Where Are They Now?' (with John Fuller), 22, June 1970: 62-63.
'Edward Pygge Reports', 24, December 1970: 80.

THE SPECTATOR

'Salvaging the Apocalypse', 23 April 1965: 540 [*The Faber Book of Twentieth-Century Verse*, edited by John Heath-Stubbs and David Wright].
'Flowers and Porpoises', 13 August 1965 [Jon Silkin, *Nature with Man*; Ted Walker, *Fox on a Barn Door: Poems 1963-64*; George MacBeth, *A Doomsday Book*; D.J. Enright, *The Old Adam*; *The Faber Book of Modern Verse*, edited by Michael Roberts; Frederick Grubb, *A Vision of Reality*].
''14 – '18 – a GCE Version', 29 October 1965: 551 [Bernard Bergonzi, *Heroes' Twilight*; Hugh D. Ford, *A Poets' War: British Poets and the Spanish Civil War*].
'Bringing Gusto to Criticism', 16-23 December 2000 [A.C. Grayling, *Hazlitt*].

STAND

'Conrad Aiken's *Selected Poems*', 5:3, 1963: 49.

THE SUNDAY TELEGRAPH

'Life in the Fast Lane to Literary Success', 3 November 1991: 111 [Diane Wood Middlebrook, *Anne Sexton: A Biography*].
'The Tough Guy of English Letters', 19 January 1992: 115 [Tom Paulin, *Minotaur: Poetry and the Nation State*].
'The Mystery of Hawthorne', 8 March 1992: 110 [Edwin Haviland Miller, *Salem Is My Dwelling Place: A Life of Nathaniel Hawthorne*].
'The Sorrows of Love and the Joys of Political Hate', 12 April 1992: 111 [*The Gonne-Yeats Letters: 1893-1938*, edited by Anna MacBride White].
'From "Ulysses" to "Penthouse"', 24 May 1992: 111.
'A Russian in Venice', 21 June 1992: 108 [Joseph Brodsky, *Watermark*].
'A Pink Lady in Public Life', 9 August 1992: 111.
'Will Gilbert Adair Turn Into Stephen Fry?', 20 September 1992: 111 [Gilbert Adair, *The Postmodernist Always Rings Twice*; Stephen Fry, *Paperweight*].
'Why Make So Much Fuss about Madonna?', 25 October 1992: 111 [Madonna, *Sex*].
'Was Robert Burns Really a Reprobate?', 8 November 1992: 110 [James Mackay, *A Biography of Robert Burns*].
'Vidal Statistics', 10 January 1993: 11.
'God and the Poems of W.H. Auden', 18 February 1993 [Anthony Hecht, *The Hidden Law: The*

Poetry of W.H. Auden].
'Short Stories, Tall Orders', 21 February 1993: 10.
'Who's Who in Philip Roth?', 14 March 1993: 9 [Philip Roth, *Operation Shylock: A Confession*].
'Did Bobby Moore Have Feet of Clay? Was There Another Side to the Golden Boy of 1966?', 9 May 1993: 9.
'The Self-Importance of Being Ernest', 20 June 1993: 9.
'Value of a Literary Valet', 12 September 1993: 11.
'Most Alcoholic of All Authors?', 10 October 1993 [Gordon Bowker, *Pusued by Furies: A Life of Malcolm Lowry*].
'Accidental Origins of Writers' Rights', 14 November 1993: 9.
'Myth-Making for Britain', 20 March 1994: 10 [Ted Hughes, *Winter Pollen: Occasional Prose*].
'Not Mad Enough to Be A Genius', 3 April 1994 [Jay Parini, *John Steinbeck: The Authorised Biography*].
'The Most Contrary of Critics', 24 April 1994: 10 [Michael Wreszin, *Dwight Macdonald: A Rebel in Defence of Tradition*].
'Letters From the Poet's Poet. Ian Hamilton Discovers the Secret Side of Elizabeth Bishop', 1 May 1994: 11.
'Gambling Against History', 8 May 1994: 10 [V.S. Naipaul, A *Way in the World*].
'Scott Fitzgerald's Big-Screen Life', 12 June 1994: 9 [Jeffrey Meyers, *Scott Fitzgerald*].
'The Man Who Knew It All: On His Centenary, Ian Hamilton Reasseses the Work and Reputation of Aldous Huxley', 24 July 1994: 9.
'Would Holden Have Liked It?', 7 August 1994: 4 [J.D. Salinger, *The Catcher in the Rye*].
'Under Green Covers', 18 September 1994: 10 [John St Jorre, *The Good Ship Venus: The Erotic Voyage of the Olympia Press*; James Campbell, *Paris Interzone: Richard Wright, Lolita, Boris Vian and Others on the Left Bank*].
'Lining Up With the Laureate', 23 October 1994: 10.
'Liverpool Down, Manchester Up', 4 December 1994: 13.
'The Rhymester Who Struck It Lucky', 19 March 1995: 11.
'Coming East or Going West', 16 April 1995: 11 [Malcolm Bradbury, *Dangerous Pilgrimages: Trans-Atlantic Mythologies and the Novel*].
'You Can't Keep a Good Myth Down', 21 May 1995: 8 [Peter Conrad, *To Be Continued: Four Stories and Their Survival*].
'The Faces Kingsley Amis Pulls', 11 June 1995: 11 [Eric Jacobs, *Kingsley Amis: A Biography*].
'Laying Down the Laws of Literature', 16 July 1995 [Ian MacKillop, *F.R. Leavis: A Life in Criticism*].
'Gawping Behind the Catwalk', 27 August 1995: 9.
'Women Beware Women', 17 September 1995 [Germaine Greer, *Slip-shod Sibyls: Recognition, Rejection and the Woman Poet*].
'Sex with Everything', 1 October 1995 [Philip Roth, *Sabbath's Theatre*].
'Gore's Love Affair with Himself', 15 October 1995: 17 [Gore Vidal, *Palimpsest: A Memoir*].
'Saving Burns from His Admirers', 29 October 1995 [Ian McIntyre, *Dirt and Deity: A Life of Robert Burns*].
'A Pro's Woes', 24 December 1995: 9.
'Why the Sixties Are Swinging Again', 4 February 1996: 7.
'Oxford's Dated New Guide to US Writers Some Reference Books Need More Than Revision', 18 February 1996: 8.
'George Orwell Versus the Publishers', 14 April 1996 [Peter Davison, *George Orwell: A Literary Life*].
'A Professor Deconstructed', 5 May 1996: 14 [Frank Kermode, *Not Entitled: A Memoir*].
'Huckleberry in Holograph', 26 May 1996: 14 [Mark Twain, *Adventures of Huckleberry Finn*].
'Telling Tales', 30 June 1996: 12.
'The Ribaldry of Robert Burns', 21 July 1996: 13.
'The All-Purpose Wife', 29 September 1996: 14 [Ann Thwaite, *Emily Tennyson*].
'Signposts of Literature', 6 October 1996: 14 [*The Oxford Guide to Contemporary Writing*, edited by John Sturrock; *The Oxford Guide to Twentieth-Century Literature in English*, edited by

Jenny Stringer; Malcolm Bradbury, *The Atlas of Literature*].
'Poet Who Came in from the Cold', 27 October 1996: 14 [Joseph Brodsky, *On Grief and Reason* and *So Forth*].
'Some Sons Do 'Ave 'Em', 10 November 1996: 15.
'The Yob's Lament', 1 December 1996: 15.
'Crack Up in Costa Rica', 19 January 1997: 14 [Joan Didion, *The Last Thing He Wanted*].
'Praise is Praise is Praise', 9 February 1997: 15 [*The Letters of Gertrude Stein and Thornton Wilder*, edited by Edward M. Burns and Ulla E. Dydo with William Rice].
'Can Our Words Be Stolen?' 2 March 1997: 13 [Neal Bowers, *Words for the Taking: The Hunt for a Plagiarist*].
'Kingsley's Corrections', 9 March 1997: 15 [Kingsley Amis, *The King's English: A Guide to Modern Usage*].
'The Goal Standard', 23 March 1997: 3; reprinted as 'Three Managers: Busby, Shankly, Stein' in *The Trouble with Money*, 1998: 221-228.
'To Be Perfectly Frank', 6 April 1997: 7.
'Performing Lawrence', 27 April 1997: 14 [Geoff Dyer, *Out of Sheer Rage: In the Shadow of D.H. Lawrence*].
'Pynchon and On and On', 4 May 1997: 14 [Thomas Pynchon, *Mason and Dixon*].
'Roth's Respectable Guy', 25 May 1997: 14 [Philip Roth, *American Pastoral*].
'Rochester As Roué', 8 June 1997: 13.
'Call of the Wild Man', 6 July 1997: 15 [Alex Kershaw, *Jack London: A Life*].
'A Polymath's Progress', 7 August 1997 [George Steiner, *Errata: An Examined Life*].
'A Sage Look at America', 17 August 1997: 12 [Gore Vidal, *Virgin Islands: Essays 1992-1997*].
'The Happy End of the Affair', 24 August 1997: 6 [Saul Bellow, *The Actual*].
'Women Who Frighten Men', 2 November 1997: 13.
'Kick and Tell Diaries', 7 December 1997: 14.
'A Mismatched Marriage', 25 January 1998: 7 [Ted Hughes, *Birthday Letters*].
'From Pet to Pariah', 15 February 1998: 7 [George Plimpton, *Truman Capote*].
'The Joy of Being Joseph Heller', 8 March 1998: 15 [Joseph Heller, *Now and Then: A Memoir from Coney Island to Here*].
'Poet of the Postbox', 29 March 1998: 14 [*The Selected Letters of Marianne Moore, edited by Bonnie Costello, Celeste Goodridge and Cristanne Miller*].
'In Timeless Prose', 26 April 1998: 15 [Jeffrey Archer, *The Eleventh Commandment*].
'Finding the Words for War', 17 May 1998 [Jean Moorcroft Wilson, *Siegfried Sassoon: The Making of a War Poet. A Biography, Vol. 1: 1886-1918*].
'Defensive Formation', 31 May 1998: 12 [Colin Shindler, *Manchester United Ruined My Life*; Alan Shearer, *My Life So Far*; Stella Orakwue, *Pitch Invaders*; Ruud Gullit, *Ruud Gullit*; Harry Harris, *Zola*].
'How Kerouac Missed the Boat', 14 June 1998: 15 [Barry Miles, *Jack Kerouac, King of the Beats: A Portrait*].
'A Punch-Up with a Poet', 5 July 1998: 14 [Les Murray, *Freddy Neptune*].
'Facts about Fictions', 27 July 1998: 12 [*Writing the Lives of Writers*, edited by Warwick Gould and Thomas F. Staley].
'The Prophet's Profit', 2 August 1998: 12 [Robin Waterfield, *Prophet: The Life and Times of Kahlil Gibran*].
'A Meeting of Bodies', 16 August 1998: 13 [*Beloved Chicago Man*, edited by Sylvie Le Bon de Beauvoir,].
'The Secretive Satirist', 23 August 1998: 15 [Victoria Glendinning, *Jonathan Swift*].
'No More Mr Tough Guy', 8 November 1998: 14 [Michael Reynolds, *Hemingway: The 1930s and The Young Hemingway*].
'Just Where Did It All Go Wrong?', 22 November 1998: 15 [Paul Theroux, *Sir Vidia's Shadow: A Friendship Across Five Continents*].
'For the Real Action, Look in the Stands', 6 December 1998: 15.
'Not Such a Harsh Frost After All', 10 January 1999: 14 [Jay Parini, *Robert Frost: A Life*].
'Between Me and We', 21 February 1999: 12 [Peter Porter, *Collected Poems, Vol. I: 1961-1981*,

Vol. II: 1984-1999; Geoffrey Hill, *The Triumph of Love*].
'A Future Without a Past', 21 March 1999: 14 [Peter Ackroyd, *The Plato Papers*].
'How Much Did He Make Up?', 4 April 1999: 13 [Nicholas Shakespeare, *Bruce Chatwin*].
'Off the Ball Incidents', 16 May 1999, 13. [David Yallop, *How They Stole the Game*].
'Reading Between the Lines', 23 May 1999: 12 [Edward Mendelson, *Later Auden*].
'Millennium Reputations', 30 May 1999: 15 [T.S. Eliot, *The Waste Land*].
'Summer Reading', 27 June 1999: 12.
'A War Poet's Battles with Peace', 4 July 1999: 14 [John Stuart Roberts, *Siegfried Sassoon (1886-1967)*].
'Homage to Catalonia', 11 July 1999: 13 [Jimmy Burns, *Barça*].
'Tough, but Not Tough Enough', 18 July 1999: 13.
'A Hard Working Mystery', 8 August 1999 [Lavinia Greacen, *J.G. Farrell: The Making of a Writer*].
'Man-U and Superman', 22 August 1999, 12: [Alex Ferguson, *Managing My Life*].
'When in Doubt, Say F', 19 September 1999: 15 [*The F Word*, edited by Jesse Sheidlower].
'Poetry's New Pecking Order', 3 October 1999: 14 [*The Oxford Book of English Verse*, edited by Christopher Ricks].
'A Scholarly Look at a Dilettante', 31 October 1999: 17 [Fred Kaplan, *Gore Vidal: A Biography*].
'The Greatest and the Rest', 28 November 1999: 16.
'Greatness Eluded Him', 12 December 1999 [David Leeming, *Stephen Spender: A Life in Modernism*].
'The Bad Book of the Film of the Book', 13 February 2000: 14 [William Cash, *The Third Woman*].
'The Martyr Who Wasn't', 2 April 2000: 12 [Erica Wagner, *Ariel's Gift; Journals of Sylvia Plath, 1950-62*, edited by Karen V. Kukil].
'A Contest to the Death', 9 April 2000: 14 [Scott Donaldson, *Hemingway vs Fitzgerald*].
'The Last Kick of His Game', 23 April 2000: 14 [Stanley Matthews, *The Way It Was*].
'In Praise of Brain Power', 14 May 2000: 15 [*The Complete Poems of William Empson*, edited by John Haffenden].
'The New Model Martin Amis', 21 May 2000: 12 [Martin Amis, *Experience*].
'A Shark with Pretty Teeth', 27 August 2000: 13 [Frances Kiernan, *Seeing Mary Plain*].
'Ali Baba is Out, Ali, Tariq Is In', 24 September 2000: 14 [*Oxford Companion to English Literature*, edited by Margaret Drabble].
'Don't Mention the Score', 1 October 2000: 13 [David Downing, *The Best of Enemies*].
'The Central Character', 22 October 2000: 15 [James Atlas, *Saul Bellow*].
'The Brilliance of a Buffoon', 29 October 2000: 15 [Adam Sissman, *Boswell's Presumptuous Task*].
'The Big Mistake of Growing Up', 5 November 2000: 11 [Margaret Ann Salinger, *Dream Catcher*].
'A Team of Mixed Ability', 3 December 2000: 15.
'Greatness Eluded Him', 12 December 2000: 14.
'The Case of the Invisible Woman', 18 February 2001: 13.
'He Wrote It to Be Famous', 4 March 2001: 13.
'An Unorthodox Eastender', 11 March 2001: 13.

THE SUNDAY TIMES

'Devolution', 13 February 1977: 15.
'Nude Magazine Cover', 20 February 1977: 32.
'Candidate for Oxford Poetry Professorship', 23 April 1978.
'Travelling Hopefully', 10 August 1980: 31.
'Origins of the Poetic Species', 28 September 1980: 42.
'The Restoration of Rochester', 12 October 1980: 43 [*The Letters of John Wilmot, Earl of Rochester*, edited and introduced by Jeremy Treglown].
'Are You Sitting Comfortably?', 16 November 1980: 43.
'Facing Up to an Optical Illusion', 30 May 1982 [Peter Conrad, *Television: The Medium and Its Manners*].

'Gore Vidal vs. The Squirrel', 22 August 1982 [Gore Vidal, *Pink Triangle and Yellow Star*].

'Pangs of Accord', 10 October 1982 [Christopher Reid, *Pea Soup*].

'The Poetry Pioneers', 31 October 1982 [*The Penguin Book of Contemporary Verse*, edited by Blake Morrison and Andrew Motion].

'The Artist as Young Bard', 12 June 1983 [Dylan Thomas, *The Collected Stories*].

'A Companionable Critic', 24 July 1983 [D.J. Enright, *A Mania for Sentences*].

'A Diarist's Kiss of Death', 7 August 1983 [Edmund Wilson, *The Forties*].

'The Manhood of Mailer', 2 October 1983 [Hilary Mills, *Norman Mailer*; Norman Mailer, *Pieces and Pontifications*].

'The Shadows of the Salon', 9 October 1983 [Frederic Prokosch, *Voices* and *The Asiatics*].

'The Launching of Ulysses', 18 March 1984 [Noel Riley Fitch, *Sylvia Beach and the Lost Generation*].

'Steinbeck the Celebrity', 8 April 1984 [Jackson J. Benson, *The True Adventures of John Steinbeck*].

'Georges Simenon and the Women', 2 September 1984 [Georges Simenon, *Intimate Memoirs*].

'Kazin's Critical Chats', 6 January 1985 [Alfred Kazin, *An American Procession*].

'The Legend of Scott and Zelda', 17 February 1985 [James R. Mellow, *Invented Lives: F. Scott and Zelda Fitzgerald*].

'Philip Larkin 1922-1985: An Appreciation by Ian Hamilton and a Poem Written by Larkin in 1981', 8 December 1985.

'Mr Bones and the Psychic Voyager', 4 February 1990 [John Berryman, *Collected Poems 1937-71* and *The Dream Songs*].

'The Grapes of Wrath', 18 February 1990.

'A Damned Serious Affair', 4 March 1990; reprinted as 'Wallace Stevens' in *Walking Possession*, 1994: 150-153 [*Opus Posthumous by Wallace Stevens*, edited by Milton J. Bates].

'All Singing, All Dancing', 4 February 1996.

'Nothing to Declare but Her Genius', 7 April 1996 [Phillip Herring, *Djuna: The Life and Works of Djuna Barnes*].

'Getting to Grips with the Words', 17 March 1996 [John Irving, *The Imaginary Girlfriend: A Memoir*].

'That Was the Year That Was', 9 June 1996.

'The One-Track Mind', 6 May 2001.

THUMBSCREW

'The Buried Life: Elizabeth Bishop', 2, 1995: 30-42.

THE TIMES

'How Well Have They Worn? – 12: *The Catcher in the Rye*', 24 March 1966.

'Signs for Southend United FC', 4 September 1968: 13.

'The Little Magazines', 13 September 1976: 8.

'Cleared of Negligence over Aircraft Crash', 25 June 1976: 2.

'The Cult of Celebrity', 11 August 1985.

'The Book and the Box: A Conversation Between Ian Hamilton and Melvyn Bragg', 29 December 1985.

'All Our Yesterdays', 8 June 1996; reprinted as 'All Our Yesterdays: Remembering the 1966 World Cup' in *The Trouble with Money*, 1998: 209-214.

'Just Mad About the Boy', 18 May 1998.

THE TIMES LITERARY SUPPLEMENT

'New Names, Old Hat', 3222, 28 November 1963: 995 [*New Poems: A PEN Anthology of Con-*

temporary Poetry, edited by Lawrence Durrell].

'Artful Make-Up', 3238, 19 March 1964: 228 [Daniel Hoffmann, *The City of Satisfactions*; Alan Dugan, *Poems 2*; Sandra Hochman, *Manhattan Pastures*].

'In Military Terms', 3238, 19 March 1964: 228.

'Crime and Merriment', 3242, 16 April 1964: 305 [Michael Baldwin, *A Mouthful of Gold*].

'Other New Novels', 3242, 16 April 1964: 305 [Michael Campbell, *The Princess in England*; Corinna Cochrane, *The Turning Point*; J.A. Michener, *Caravans*].

'Syllables Under Stress', 3243, 23 April 1964: 344 [B.S. Johnson, *Poems*; Phillip Callow, *Turning Point*; Keith Wright, *Western Time*].

'No Ideas but in Things', 3245, 7 May 1964: 396 [William Carlos Williams, *Pictures from Breuguel and Other Poems*; Elder Olson: *Collected Poems*; William Dickey, *Interpreter's House*].

'Rustic and Urbane', 3260, 20 August 1964: 748 [James Dickey, *Helmets*; John Updike, *Telephone Poles*; Blas de Otero, *Twenty Poems*].

'One Man's River', 3263, 10 September 1964: 842 [William Carlos Williams, *Paterson*, Books 1-V].

'At the Heel of the Hunt', 3269, 22 October 1964: 960 [Thomas Blackburn, *A Breathing Space*; Brian Guinness, *The Rose in the Tree*].

'Soft Finger', 3270, 29 October 1964: 980 [James Dickey, *The Suspect in Poetry*].

'Uplift in Old Sustainers', 3270, 29 October 1964: 980 [Richard Eberhart, *The Quarry*; M.L. Rosenthal, *Blue Boy on Skates*].

'Poetry Puts Ox to Rights', 3289, 11 March 1965: 196 [Marianne Moore, *The Arctic Ox*; David Ignatow, *Figures of the Human*; Oscar Williams, *Selected Poems*].

'Sweating It Out', 3323, 4 November 1965: 982 [I.M. Parsons, *Men Who March Away: Poems of the First World War*].

'Hot Money', 3324, 11 November 1965: 1003.

'Songs Among the Ruins', 3326, 25 November 1965: 1068 [reprinted in *A Poetry Chronicle*, 1973: 11-18].

'Dutiful Heirs', 3329, 16 December 1965: 1179.

'Periodical Studies', 3334, 20 January 1966: 63.

'Any Questions', 3339, 24 February 1966: 143.

'One Man's Worship', 3340, 3 March 1966: 167.

'A Machine & Sympathy', 3342, 17 March 1966: 223.

'Well-Bred', 3342, 17 March 1966: 224.

'Ps & Qs', 3349, 5 May 1966: 387.

'Now Read In', 3350, 12 May 1966: 387.

'Ancestral Figure', 3353, 2 June 1966: 496 [*Adam*, No. 300, edited by Miron Grindea].

'Speak Easy', 3353, 2 June 1966: 494.

'The Hungry Writer', 3355, 16 June 1966: 496.

'Dreams and Responsibilities', 3357, 30 June 1966: 555.

'The Days of the Calendar', 3360, 21 July 1966: 635.

'Poet Zoo', 3364, 18 August 1966: 743.

'Off Campus', 3370, 29 September 1966: 899.

'The Panel Game', 3373, 20 October 1966: 959.

'The Panel Game, II', 3376, 10 November 1966: 1023.

'The Shock of Recognition', 3379, 1 December 1966: 1116 [Peter Fryer, *Private Cases – Public Scandal*; Lenny Bruce, *How to Talk Dirty and Influence People*; Siné, *Massacre*].

'Doggerel in a Manger', 3382, 22 December 1966: 1189.

'Objectionable', 3388, 2 February 1967: 87.

'Macbird', 3389, 9 February 1967: 107.

'On the Shelf: Poetry in the Public Library', 3393, 9 March 1967: 177.

'Responsibilities', 3395, 23 March 1967: 243.

'Poetry in Mss', 3400, 27 April 1967: 357.

'Foul Play?', 3400, 27 April 1967: 357.

'The Dons Have It', 3403, 18 May 1967: 419.

'Gone with the Wind', 3405, 1 June 1967: 485 [Brigid Brophy, Michael Levey, Charles Osborne,

Fifty Writers We Could Do Without].
'Visualizing', 3405, 1 June 1967: 487.
'Poetry International', 3410, 6 July 1967: 599.
'Limits of Literature', 3413, 27 July 1967: 651.
Editorial, 3413, 27 July 1967: 672.
Editorial, 3423, 5 October 1967: 938.
'Uncollected', 3439, 25 January 1968: 85.
'Public Relations', 3448, 28 March 1968: 317.
'The Little Magazine – IV: *The Criterion*', 3452, 25 April 1968: 430 [reprinted as 'The Straight and Narrow' in *The Little Magazines*, 1976: 67-80].
'TLS6', 3456, 23 May 1968: 529.
'Ten Per Centers', 3463, 11 July 1968: 729.
'Mincing Words', 3465, 25 July 1968: 767.
'Picture Books', 3471, 9 September 1968: 945.
'Plugging the Gaps', 3473, 19 September 1968: 1051.
'Poor Relations', 3477, 17 October 1968: 1251.
'T.S. Eliot and the *TLS*', 3480, 7 November 1968: 1251.
'Many Thanks', 3487, 26 December 1968: 1455.
'Penguin 3000', 3504, 24 April 1969: 438.
'Between Mammon and the Muse', 3517, 24 July 1969: 791.
'Packaged for Gluesville', 3517, 24 July 1969: 808 [Mario Puzo, *The Godfather*, Norman Bogner, *The Madonna Complex*].
'Fools Rush In', 3520, 14 August 1969: 897 [Barbara Skelton, *A Love Match*].
'Altering the Modes of Consciousness: The Ecstatic, Infinite Idealism of Hart Crane', 3527, 2 October 1969: 1117 [*The Complete Poems and Selected Prose and Letters of Hart Crane*, edited by Brom Weber; R.W. Butterfield, *The Broken Arc: A Study of Hart Crane*].
'Cut Short', 3532, 6 November 1969: 1273 [V.S. Pritchett, *Blind Love and Other Stories*].
'Little Magazines in Reprint: the Profits of Patronage', 3546, 12 February 1970: 177.
'Surviving Most Subtilly', 3578, 25 September 1970: 1075 [Dan Jacobson, *The Rape of Tamar*].
'The Poet at Home', 3578, 25 September 1970: 1075 [Roy Fuller, *The Carnal Island*].
'On Not Rocking the Boat', 3581, 16 October 1970: 1183 [John Updike, *Bech: A Book*].
'Ireland Intensified', 3587, 27 November 1970: 1378 [John McGahern, *Nightlines*].
'A Mouthful of Blood', 3593, 8 January 1971: 8; reprinted as 'Ted Hughes: *Crow*' in *A Poetry Chronicle*, 1973: 165-170.
'Leisurely Ways', 3596, 29 January 1971: 113 [Anthony West, *David Rees Among Others*].
'Incestuous Undertones', 3599, 19 February 1971: 207 [*Wagner Literary Magazine*, Nos. 1-4; *Angel Hair*, Nos. 106; *Neon*, Nos. 1-4; *Folder*, 1-4; *City Lights Journal*, Nos. 1-2; *The San Francisco Earthquake*, Vol. 1: 1967-1968].
'Interment of the Intellectual', 3599, 19 February 1971: 206 [*Poetry London*, 5 Volumes; *Art and Letters, July 1917 to Spring 1920*].
'The Talented Miss Highsmith', 3630, 24 September 1971: 1147.
'Nowhere to Go', 3632, 8 October 1971: 1199 [V.S. Naipaul, *In a Free State*].
'Viewpoint', 3676, 11 August 1972: 658.
'Viewpoint', 3683, 6 October 1972: 194.
'Viewpoint', 3706, 16 March 1973: 294.
'Viewpoint', 3718, 8 June 1973: 642.
'Turnstile Press', 3772, 27 June 1974: 669.
'Fiction and the Voting Public' (as 'Edward Pygge'), 3787, 4 October 1974: 1076.
Editorial, 3826, 11 July 1975: 760.
'The Call of the Cool', 4138, 23 July 1982: 782 [Thom Gunn, *The Passages of Joy* and *The Occasions of Poetry*].
'Among the Muckers', 4154, 12 November 1982: 1243 [*Short Stories from the Second World War*, edited by Dan Davin].
'Heading for a Showdown', 4252, 28 September 1984: 1076 [John Pikoulis, *Alun Lewis: A Life*].
'Dense But Democratic', 4260, 23 November 1984: 1348 [*Raritan*].

'Striving and Stranded', 19 August 1988; reprinted as 'Jean Stafford' in *Walking Possession*, 1994: 22-26 [David Roberts, *Jean Stafford: A Biography*].

'Posing on a Titghtrope', 4480, 10 February 1989: 131 [Michael Shelden, *Friends of Promise: Cyril Connolly and the World of* Horizon].

'A Talent of the Shallows', 4511, 15 September 1989: 999; reprinted as 'Richard Wilbur' in *Walking Possession*, 1994: 117-122 [Richard Wilbur, *New & Collected Poems*].

'Bonny Prince Charlatan', 4522, 17 December 1989: 1335 [*Tambimuttu: A Bridge Between Two Worlds*, edited by Jane Williams].

'Changing to Neutral', 4633, 17 January 1992: 18-19 [IH recalls his years as poetry and fiction editor at the *TLS* for the paper's 90th anniversary issue].

'Mocking the Meat It Feeds on', 4657, 3 July 1992: 21 [Robert Altman's film, 'The Player'].

'Self's the Man', 4696, 2 April 1993: 3-4; reprinted as 'Philip Larkin: 3. The Biography' in *Walking Possession*, 1994: 137-145; and reprinted again in *The Trouble with Money*, 1998: 321-329 [Andrew Motion, *Philip Larkin: A Writer's Life*].

'The Embarrassing Pursuit', 4752, 29 April 1994: 16-18 [IH discusses his research for *Robert Lowell: A Biography*.

'Edmund Wilson's Wounds', 4830, 27 October 1995: 4-5; reprinted in *The Trouble with Money*: 31-39 [Jeffrey Meyers, *Edmund Wilson: A Biography*; *From the Uncollected Edmund Wilson*, selected and introduced by David Castronovo].

'The Road Not Taken', 4891, 27 December 1996: 24 [Keith Ovenden, *A Fighting Withdrawal: The Life of Dan Davin: Writer, Soldier, Publisher*].

'"These are Damned Times"', 11 July 1997; reprinted as 'Arnold's Letters, Finally' in *The Trouble with Money*, 1998: 180-192 [*The Letters of Matthew Arnold, Vol. Two: 1860-1865*, edited by Cecil Y. Lang].

'Dreaming On Down Under', 5060, 24 March 2000: 36 [Patricia Dobrez, *Michael Dransfield's Lives*].

'Some Splintered Garland', 5085, 15 September 2000: 6-7 [Paul Mariani, *The Broken Tower: The Life of Hart Crane*; *The Complete Poems of Hart Crane*, edited by Marc Simon].

'Holding On', 9-15 October 2000; reprinted as 'Andrew Motion' in *Walking Possession*, 1994: 162-165 [Andrew Motion, *Natural Causes*].

VANITY FAIR

'What Made Salinger So Mad?', 51:5, May 1988: 158-168 [Excerpt from *In Search of J.D. Salinger*].

VOGUE

'The Secret History', 1994 [Jan Marsh, *Christina Rossetti: A Writer's Life*].

'Chunnel Vision', 185:3, March 1995: 286-290; reprinted as 'Chunnel Crossing' in *The Trouble with Money*, 1998: 243-249.

WASHINGTON POST BOOK WORLD

'James Merrill and the Spirit of Poetry', 27 March 1983: 8; reprinted as 'James Merrill' in *Walking Possession*, 1994: 146-149 [James Merrill, *The Changing Light at Sandover; From the First Nine*; and *James Merrill: Essays in Criticism*, edited by David Lehman and Charles Berger].

'At the Right Place at the Right Time', 19 February 1984: 3 [*H.D. Collected Poems 1912-1944*, edited by Louis L. Martz; Barbara Guest, *Herself Defined: The Poet H.D. and Her World*].

'Portrait of the Poet as a Letter Writer', 4 May 1986: 1 [Dylan Thomas: *The Collected Letters*, edited by Paul Ferris].

'The Indian Summer of Edmund Wilson', 14 September 1986: X5 [Edmund Wilson, *The Fifties:*

From Notebooks and Diaries of the Period, edited by Leon Edel].

MAGAZINES EDITED

The Scorpion, 1955 [2 issues].

Tomorrow, 1959-1960 [4 issues].

The Review, 1962-1972 [30 issues].

The New Review, 1974-1979 [50 issues].

TELEVISION SHOWS HOSTED

Bookmark, BBC TV, 1984-1987
(AN ASTERISK INDICATES THAT IH INTERVIEWED AND SCRIPTED THE FILM OR STUDIO ITEM.)

9 September 1984: Martin Amis, T.S. Eliot*, Agatha Christie
24 October 1984: J.G. Ballard*, Seamus Heaney*, D.H. Lawrence
21 November 1984: Virginia Woolf, James Baldwin
19 December 1984: Mirror Poetry (Kingsley Amis), Dr. Johnson, Mark Twain
21 January 1985: Alison Lurie*, Austin, Texas, Ezra Pound*
20 February 1985: Rosamond Lehmann, John Cheever, Edward Fitzgerald*
20 March 1985: The Tenth Man, A Passage to India, Richardson's Pamela*
17 April 1985: Dorothy Wordsworth, Esperanto, Stratis Haviaras
22 May 1985: Keith Douglas*, Mario Vargas Llosa
26 September 1985: Italo Calvino*, Simon Gray*, Clive Sinclair*
17 October 1985: Primo Levi, Koestler Awards (Prison Writing)
14 November 1985: V.S. Pritchett*, Miss Read, Grace Paley*
19 December 1985: Roald Dahl, Shirley Hughes, Janni Howker
16 January 1986: Angus Wilson*, H.R.F. Keating, Simon Burt
13 February1986: J.M. O'Neill, Margaret Forster, R.S. Thomas*
13 March 1986: Ruth Rendell, William Trevor*, Edmund White
10 April 1986: Dannie Abse*
8 May 1986: A. Alvarez, Timothy Mo*, S-Z Dictionary
2 October 1986: A.N. Wilson*, Joseph Brodsky
30 October 1986: Jonathan Raban, Joseph Skvorecky*, Ted Albeury
31 October 1986: Fay Weldon Special
27 November 1986: James Clavell, George Lamming
8 January 1987: Peter Reading*, Pat Barker, Kazuo Ishiguro*
5 February 1987: Nurrudin Farah, Don Mattera
5 March 1987: Spalding Gray, Peter Taylor*
7 May 1987: Yorkshire Ripper, Melvyn Bragg, Christine Brooke-Rose

OTHER TELEVISION AND RADIO APPEARANCES

New Release, 16 February 1967, 'The Film of the Book' [About publication of a first novel].
Omnibus, George Orwell, 10 January 1970, BBC TV [IH interviewed about George Orwell].

162

Books and Writers, 22 June 1970, BBC Radio [IH interviewed about his new collection of poems, *The Visit*].
The Living Poet, 16 March 1970, BBC Third Programme [IH introduces and reads a selection of his poems].
Second House, 5 January 1974, BBC TV [Melvyn Bragg profile of John Fuller, including interview with IH].
Kaleidoscope, 5 April 1974, BBC Radio [IH interviewed about the aims of *The New Review*].
Second House, 20 April 1974, BBC TV [IH interviewed about *The New Review*].
Bookmark, 28 September 1983, BBC TV [IH previews the six novels nominated for the Booker Prize].
Omnibus, 'The Other Side of Paradise', 5 November 1985 [IH scripts and presents a 50' documentary on F. Scott Fitzgerald].
Poetry Please, 23 January 1994, BBC Radio 4 [IH introduces a selection of listeners' requests for American poetry].
Bookmark, 'Lifers', 9 March 1996, BBC TV [IH interviewed about J.D. Salinger biography and biography in general].
Night Waves, 11 March 1998, BBC Radio 3 [IH talks to Tony Palmer about *A Gift Imprisoned: The Poetic Life of Matthew Arnold*].
Critic!, 12 April 1998, BBC, Radio 3 [Tom Paulin and Ian Hamilton discuss William Hazlitt and Matthew Arnold].
Twenty Minutes, 'Against Oblivion', 22 March 2000, BBC Radio 3 [IH on Charlotte Mew and Hart Crane (adapted from his book, *Against Oblivion: Some Lives of the 20th Century Poets*)].
Twenty Minutes, 'Against Oblivion', 24 March 2000, BBC Radio 3 [IH on Norman Cameron and Weldon Kees (adapted from his book, *Against Oblivion: Some Lives of the 20th Century Poets*)].

INTERVIEWS

'Four Conversations: Thom Gunn, Philip Larkin, Christopher Middleton and Charles Tomlinson', *London Magazine*, 4:8, 4 November 1964: 64-85.
'A Conversation with Edgell Rickword', *The Review*, 11-12, The Thirties – A Special Number, August 1964: 17-21.
'A Conversation with Claud Cockburn', *The Review*, 11-12, The Thirties – A Special Number, August, 1964: 51-53.
'A Conversation with Edward Upward', *The Review*, 11-12, The Thirties – A Special Number, August 1964: 65-67.
'A Conversation with James Reeves', *The Review*, 11-12, The Thirties – A Special Number, August 1964: 68-70.
'A Conversation with Geoffrey Grigson', *The Review*, 22, June 1970: 15-26.
'A Conversation with Stephen Spender', *The Review*, 23, September-November 1970: 19-32.
'A Conversation with Alan Ross', *The Review*, 25, Spring 1971: 39-50.
'A Conversation with Robert Lowell', *The Review*, 25, Summer 1971: 10-29; reprinted in *Modern Occasions*, 2:1, Winter 1972: 28-48; reprinted in *American Poetry Review*, 7, September-October 1978: 23-27; reprinted in *Robert Lowell: Interviews and Memoirs*, edited by Jeffrey Meyers, University of Michigan Press, Ann Arbor, Michigan, 1988.
'Going Public', *The New Review*, 3:33, December 1976: 31-37 [An interview with Clive James].
'Simon Gray in Conversation with Ian Hamilton', *The New Review*, 3:34/35, January-February 1977: 39-46.
'Patricia Highsmith Talks to Ian Hamilton', *The New Review*, 4:41, August 1977: 31-36.
'Dan Jacobson Talks to Ian Hamilton', *The New Review*, 4:43, October 1977: 25-29.
'Melvyn Bragg Talks to Ian Hamilton', *The New Review*, 4:44, November 1977: 3-11.
'Goodbye to All That', *The New Review*, 4:48, March 1978: 11-18 [An interview with Al Alvarez].

'Points of Departure', *The New Review*, 5:2, Autumn 1978: 9-21 [An interview with Ian McEwan].
'Without a Place: V.S. Naipaul in Conversation with Ian Hamilton', *Times Literary Supplement*, 7 July 1971: 897-898; reprinted as 'Without a Place: V.S. Naipaul Interviewed' in *Savacou: A Journal of the Caribbean Artists' Movement*, 1974: 9-10, 120-126; and reprinted under its original title in *Conversations with V. S. Naipaul*, edited and introduced by Feroza Jussawalla (University Press of Mississippi, Jackson, Mississippi, 1997: 14-21).
'Ian Hamilton Talks to Philip Roth about the Confusions of Life and Fiction', *The Sunday Times*, 19 February 1984.
'Poet of Unhappiness', 23 September 1984 [An interview with Peter Ackroyd].
'A Confusion of Realms: Interview with Philip Roth', *Nation*, 240, 1985: 679-681.
'Triumph of the Downside', *The Guardian*, 20 February 1999 [An interview with, and profile of, Peter Porter].

SECONDARY WORKS

BOOKS

Another Round at the Pillars: Essays, Poems and Reflections on Ian Hamilton, edited by David Harsent, with contributions from Julian Barnes, Blake Morrison, Al Alvarez, Andrew Motion, Harold Pinter, Peter Dale, Hugo Williams, Douglas Dunn, Karly Miller, Alan Jenkins, David Harsent, Christopher Reid, Ian McEwan, Craig Raine, Dan Jacobson, Simon Gray, Peter Porter, Michael Hofmann, John Fuller, Charles Osborne, Michael Fried, Clive James and Colin Falck (Cargo Press, Tregarne, 1999).

ARTICLES / ESSAYS / ENTRIES

Falck, Colin, 'The State of Poetry – a Symposium', *The Review*, 29-30, Spring-Summer 1972: 70-73.
'Hamilton, (Robert) Ian, 1938-', *Contemporary Authors*, Vol. 106, Gale Research, Detroit, Michigan, 1982: 223-224.
Cookson, William, 'Ian Hamilton (24 March 1938-)', *Dictionary of Literary Biography*, 40, Gale Research, Detroit, Michigan, 1985.
Wiloch, Thomas, 'Hamilton, (Robert) Ian, 1938-', *Contemporary Authors*, New Revision Series, Vol. 41, Gale Research, Detroit, Michigan, 1994: 198-200.
Maldive, Pierre, 'Hamilton, Ian (1938-)', *The Oxford Companion to 20th Century Poetry*, edited by Ian Hamilton (OUP, Oxford, 1996).
Sedgwick, Fred, 'Hamilton, (Robert) Ian', *Contemporary Poets*, edited by Thomas Riggs, St James Press, Detroit, Michigan, 1996: 435-436.
Williams, Hugo, 'Freelance', *Times Literary Supplement*, 4960, 24 April 1998: 16.
Williams, Hugo, 'Mr. Write', *Esquire*, May 1998: 192-193.
'Hamilton, (Robert) Ian, 1938', *Contemporary Authors*, New Revision Series, Vol. 67, 1998: 195-198.
Dale, Peter, 'Oxford Poetry: Ian Hamilton', *Oxford Today*, Michaelmas Issue, 2001: 54.

TELEVISION PROGRAMMES

Ian Hamilton: A Writing Life, BBC 4, 8 May 2002 [Producer, Patricia Wheatley].

INTERVIEWS

Horder, John, 'The Poetaster Turned Poet', *Guardian*, 5 June 1970: Arts, 8. [This bibliography does not include published letters from, to, or concerning IH; however, it seems only right to point out that he so thoroughly disapproved of Horder's piece that he sent *The Guardian* a letter, the crucial part of which reads as follows: 'The seven paragraphs which purport to quote me verbatim so grotesquely misrepresent what I in fact said to Mr Horder that it would take me at least as much space to set the record straight. I must therefore repudiate the document in its entirety.']

'A Conversation with Ian Hamilton', *American Poetry Review*, 7:5, September–October 1978: 23-27. [Reprinted from *The Review*, 1971, and *Modern Occasions*, 1972].

Weatherby, W.J., '"The 24-Hour a Day Poet": Ian Hamilton Talks to W.J. Weatherby About His Life of Robert Lowell', *Guardian*, 16 December 1982: 10.

Stead, D., 'Guilty Five Times a Week', *New York Times Book Review*, May 1990: 2.

Dale, Peter, 'Ian Hamilton in Conversation with Peter Dale', *Agenda*, 31:2, Summer 1993: 7-21.

LeStage, Greg, 'Pick Me Flowers for Vietnam', *Poetry Review*, 87:4, 1997: 28-32.

Cambridge, Gerry, *The Dark Horse*, 3, 1997.

REVIEWS

BOOKS

POETRY

PRETENDING NOT TO SLEEP (1964)

Alvarez, A., *Observer*, 20 December 1964.

Ricks, Christopher, *New Statesman*, 15 January 1965.

Hobsbaum, Philip, 'New Poetry', BBC Third Programme, produced by George MacBeth, broadcast 16 January 1965.

Dale, Peter, 'Book Reviews', *Agenda*, 4:1, April-May 1965: 49-52.

Howard, Richard, *Poetry* (Chicago), June 1967.

THE VISIT (1970)

Bookseller, 21 February 1970.

Dodsworth, Martin, 'A Painful Shot in the Arm', *Observer*, 31 May 1970: Review, 30.

Fuller, John, 'The Larger Deception', *Listener*, 4 June 1970.

Brownjohn, Alan, 'Present Tense', *New Statesman*, 12 June 1970: 844.

Lloyd Evans, Barbara, 'Poetry Today: Are Contemporary Poets Dodos or Phoenixes?', *Birmingham Post*, 6 June 1970.

Ehrenpreis, Irvin, 'Moments of Suffocation', *Times Literary Supplement*, 3566, 2 July 1970: 703.

Porter, Peter, 'Restraint or Prodigality', *Guardian*, 2 July 1970: 9.

Jay, David, 'Surface Calm', *Times Educational Supplement*, 3 July 1970.

Fried, Michael, 'Strictly Personal', *Spectator*, 22 August 1970: 187.

Dale, Peter, 'The Poetry of Ian Hamilton', *Agenda*, 9:1, Winter 1971: 38-44.

Fifty Poems (1988)

de Jongh, Nicholas, 'A Gamekeeper's Bag', *Guardian*, 21 January 1988.

Mackinnon, Lachlan, *Times Literary Supplement*, 4426, 29 January 1988: 115.

Jenkins, Alan, 'Hand to mouth', *Observer*, 31 January 1988.

Billington, Rachel, 'Poetry in Motion', *Financial Times*, 20 February 1988.

Profumo, David, *Sunday Times*, 21 February 1988: G10.

Morrison, Blake, 'Every Three Years', *London Review of Books*, 10:5, 3 March 1988: 13-14.

Jennings, Elizabeth, 'Occasional Verse', *Independent,* 17 March, 1988.
Dunn, Douglas, 'Caribbean Beat', *Punch,* 25 March 1988: 47.
Hofmann, Michael, 'An Oriental Air', *New Statesman,* 25 March 1988: 28.
Abse Dannie, 'Poet As His own Critic', *Evening Standard,* 7 April 1988.
Booth, Martin, 'Transcending the Pain', *Tribune,* 22 April 1988.
Eagleton, Terry, 'Poetry Chronicle', *Stand,* Spring 1990.
Surple, John, 'Ian Hamilton', *Agenda,* 31:2, Summer 1993: 107-111.

Steps (1997)

Sansom, Ian, *Poetry Review,* 87:4, 1997: 32.
Gregson, I., *Stand,* 39:3, Summer 1998: 47.

Sixty Poems (1998)

Sanderson, Mark, 'A Hard Man to Please', *Sunday Telegraph,* 18 April 1999: Review, 12.
Greenlaw, Lavinia, 'Heads Off', *New Statesman,* 26 April 1999: 47.
Brownjohn, Alan, 'A Hard Act', *Sunday Times,* 9 May 1999: Art and Books, 10.
Waling, Steven, *City Life (What's on in Manchester),* 26 May 1999: 55.
Kellaway, Kate, 'Who Turned the Page?', *Prospect,* May 1999: 65.
Murray, Nicholas, 'Brief but Feelingful', *Times Literary Supplement,* 5018, 4 June 1999: 25.
Spivey, Nigel, 'Lest the Tribute Turn to Gush', *Daily Telegraph,* 12 June 1999: Arts & Books, 4.
Campbell-Johnston, Rachel, 'Poetry of the Month', *Times,* 31 July 1999: Metro, 18.

PROSE

THE POETRY OF WAR *1939-45* (1965)

Furbank, N., 'Poets in Battledress', *Guardian,* 19 November 1965.
Wall, Stephen, 'Rigours of War', *Listener,* 2 December 1965: 912-913.
Jennings, Elizabeth, 'War and Peace', *Spectator,* 31 December 1965: 868-869.
Read, Herbert, 'Selected Books', *London Magazine,* 5:9, December 1965: 75-78.
'Alvarez, A., 'Up-to-Date Aesthete', *Observer,* 2 January 1966.
Carey, John, 'Quiet Voices', *New Statesman,* 18 February 1966.
Times Literary Supplement, 10 March 1966: 186-188.

ALUN LEWIS: SELECTED POETRY AND PROSE (1966)

Alvarez, A., 'Poets on the Battlefield', *Observer,* 13 November 1966.
Cox, C.B., 'Poets at War', *Spectator,* 18 November 1966: 654.
Carey, John, 'Keith Douglas and Alun Lewis', *New Statesman,* 18 November 1966: 745.
Graham, Martin, 'A Human Scale', 1 December 1966: 816, 818.
'Poetry of Hitler's War', *Times,* 1 December 1966.
Symons, Julian, 'Simplified by Death', *Times Literary Supplement,* 3379, 1 December 1966.
Burgess, Anthony, 'War and the Wheatsheaf', *Sunday Times,* 18 December 1966.
Fuller, Roy, 'Alun Lewis & His Place', *Encounter,* 28:4, April 1967: 72-73.

THE MODERN POET: ESSAYS FROM 'THE REVIEW' (1969)

Potter, Dennis, 'Poets Squatting Round the Mat', *Times,* 25 January 1969.

Bergonzi, Bernard, 'Critical Condition', *New Society*, 30 January 1969.
Symons, Julian, 'Detectives of the Spurious', *Times Literary Supplement*, 3492, 30 January 1969.
Donoghue, Denis, 'Satisfaction', *Listener*, 6 February 1969.
Thwaite, Anthony, 'Pygge's Pokes', *New Statesman*, 7 February 1969.
Toynbee, Philip, 'Back to the Fountain-Head', *Observer*, 23 February 1969.
Kavanagh, P.J., 'The Modern Critic', *Guardian*, March 1969.
Seymour-Smith, Martin, 'Lament for the Makers', *Spectator*, 12 July 1969.
Barfoot, C.C., 'Reviews – Literature', *DQR: The Dutch Quarterly Review of Anglo-American Letters*, 1:2, 1971: 107-109.

A Poetry Chronicle: Essays and Reviews (1973)

Fenton, James, 'Against the Tide', *New Statesman*, 12 January 1973: 59-60.
Dodsworth, Martin, 'What's Good is Well-Made', *Times Literary Supplement*, 3707, 23 March 1973.
Fuller, Roy, 'Who Needs a Poetry Reviewer?', *Encounter*, 40, May 1973: 72.
Stanford, Derek, *Books and Bookmen*, June 1973.
Choice: Current Reviews for Academic Libraries, February 1974: 1866.
Davie, Donald, *Poetry Nation*, 2, 1974: 72-80.

Robert Frost: Selected Poems (1973)

Wright, C., 'Bad and Best', *Times Literary Supplement*, 3737, 19 October 1973.

The Little Magazines (1976)

James, Clive, 'Hamilton Academicals', *Observer*, 29 August 1976: 22.
Lewis, Jeremy, 'Seeing the Light', *Times*, 13 September 1976.
de Jongh, Nicholas, 'Small Wonders', *Guardian*, 17 September 1976.
Gransden, K.W., 'Ten-Year Sentences', *Listener*, 23 September 1976: 381.
Bradbury, Malcolm, 'The Shock Troops of Modernism', *Times Literary Supplement*, 3892, 15 October 1976: 1297-1298.
Freeman, John, 'Reviews', *Anglo-Welsh Review*, 26:59, Autumn 1977: 74-77.
Bergonzi, Bernard, *Modern Language Studies*, 74, 1979: 932-933.

Robert Lowell: A Biography (1982; 1983)

Davison, Peter, 'Robert Lowell's Terrible Heroism', *Boston Globe*, 11 July 1982: B10, B12.
Kirkus Reviews, 1 October 1982.
'Robert Lowell: A Biography', *Publishers Weekly*, 15 October 1982: 51.
Hunter, William B., Jr., 'The Waste of Robert Lowell', *Houston Chronicle*, 1 November 1982.
Shapiro, Karl, 'Exploring the Myth and Psyche of Robert Lowell', *Chicago Tribune, Bookworld*, 7 November 1982: 1-2.
Maddocks, Melvin, 'Wild Man', *Time*, 8 November 1982: K20, K24.
Sachs, Lloyd, 'A Mad Art Beyond Revenge', *Chicago Sun Times*, 14 November 1982: 25.
Spender, Stephen, 'Life Studies in Poetry, History and Madness', *Washington Post Book World*, 14 November 1982: 1, 9.
Booklist, 15 November 1982.
Strouse, Jean, 'A Life of Lord Weary', *Newsweek*, 15 November 1982: 105.
Stone, Laurie, 'Genius at Work: Some Kinds of Love', *Village Voice*, 16 November 1982: 1, 43-46.

O'Neill, Catherine, 'Revealing Shadows Hovered Over Poet', *USA Today*, 19 November 1982.

Davis, Patricia, 'Who Was That Poet?', *San Diego Union*, 21 November 1982.

Merritt, Robert, 'Passionate Poet, Tormented Man', *Richmond Times* (Virginia), 21 November 1982.

Schapiro, Nancy, '"From Lout to Man of Sensibility"', *St. Louis Post-Dispatch*, 21 November 1982.

Ellmann, Richard, *New York Times Book Review*, 28 November 1982: 1, 14.

Seidenbaum, Art, 'Poetry Plus Pain in an Outsized and Wondrous Balance', *Los Angeles Times*, 28 November 1982: Book Review, 2.

Whitman, Alden, 'Robert Lowell: A Poet in Pain', *Dallas News*, 28 November 1982.

Koenig, Rhoda, 'Loves of a Poet', *New York*, 29 November 1982: 76-77.

Rovit, Earl, 'Book Review: Literature', *Library Journal*, 107, 1 December 1982: 2258.

Vendler, Helen, 'American Poet', *New York Review of Books*, 2 December 1982: 3-5.

Howes, Victor, 'A Poet's Contradictory Life', *Christian Science Monitor*, 3 December 1982: B4.

Duhamel, P. Albert, 'Lowell's Tragic Life', *Boston Herald*, 5 December 1982.

Mott, Michael, 'Lowell Biography Begs Question of Risk, Art', *Baltimore Sun*, 5 December 1982. *New York Times*, 5 December 1982: 16.

Staten Island Advance, 5 December 1982.

Walters, Colin, 'Poetic Agonies, Ecstasy', *Washington Times*, 7 December 1982: 2C, 15C.

Lehmann-Haupt, Christopher, 'Books of the Times', *New York Times*, 9 December 1982: C25.

Starr, William, 'Notable Biographies', *State*, (Columbia, South Carolina), 12 December 1982.

Pettingell, Phoebe, 'On Poetry: Mad, Bad and Dangerous', *New Leader*, 13 December 1982: 24-25.

Basbanes, Nicholas, 'What's in a Name? Lot's, If It's Robert Lowell', *Worcester Gazette* (Massachussetts), 15 December 1982.

Torkelson, Lucile, 'Much Wrong with Lowell – But Not His Poetry', *Milwaukee Sentinel*, 17 December 1982.

Brochu, Pam Miller, 'Story of Lowell's High-Speed Life Sheds Light on Enduring Poetry', *Tribune & Herald* (Duluth), 19 December 1982: 10, 34.

Carson, Herbert L., 'Flawed Man and Anguished Poet', *Grand Rapids Michigan Press*, 19 December 1982.

Clark, Patricia, 'Poet's Gifts Were Considerable, but There Was a Flaw In the Motor', *Houston Post*, 19 December 1982: 22F.

King, Nina, 'What Price Poetic Glory?', *Newsday*, 19 December 1982.

Morin, Edward, 'Deteriorating Genius', *Detroit News*, 19 December 1982: 2-K.

Schott, Webster, 'Robert Lowell, Kamikaze Poet', *Plain Dealer* (Cleveland, Ohio), 19 December 1982: Books, 18-C.

Whitman, Alden, 'The Dark-Spirited Bard Who Was Called Caliban', *Los Angeles Herald Examiner*, 19 December 1982: F5-6.

Shaw, Jane, S., 'Robert Lowell: The Dark Side of Genius', *Business Week*, 20 December 1982: 8.

Lehmann-Haupt, Christopher, 'Poet Robert Lowell Subject of Biography', *Blade* (Toledo, Ohio), 26 December 1982.

Simon, John, 'Cursed and Blessed', *New Republic*, 3545, 27 December 1982: 29-32.

Wolcott, James, 'The Limits of Poetic License', *Harper's*, 265, December 1982: [52].

Cotter, James Finn, 'Robert Lowell', *America*, 148, 1-8 January 1983: 18-19.

Eder, Richard, 'Lowell's Poetry, Pain in Balance', *Indianapolis Star*, 2 January 1983.

Prescott, Peter S., 'The Best of a Middling Lot', *Newsweek*, 3 January 1983: 58.

Baskin, Bernard, 'Lowell: The Man Who Snubbed LBJ', *Hamilton Spectator* (Canada), 8 January 1983.

Brady, Charles A., 'Lowell Preferred to Be a Frog', *Buffalo News*, 9 January 1983.

Meece, Gary, 'Along a Trail of Victims', *Commercial Appeal* (Memphis, Tennessee), 9 January 1983: G3.

Secrest, Meryle, *Courier-Journal* (Louisville, Kentucky), 9 January 1983.

Seib, Kenneth, 'Biography of a Brilliant but Troubled Poet', *The Fresno Bee*, 9 January 1983: E4.

Gervais, Marty, 'Robert Lowell: The Full Story', *Windsor Star* (Canada), 15 January 1983: C9.

Paddock, Polly, 'Making Rhyme and Reason out of Lowell', *Observer* (Charlotte, North Carolina), 16 January 1983.
Zaller, Robert, 'The Poet as Connoisseur of Madness', *Miami Herald,* 16 January 1983.
Dunne, Michael, 'Study of Lowell: The Biography', *Tennesseean* (Nashville), 23 January 1983.
Overmyer, Janet, 'Lowell's Pathetic Genius Described', *Columbia Dispatch,* 28 January 1983.
Bond, Carolyn, 'Furies Muscled In', *Whig Standard Magazine,* 29 January 1983: 18.
Petersen, Donald, 'The Legacy of Robert Lowell', *New Criterion,* January 1983: 9-29.
Stern, Richard, 'Obsessed with Writing', *Chicago,* January 1983: 78-79.
Patton, Priscilla, 'A Candid Look at Robert Lowell', *Brian College Station Eagle* (Texas), 12 February 1983.
Evening Post (Charleston), 18 February 1983.
Rolfe, John, 'Lowell Book Probes Life of a Public Poet', *Telegram* (Portland, Maine), 20 February 1983.
McCabe, Bernard, 'The Luckiest Poet', *Nation,* 236, 26 February 1983: 246-248.
Adams, Phoebe-Lou, 'Short Reviews: Robert Lowell', *Atlantic Monthly,* 251:2, February 1983: 105.
Vogue, February 1983.
Lovering, Joseph, P., *Best Sellers* (University of Scranton, Pennsylvania), February 1983: 427.
Naiden, James, 'A Portrait of Robert Lowell', *Minneapolis Tribune,* 6 March 1983: 16G-17G.
Mallon, Thomas, 'CAL', *National Review,* 35, 18 March 1983: 333-334.
'Recent Arrivals', *Christian Century,* 26 March 1983.
Choice: Current Reviews for Academic Libraries, 20, March 1983: 984.
Shaw, Robert B., 'A Life Studied', *Inquiry,* March 1983: 35-36.
Tillinghast, Richard, 'The Life of Robert Lowell', *Boston Review,* March-April 1983.
Reynolds, Stanley, 'Boston Strangler', *Punch,* 4 May 1983.
Kazin, Alfred, 'The Case History of Cal', *Times Literary Supplement,* 4179, 6 May 1983: 447-448.
Alvarez, A., 'Expense of Spirit', *Observer,* 8 May 1983: 30.
Carey, John, 'The Sport of a Mad Master', *Sunday Times,* 8 May 1983: 45.
Grigson, Geoffrey, 'Scarcely a Poet', *Standard* (London), 11 May 1983: 14.
Adcock, Fleur, 'The Cal Story', *New Society,* 12 May 1983: 236.
Jennings, Elizabeth, 'Most Gifted Poet', *Telegraph,* 12 May 1983.
Ratcliffe, Michael, 'Seriously Crazy Times', *Times,* 12 May 1983.
Shrimpton, Nicholas, 'I Was a Reincarnation of the Holy Ghost', *Listener,* 12 May 1983: 22-23.
Lucas, John, 'Lord Weary', *New Statesman,* 13 May 1983: 25-26.
Thwaite, Anthony, 'Madness and Authority', *Spectator,* 14 May 1983: 21.
Miller, Karl, 'Some Names for Robert Lowell', *London Review of Books,* 5:9, 19 May-2 June 1983: 7-10.
'Public Property', *Economist,* 287, 21 May 1983: 113.
Williams, Hugo, 'Lowell Life', *Tatler,* May 1983: 129-130.
Hecht, Anthony, 'Le Byron de Nos Jours', *Grand Street,* 2, Spring 1983: 32-48.
'Robert Lowell: A Biography', *Antioch Review,* 41:2, Spring 1983: 250.
Gowrie, Grey, 'Poor Passing Facts', *Literary Review,* 61, July 1983: 2-4.
Harmon, William, 'Analysts or Annalists', *Kenyon Review,* 5:3, Summer 1983: 112-117.
Meyers, Jeffrey, 'Cosmic Sorrows', *Virginia Quarterly Review,* 59, Summer 1983: [516].
Pratt, William, *World Literature Today,* 57:3, Summer 1983: 463-464.
'Robert Lowell: A Biography', *Publishers Weekly,* 19 August 1983: 77.
Dunn, Douglas, 'Infinite Mischief', *Encounter,* 61, September-October 1983: 68.
Gelpi, Albert, 'Book Reviews', *American Literature,* 55, October 1983: 481-484.
Cantor, Jay, *New England Quarterly,* 56:4, December 1983: 606-609.
Levi, Peter, *PN Review,* 10:1, 1983: 24-26.
Pinsker, Sanford, *Literary Review* (Fairleigh Dickinson University, New Jersey), 1983: 259-261.
Richman, Robert, 'The Saddest Story', *American Scholar,* 53, Spring 1984: 266-274.
Crowley, S.M., *Religion and Literature,* 16:3, 1984: 73-83.
Neill, E., 'Pity the Monster – Reflections on a Biography of Lowell', *Critical Quarterly,* 27:3, 1985: 53-62.

Spears, Monroe K., *Southern Review*, 20, 1985: 221-231.

Waddell, William S. Jr., *Modern Language Studies*, 15:4, 1985: 370-372.

THE NEW REVIEW ANTHOLOGY (1985)

Christiansen, Rupert, 'The Last Party', *New Statesman*, 1 November 1985: 31.

James, Clive, 'Clive James Writes About Literary Magazine', *London Review of Books*, 7:19, 7 November 1985: 8-9.

Berry, Neil, 'From the Middle Ground', *Times Literary Supplement*, 4312, 22 November 1985.

Pulik, Ruth, *UNISA English Studies: Journal of the Department of English, University of South Africa* (Pretoria), 24:2, September 1986: 54-55.

IN SEARCH OF J.D. SALINGER (1988)

Stuttaford, Genevieve, 'Nonfiction: J. D. Salinger: A Writing Life', *Publishers Weekly*, 27 June 1986: 80.

Young, Tracy, 'J.D. Salinger: a Writing Life', *Vogue*, August 1986: 196.

'J.D. Salinger Sues to Bar Biography', *New York Times*, 4 October 1986: 8 [Legal case involving *J. D. Salinger: A Writing Life*].

Streitfeld, David, 'Salinger's Articles of Privacy', *Washington Post*, 22 October 1986: C1 [Legal case involving *J. D. Salinger: A Writing Life*].

Yen, Marianne, 'Judge Grants Restraint Order on Salinger Bio', *Publishers Weekly*, 24 October 1986: 13 [Legal case involving *J. D. Salinger: A Writing Life*].

'J.D. Salinger Sues to Bar Biography', *New York Times*, 4 October 1986: 8 [Legal case involving *J. D. Salinger: A Writing Life*].

Streitfeld, David, 'Salinger Loses Bid for Injunction Against Biography', *Washington Post*, 6 November 1986: D1 [Legal case involving *J. D. Salinger: A Writing Life*].

Streitfeld, David, 'Salinger Wins Delay on Biography', *Washington Post*, 8 November 1986: D3 [Legal case involving *J. D. Salinger: A Writing Life*].

Hitchens, Christopher, 'American Notes', *Times Literary Supplement*, 4363, 14 November 1986: 1276.

Streitfeld, David, 'Court to Hear Salinger Appeal', *Washington Post*, 19 November 1986: B4 [Legal case involving *J. D. Salinger: A Writing Life*].

McDowell, Edwin, 'Salinger Book's Fate Cloudy', *New York Times*, 20 November 1986: 16 [Legal case involving *J. D. Salinger: A Writing Life*].

Streitfeld, David, 'Salinger's Privacy Claim', *Washington Post*, 4 December 1986: C8 [Legal case involving *J. D. Salinger: A Writing Life*].

Lubasch, Arnold H., 'Salinger Biography Is Blocked', *New York Times*, 30 January 1987: 1 [Legal case involving *J. D. Salinger: A Writing Life*].

Streitfeld, David, 'Salinger Wins Injunction', *Washington Post*, 30 January 1987: C1 [Legal case involving *J. D. Salinger: A Writing Life*].

Streitfeld, David, 'Rehearing Sought in Salinger Case', *Washington Post*, 4 February 1987: D3 [Legal case involving *J. D. Salinger: A Writing Life*].

McDowell, Edwin, 'Publisher to Seek Rehearing on Salinger Biography Ban', *New York Times*, 5 February 1987: 24 [Legal case involving *J. D. Salinger: A Writing Life*].

Press, Aric, 'Whose Mail Is It, Anyway? J.D. Salinger Bests a Biographer in Court', *Newsweek*, 9 February 1987: 58 [Legal case involving *J. D. Salinger: A Writing Life*].

'Return to Sender; Salinger Throws a Writer's Block', *Time*, 9 February 1987: 62 [Legal case involving *J. D. Salinger: A Writing Life*].

Yardley, Johnathan, 'The Catcher in the Right', *Washington Post*, 9 February 1987: D2 [Legal case involving *J. D. Salinger: A Writing Life*].

Streitfeld, David, 'Salinger Reconsideration Asked', *Washington Post*, 13 February 1987: B2 [Legal case involving *J. D. Salinger: A Writing Life*].

Yen, Marianne, 'Random House Seeks Review of Salinger Decision', *Publishers Weekly*, 13 February 1987: 24 [Legal case involving *J. D. Salinger: A Writing Life*].

Yen, Marianne, 'AAP Files Amicus Brief for Random House in Appeal of Salinger Desicion', *Publishers Weekly*, 27 February 1987: 90 [Legal case involving *J. D. Salinger: A Writing Life*].

Delbanco, Andrew, 'Holden Caulfield Goes to Law School', *New Republic*, 196:10, 9 March 1987: 27-30 [Legal case involving *J. D. Salinger: A Writing Life*].

'Salinger Copyright Claim Blocks Letter Use in Book', *News Media & the Law*, 11:2, Spring 1987: 41-42 [Legal case involving *J. D. Salinger: A Writing Life*].

Hoban, Phoebe, 'The Salinger File: Fighting for His Privacy, America's Most Elusive Author Is Flushed From His Refuge', *New York*, 15 June 1987: 36 [Legal case involving *J. D. Salinger: A Writing Life*].

Diviney, Catherine A., 'Guardian of the Public Interest: an Alternative Application of the Fair Use Doctrine in Salinger V. Random House, Inc.', *St. John's Law Review*, 61:4, Summer 1987: 615-628 [Legal case involving *J. D. Salinger: A Writing Life*].

Fields, Howard, 'AAP and Seven Authors Ask to Join Random House in Salinger Appeal', *Publishers Weekly*, 25 September 1987: 11 [Legal case involving *J. D. Salinger: A Writing Life*].

Teachout, Terry, 'Salinger Then and Now', *Commentary*, 84:3, September 1987: 61 [Legal case involving *J. D. Salinger: A Writing Life*].

Murphy, Christopher A., 'The Author's Interests in Unpublished Materials', *Columbia - VLA Journal of Law & the Arts*, 12:1, Autumn 1987: 103-129 [Legal case involving *J. D. Salinger: A Writing Life*].

'Ruling Stands Against Book on Salinger', *New York Law Journal*, 198, 6 October 1987: 1 [Legal case involving *J. D. Salinger: A Writing Life*].

Blau, Eleanor, 'Supreme Court Refuses to Review Salinger Ruling', *New York Times*, 6 October 1987: 17 [Legal case involving *J. D. Salinger: A Writing Life*].

Reuter, Madalynne, 'High Court Won't Rule on "Salinger"', *Publishers Weekly*, 16 October 1987: 13 [Legal case involving *J. D. Salinger: A Writing Life*].

Zissu, Roger L., 'Salinger and Random House: Good News and Bad News', *Journal of the Copyright Society of the U.S.A.*, 35:1, October 1987: 13-16 [Legal case involving *J. D. Salinger: A Writing Life*].

Margolic, David, 'Whose Words Are They, Anyway?', *New York Times*, 1 November 1987: 1 [Legal case involving *J. D. Salinger: A Writing Life*].

Gillespie, Elgy, 'Catcher in the Court', *New Statesman*, 13 November 1987: 13 [Legal case involving *J. D. Salinger: A Writing Life*].

Zissu, Roger L., 'Fears, Criticisms of Salinger Opinion Result From Misreading of Decision', *The National Law Journal*, 10:16-17, 28 December 1987: 24 [Legal case involving *J. D. Salinger: A Writing Life*].

McDowell, Edwin, 'Writer, Twice Restrained, Has New Salinger Book', *New York Times*, 19 February 1988: 34.

Goldstein, William, 'Random to Issue New Version of Embattled Salinger Biography', *Publishers Weekly*, 26 February 1988: 102.

Zissu, Roger L., 'Fears, Criticisms of Opinion Result From Misreading of Decision', *Journal of the Copyright Society of the U.S.A.*, 35:3, April 1988: 189-195 [Legal case involving *J. D. Salinger: A Writing Life*].

Lehmann-Haupt, Christopher, 'A Frustrated Hunter on the Trail of J. D. Salinger', *New York Times*, 19 May 1988: 29.

Stuttaford, Genevieve, 'Nonfiction', *Publishers Weekly*, 20 May 1988: 80.

Clemons, Walter, 'The Phantom of Cornish', *Newsweek*, 111:21, 23 May 1988: 73.

Koenig, Rhoda, 'Search and Destroy', *New York*, 21:21, 23 May 1988: 93-94.

Sheppard, R. Z., 'Trespassers Will Be Prosecuted', *Time*, 131:21, 23 May 1988: 74.

Moran, Terence, 'In Search of J.D. Salinger', *Legal Times*, 11:1, 30 May 1988: 34.

Richler, Mordecai, 'Rises at Dawn, Writes, Then Retires', *New York Times Book Review*, 5 June 1988: 7.

Chambers, Andrea and Jonathan Cooper, 'In Search of J.D. Salinger: Biographer Ian Hamilton Discovers a Subject Who Didn't Want to Be Found', *People Weekly*, 29:22, 6 June 1988: 50.

Yardley, Jonathan, 'Of Salinger & Sour Grapes', *Washington Post,* 8 June 1988: C2.

Harris, Mark, 'J. D. Salinger Has Won', *Los Angeles Times,* 12 June 1988: 3.

Cryer, Dan, 'Salinger Reclusive As Ever Despite Search', *Newsday,* 13 June 1988: 6.

Winship, Frederick, 'Ian Hamilton's Losing Match with J. D. Salinger', *UPI,* 21 June 1988.

Peary, Gerald, 'A Novelist in Hiding', *Maclean's,* 101:27, 27 June 1988: 56.

Udovitch, Mim, 'So Sue Me: Mixed Messages from J. D. Salinger', *Village Voice,* 33:27, 5 July 1988: 49.

Cockburn, Alexander, 'Peepers and Pokers', *Interview,* 18:7, July 1988: 95-96.

Gargan, William, 'Book Review: Literature', *Library Journal,* 113:12, July 1988: 81.

Warner, Judy, 'In Search of Ian Hamilton', *National Review,* 40:15, 5 August 1988: 48.

Lee, Michael, 'A Game Called Catcher in the Wry', *National Catholic Reporter,* 24:37, 12 August 1988: 9.

Glendinning, Victoria, *Times,* 17 September 1988.

'Lives of the Famous: Private, Keep Out', *Economist ,* 17 September 1988: 108-110.

Gross, John, 'The Book About the Book That Salinger Escaped From', *Sunday Telegraph,* 18 September 1988.

Profumo, David, 'The Greta Garbo of American Letters', *Sunday Times,* 18 September 1988.

Raban, Jonathan, 'Catcher on the Sly', *Observer,* 18 September 1988.

Barnacle, Hugo, 'Enough for one life', *Independent,* 20 September 1988.

Folkenflik, Robert, 'Ferret in the Rye', *Listener,* 22 September 1988: 23-24.

Angier, Carole, 'Shoot the Biographer', *New Statesman & Society,* 1:16, 23 September 1988: 33-34.

Lewis, Roger, 'He Wants to Be Alone', *Punch,* 23 September 1988: 49-50.

Morton, Brian, 'Desperately Seeking Salinger', *Times Educational Supplement,* 3769, 23 September 1988: 27.

Ford, Mark, 'Author, Author', *Times Literary Supplement,* 4461, 30 September 1988: 1066.

Catling, Patrick Skene, 'People Who Live in Glass Houses May Remain Invisible', *Spectator,* 1 October 1988: 33-34.

Barnes, Julian, 'Salinger Affair', *London Review of Books,* 10:19, 27 October 1988: 3.

Sheed, Wilfrid, 'The Exile', *New York Review of Books,* 35:16, 27 October 1988: 35.

Goddard, John, *Books Canadian,* 17, October 1988: 29.

Johnson, George Sim, 'Book Reviews', *American Spectator,* 21:10, October 1988: 38-39.

Cockburn, Alexander 'Peepers and Pokers', *Interview Magazine,* 18:8, 1988.

Bellman, S. I., *Choice: Current Reviews for Academic Libraries,* 26, February 1989: 939.

Washington Post Book World, 27 August 1989: 12.

Whalen-Bridge, John, *Modern Fiction Studies,* 35:2, Summer 1989: 299-300.

Benson, Jackson J., 'Book Reviews', *American Literature,* 61:3, October 1989: 465-468.

Sheppard, R. Z., 'Foul Weather for Fair Use', *Time,* 30 April 1990: 86.

Silverberg, Mark, 'A Bouquet of Empty Brackets: Author-Function and the Search for J. D. Salinger', *Dalhousie Review,* 75:2, Summer-Fall 1995: 222-246.

Soho Square (2) (1989)

Coe, Jonathan, 'My Wife', *London Review of Books ,* 11:24, 21 December 1989: 20-21.

Menand, Louis, Memoirs, Dramas, Reflections', *Times Literary Supplement,* 4525, 22 December 1989: 1411.

Hughes-Hallett, Lucy, 'A Picker-Up of Considered Trifles', *Spectator,* 20 January 1990: 28.

Writers in Hollywood (1990)

Ward, Robert, 'As Good As Their Words', *Los Angeles Times,* 1 April 1990: 1.

Wiener, Thomas, 'Book Review: Performing Arts', *Library Journal,* 115:6, 1 April 1990: 117.

Stuttaford, Genevieve, 'Nonfiction', *Publishers Weekly,* 6 April 1990: 110.

Feeney, Mark, 'Wordsmiths for the Silver Screen', *Boston Globe*, 6 May 1990: B51.
Walters, Colin, 'Hollywood Story Has Thin Script', *Washington Times*, 14 May 1990: E6.
Hunter, Frederic, 'Hollywood's Write Stuff', *Christian Science Monitor*, 21 May 1990: 14.
Lehmann-Haupt, Christopher, 'Putting Words in the Actors' Mouths', *New York Times*, 21 May 1990: 14.
'War of the Words in Hollywood', *USA Today*, 25 May 1990: 6.
Sigal, Clancy, 'Life Among the "Thickheads"', *New York Times Book Review*, 27 May 1990: 2.
Hampton, Christopher, 'Stuck Together in Tinsel Town', *Sunday Telegraph*, 10 June 1990.
Latham, Aaron, 'Credits Where Credit Is Due', *Washington Post Book World*, 10 June 1990: 4-5.
Taylor, D. J., 'Stars and Bars', *Sunday Times*, 10 June 1990.
Truss, Lynne, 'More Cents than Sense', *Listener*, 14 June 1990: 29.
Wood, Michael, 'Bonded by the Bottle', *London Review of Books*, 12:11, 14 June 1990: 21.
French, Sean, 'Refuge for Writers', *New Statesman & Society*, 3:105, 15 June 1990: 33-34.
Leader, Zachary, 'Pride and Professionalism', *Times Literary Supplement*, 4550, 15 June 1990: 630.
Andrews, Nigel, 'The Not So Lost Race of the Movie World', *Financial Times*, 16 June 1990.
Critics' Forum: Review discussion on BBC Radio 3, 23 June 1990.
Mortimer, John, 'Two Thousand Dolours', *Spectator*, 23 June 1990: 32.
Klepp, L.S., *Entertainment Weekly*, 29 June 1990.
Green, William, 'Hackery Packery', *Punch*, 6 July 1990: 48.
Katzmann, Pat, *San Francisco Chronicle*, July 1990.
Stimson, Mansel, *Film*, July-August 1990.
'Literati', *Variety*, 340:4, 1 August 1990: 80.
Allen, W.H., *Film Review Annual*, 1990-1.
Dardis, Tom, 'Writers in Hollywood', *America*, 164:8, 2 March 1991: 252-253.
Kalson, Albert E., 'The Americas', *Modern Fiction Studies*, 37:2, Summer 1991: 259.
McGilligan, Patrick, 'Reviews', *Film Quarterly*, 45:1, Autumn 1991: 46-47.
Ceplair, Larry, 'Book Reviews', *Cineaste*, 18:4, December 1991: 53.

THE FABER BOOK OF SOCCER (1992)

O'Hagan, Simon, 'Poetry and Pros', *Independent on Sunday*, 9 February 1992.
O'Keefe, Brendan, 'We Wuz Robbed', *Observer*, 9 February 1992.
Read, Benedict, 'West Ham Three – Arsenal Nil', *Sunday Telegraph*, 16 February 1992.
White, Jim, 'The Cultured Pass', *Independent*, 17 February 1992.
Fletcher, Martin, 'Set Pieces', *New Statesman & Society*, 5:190, 21 February 1992: 41.
Flusfeder, David, 'Literary Goals', *G.Q.*, March 1992.
Ford, Mark, 'Perishing Genius', *Times Literary Supplement*, 4648, 1 May 1992: 32.

KEEPERS OF THE FLAME (1992; 1993)

Motion, Andrew, *Observer*, 4 October 1992.
Fraser, Antonia, 'Private Faces in Public Places', *Times*, 8 October 1992.
Thwaite, Anthony, *Sunday Telegraph*, 11 October 1992.
Miller, Karl, *Guardian*, 13 October 1992.
Binding, Paul, 'Shilling Lives', *New Statesman & Society*, 5:224, 16 October 1992: 40-41.
Treglown, Jeremy, 'Beware the Biographer', *Times Literary Supplement*, 4674, 30 October 1992: 9.
Symons, Julian, 'Burnt Offerings', *Sunday Times*, 1 November 1992.
Sutherland, John, 'After-Lives', *London Review of Books*, 14:21, 5 November 1992: 8-9.
Lee, Hermione, *Independent on Sunday*, 10 November 1992.
Keates, Jonathan, *Independent*, 25 November 1992.
Christiansen, Rupert, 'Hanging Out the Washing', *Spectator*, 5 December 1992: 45.

173

Braybrooke, Neville, *The Tablet*, 6 March 1993.
Belsey, Andrew, *Journal of Media Law and Practice*, 14, 1993: 83-84.
Stuttaford, Genevieve, 'Nonfiction: Keepers of the Flames', *Publishers Weekly*, 14 February 1994: 74.
Lehman, David, 'Over Their Dead Bodies', *New York Times Book Review*, 27 March 1994: 20.
Yardley, Jonathan, 'Their Precious Reputations', *Washington Post Book World*, 10 April 1994: 3.
Mallon, Thomas, 'Books', *New Criterion*, 12:10, June 1994: 80-84.
Black, Barbara, 'Literary Fame and Misfortune Go Hand in Hand', *Gazette* (Montreal), 23 July 1994: H2.
Hulbert, Ann, 'The Soul and Discretion', *New Republic*, 211:8-9, 22-29 August 1994: 40.
Glendinning, Victoria, 'Whose Life Is It Anyway?', *Los Angeles Times*, 23 October 1994: 2.
West, James L. W., 'Biography and Literary Estates', *Sewanee Review*, 103:1, Winter 1995: xx-xxi.

GAZZA ITALIA (1993)
GAZZA AGONISTES (1994; 1998)

Crickmer, Clive, 'Samson and Gazza!', *Daily Mirror*, 4 October 1993.
Young, Robin, 'Gazza's Poetry On the Ball Makes Him a Literary Hero', *Times*, 4 October 1993.
Herbert, Susannah, *Sunday Telegraph*, 28 November 1993.
Barnes, Simon, 'Yes, But Who Is Gazza?', *Times*, 28 May 1994.
Hofmann, Michael, 'Main Man', *London Review of Books*, 16:13, 7 July 1994: 6.
Thomas, Dave, 'Gazza's Grief', *Times*, 24 October 1998.
Glanville, Brian, 'Book Review', *Sunday Times*, 1 November 1998.

WALKING POSSESSION (1994; 1996)

Wright, Michael, 'Rarity Among Critics', *Times*, 5 May 1994.
Ford, Mark, 'Unimpressed but Not Unappeased', *Times Literary Supplement*, 4754, 13 May 1994: 23.
Sexton, David, 'The Gazza of Criticism?', *Sunday Telegraph*, 15 May 1994.
Taylor, D. J., 'For Love and Money', *Sunday Times*, 22 May 1994.
Hofmann, Michael, 'Main Man', *London Review of Books*, 16:13, 7 July 1994: 6.
Armstrong, Isobel, 'Decades in the Making', *Times Educational Supplement*, 4074, 29 July 1994: 18.
Stuttaford, Genevieve, 'Nonfiction: Walking Possession', *Publishers Weekly*, 8 July 1996: 68.
Johnson, Denise, 'Reviews: Literature', *Library Journal*, 121:15, 15 September 1996: 69.
Seaman, Donna, 'Nonfiction', *Booklist*, 93:2, 15 September 1996: 204.
Firchow, Peter, 'Essays', *World Literature Today*, 71:3, Summer 1997: 596-597.
Simon, John, 'Supreme Nonfiction', *New Criterion*, 15:5, 1997: 63-68.
Pinsker, Sanford, 'Essayists, Obsessions and Hardcovers', *Georgia Review*, 51:3, Autumn 1997: 549-556.
Kirsch, Adam, *Harvard Review*, 12, 1997: 221-222.

THE OXFORD COMPANION TO TWENTIETH-CENTURY POETRY (1994)

Cunningham, Valentine, *Observer*, 6 February 1994.
Scammell, William, 'Swans, Geese and Ugly Ducklings', *Independent on Sunday*, 6 February 1994.
Sexton, David, 'Intimations of Immortality', *Sunday Telegraph*, 6 February 1994.

Spender, Stephen, 'The Oxford Companion to Twentieth Century Poetry in English', *Times*, 7 February 1994.
Horovitz, Michael, 'Gents at Work', *New Statesman & Society*, 7:289, 11 February 1994: 37.
Corke, Hillary, 'You Taught Me the Language', *Spectator*, 12 February 1994: 24.
Potts, Robert, 'Poetries in Englishes', *Times Literary Supplement*, 4742, 18 February 1994: 9.
Gowrie, Grey, 'The Special Relationship', *Daily Telegraph*, 26 February 1994.
Porlock, Harvey, 'On the Critical List', *Sunday Times*, 6 March 1994.
Booklist, 90:16, 15 April 1994: 1557.
Dollard, Peter, 'Book Reviews: Reference', *Library Journal*, 119, 15 April 1994: 68.
Day, Aidan, 'Dylan, Rap and Angry Penguins', *Times Higher Education Supplement*, 1122, 6 May 1994: 32.
Craven, Peter, 'Hamilton's 1500', *The Age* (Melbourne, Australia), 14 May 1994.
Vendler, Helen, 'The Three Acts of Criticism', *London Review of Books*, 16:10, 26 May 1994: 5-6.
Bravard, R. S., *Choice: Current Reviews for Academic Libraries*, 32:1, September 1994: 74.
Craig, Patricia, *Honest Ulsterman* (Belfast), 98, 1994: 105-107.
Poole, Richard, *Poetry Wales*, 30:1, 1994: 2-4.
'At a Glance', *School Library Journal*, 41:3, March 1995: 238.
North, Michael, 'Book Review', *Modernism/Modernity*, 2:2, April 1995: 86-88.
Haberer, Adolphe, *Études Anglaises* (Paris), 48:3, July-30 September 1995: 343-344.
McIlvaine, Eileen, 'Selected Reference Books of 1994', *College & Research Libraries*, 56:5, September 1995: 433.

A Gift Imprisoned (1998; 1999)

Gross, John, 'Return to Dover Beach', *Sunday Telegraph*, 8 March 1998.
Eagleton, Terry, 'Dreaming Uninspired', *Times Higher Education Supplement*, 1323, 13 March 1998: 22.
Taylor, D. J., 'Counterpoints', *New Statesman*, 13 March 1998: 53.
Hughes, Kathryn, 'Driven to Duty by His Father's Memory', *Daily Telegraph*, 14 March 1998.
Scott, Peter, 'Elusive Poet and Dutiful Victorian', *Financial Times*, 14 March 1998.
Conrad, Peter, 'Rhyme and Punishment', *Observer*, 15 March 1998.
Tomalin, Claire, 'In His Father's Shadow', *Sunday Times*, 15 March 1998.
Sutherland, John, 'Enisled', *London Review of Books*, 20:6, 19 March 1998: 7-8.
Murray, Nicholas, 'Rare Case of a Poet Who Doubted His Own Genius', *Literary Review*, March 1998.
Morrison, Blake, 'Poet Beached at Dover', *Independent on Sunday*, 5 April 1998.
Nye, Robert, 'Parting Lines of a Divine Dandy', *Times*, 5 April 1998.
Adams, Jad, 'How Matthew Lost His Muse', *Times Educational Supplement*, 4266/4267, 10 April 1998: Friday Supplement, 10.
'Dr. Arnold's Boy', *Economist*, 347:8064, 18 April 1998: 13.
Pierce, Peter, *The Bulletin with Newsweek*, 117:6137, 25 August 1998: 69.
Imlah, Mick, 'A Poet Aged Before His Time', *Times Literary Supplement*, 4979, 4 September 1998: 4.
MacKinnon, Lachlan, 'School Inspector Marked for Life', *Independent*, 1998.
Lane, Anthony, 'Poetry and Principle', *New Yorker*, 74:44, 1 February 1999: 74.
Driscoll, Kevin, 'The Poet Is Dead. We Have Lost a Poet', *Washington Times*, 21 March 1999: B6.
Kimball, Roger, 'The Divided Victorian', *Wall Street Journal*, 25 March 1999: 24.
Jenkins, Nicholas, 'The Story of A', *New York Times Book Review*, 20 June 1999: 12.
Vendler, Helen, 'The Unburied Life', *New Republic*, 21 June 1999: 48.
Carduff, Christopher, 'Book Notes', *New Criterion*, 17:10, June 1999: 90.
Mermin, Dorothy, 'Reviews', *Nineteenth-Century Literature*, 54:1, June 1999: 110-113.

Hoagwood, T., *Choice: Current Reviews for Academic Libraries*, 37, September 1999: 143.
Machann, Clinton, 'Matthew Arnold', *Victorian Poetry*, 37:3, Autumn 1999: 366.
Bryant, Hallman, 'Honour Thy Father', *South Carolina Review*, 33:1, Autumn 2000: 213-219.

ANTHONY THWAITE IN CONVERSATION WITH PETER DALE AND IAN HAMILTON (1999)

Crotty, Patrick, 'Poets on the Parish', *Times Literary Supplement*, 5091, 27 October 2000: 27.
Share, Don, 'Interviewing', *Essays in Criticism*, 50:4, October 2000: 378.

THE PENGUIN BOOK OF TWENTIETH-CENTURY ESSAYS (1999)
THE BOOK OF TWENTIETH-CENTURY ESSAYS (2000)

Scruton, Roger, 'An Assay into Essay Finds the Best of a Form Which Won't Be Ignored', *Times*, 26 August 1999.
Palmer, Alasdair, 'Culture of Complaint', *Sunday Telegraph*, 19 September 1999.
Banville, John, 'A Craftily Assembled Collection', *Irish Times*, 25 September 1999.
Hillier, Bevis, 'Why Did He Leave Out E.M. Forster?', *Spectator*, 25 September 1999.
Lewis, Jeremy, 'A Worthy Enthusiasm', *Literary Review*, September 1999.
Grayling, A.C., 'A Touch of the Indefinable Thing', *Weekend Financial Times*, 9 October 1999.
Adams, Tim, 'The Secret of the Universe? It's a Banana ...', *Observer*, 10 October 1999.
Fearn, Nicholas, 'A Sense of an Ending', *New Statesman*, 6 December 1999: 77.
Thomson, Ian, *Independent*, 1999.
'Reviews', *Contemporary Review*, 276:1608, January 2000: 54.
Lezard, Nicholas, 'Nice Shorts', *Guardian*, 24 April 2000.
'The Book of 20th-Century Essays', *Publishers Weekly*, 21 August 2000: 60-61.
Christensen, Bryce, 'The Book of Twentieth-Century Essays', *Booklist*, 97:1, 1 September 2000: 57.
Paumier Jones, Mary, 'The Book of Twentieth-Century Essays', *Library Journal*, 125:14, 1 September 2000: 206.
Birkerts, Sven, 'State of the Art: The Essay', *Washington Post Book World*, 19 November 2000.
Carey, Leo, 'Thinking Men', *New Yorker*, 76:41, 8 January 2001: 16.
Butscher, Edward, 'Essays of Our Time and Clime', *Georgia Review*, 55, Spring 2001: 170.

DONALD HALL IN CONVERSATION WITH IAN HAMILTON (2000)

Crotty, Patrick, 'Poets on the Parish', *Times Literary Supplement*, 5091, 27 October 2000: 27.

AGAINST OBLIVION (2002)

Adams, Tim, 'Chapter and Verse: Ian Hamilton's Valedictory Work', *Observer*, 17 March 2002: Review, 15.
Thwaite, Anthony, 'Survival of the Poetic', *Sunday Telegraph*, 17 March 2002: 12.
Gray, Simon, *Front Row*, BBC Radio 4, 20 March 2002.
Wroe, Ann, *Daily Telegraph*, 23 March 2002: 3.
Carey, John, 'Reading Between the Lines: What Makes a Poet's Work Survive?', *Sunday Times*, 24 March 2002.
Herbert, W.N., 'Against Oblivion: Poetry's Judge, Jury and Executioner', *Scotland on Sunday*, 24 March 2002: 5.
Hulse, Michael, 'Editor's Choice', *Leviathan Quarterly*, 3, March 2002: 72.
Potts, Robert, 'A Passionate Partisan', *New Statesman*, 1 April 2002: 51-52.
Hofmann, Michael, 'Poet with a Chilling Turn of Prase', *Evening Standard*, 8 April 2002: 53.

MAGAZINES

THE REVIEW

Bergonzi, Bernard, 'The Poet's Reasons', *Guardian*, April 1962.
Enright, D.J., 'Frogs', *New Statesman*, Spring 1962.
'Language and the Self', *Times Literary Supplement*, 29 June 1962.
Kermode, Frank, 'Eliot on Herbert', *Guardian*, 14 December 1962.
Braybrooke, Neville, 'Reviewing the Reviews', *Time & Tide*, 21-27 February 1963.
Dale, Peter, 'Experience and Experiencing', *Isis*, 6 March 1963: 18, 20, 23.
Kell, Richard, 'The Fruits of Obsession', *Guardian*, Autumn 1963.
'Don't Bury the Hatchet', *Times Literary Supplement*, 13 February 1964.
'Little Magazines', *New Statesman*, 21 February 1964.
'Literary Periodicals', *Times Literary Supplement*, 26 March 1964.
Daniel, John, 'The Little Magazines', *Guardian*, Spring 1964.
'The Thirties and the Under-Thirties', *Guardian*, July 1964.
Stephen Spender, 'A High-Pitched Scream', *Listener*, 13 August 1964.
Toynbee, Philip, 'Hurrah for the Republic?', *Observer*, 16 August 1964.
John Horner, 'And the Same Old Mix ...', *Spectator*, Summer 1964.
Connolly, Cyril, 'Battles of the Thirties', *Sunday Times*, 20 December 1964.
Allen, Walter, 'Letter from London', *New York Times Book Review*, 24 January 1965.
'Reducing the Risks', *Times Literary Supplement*, 10 October 1968.
Boston, Richard, 'The Razor's Edge', *Guardian*, 30 August 1972: Arts, 8.

THE NEW REVIEW

Andrews, Lyman, 'First Steps', *Sunday Times*, 7 April 1974.
Morrison, Blake, *Times Literary Supplement*, June 1978.

RADIO PROGRAMMES

TWENTY MINUTES, BBC RADIO 3 BROADCASTS, 22 AND 24 MARCH 2000

Warner, Val, 'Poetry's Maw', *PN Review*, 134, 26:6

OBITUARIES AND TRIBUTES

Morrison, Blake, 'Obituary: Ian Hamilton', *Guardian*, 29 December 2001: 18.
'Ian Hamilton: Poet, Biographer', *Milwaukee Journal Sentinel*, 30 December 2001: 5B.
'Ian Hamilton, 61, Noted Biographer, Poet, Critic', *Newsday* (New York), 30 December 2001: A51.
'Deaths Elsewhere', *Baltimore Sun*, 31 December 2001: 4B.
'Ian Hamilton', *Times*, 31 December 2001.
'Ian Hamilton Poet and Editor of *The Review* and *The New Review* Who Wrote Biographies of Robert Lowell and J.D. Salinger', *Daily Telegraph*, 31 December 2001: 23.
'Obituaries: Ian Hamilton', *Scotsman*, 31 December 2001: 14.
Oliver, Myrna, 'Obituaries: Ian Hamilton, 63', *Los Angeles Times*, 31 December 2001: 9.
Sexton, David, 'Literary Critic Hamilton Dies at 63', *Evening Standard*, 31 December 2001.
Cambridge, Gerry, 'Ian Hamilton: Poet, Biographer, Editor, and Critic', *Herald* (Glasgow), 1 January 2002: 14.

Josyane, Savigneau, 'Ian Hamilton; le Biographe du Mythique J. D. Salinger', *Le Monde*, 1 January 2002.
Miller, Karl, 'The Gaffer', *Independent*, 1 January 2002: 10.
'Dichter en Schrijver Hamilton Overleden', *De Standaard*, 2 January 2002: 11.
'Das Spiel ist Aus', *Suddeutsche Zeitung*, 3 January 2002: 17.
Dennehy, Luke, 'Author Fought to Publish', *Herald Sun*, 3 January 2002: 72.
'Mort de Ian Hamilton', *Liberation*, 3 January 2002: 4.
Pearce, Edward, 'Obituary: Ian Hamilton', *Independent*, 4 January 2002: 6.
'Distinguished Biographer, Critic, Poet and Editor', *Irish Times*, 5 January 2002: 16.
Martin, Douglas, 'Ian Hamilton, 63, Whose Salinger Book Caused a Stir, Dies', *New York Times*, 7 January 2002: 6. [A correction to information given in this obituary was printed on 11 January 2002: 2].
McEwan, Ian, 'Poetry and Pillar Talk', *Guardian*, 8 January 2002: 8-9.
Porter, Peter, 'Remembering Ian Hamilton, 1938-2001', *Times Literary Supplement*, 5155, 18 January 2002: 19.

THE HAMILTON ARCHIVES

PRINCETON UNIVERSITY LIBRARY, MANUSCRIPTS DIVISION, DEPARTMENT OF RARE AND SPECIAL COLLECTIONS, PRINCETON, NEW JERSEY, USA.

COLLECTION NO. C0714

Working Papers for *J.D. Salinger: A Writing Life*. There are three boxes of material, containing writings, legal papers and correspondence relating to this book, a listing of which is to be found on the university's website, at:

http://infoshare1.princeton.edu/libraries/rbsc/aids/hamilton-ian.html

BRITISH LIBRARY, ST PANCRAS, LONDON

General correspondence from the 1960s to the late 1980s; research, manuscript and typescript material, as well as some correspondence relating to *A Gift Imprisoned: The Poetic Life of Matthew Arnold*, *Gazza Agonistes*, *Keepers of the Flame*, *In Search of J.D. Salinger*, *Writers in Hollywood*, *Robert Lowell: A Biography*, *The Little Magazines*, *The Oxford Companion to Twentieth Century Poetry*, *The Review*, *The New Review*. This archive is still being catalogued, and is not yet open, although the library says that access can be granted in special cases. Written applications should be made to Chris Fletcher.

NATIONAL SOUND ARCHIVE, BRITISH LIBRARY, ST PANCRAS, LONDON

COLLECTION NO. C393

The holding comprises open reel tapes and audio cassettes, featuring IH in conversation with various figures. The open reel tapes contain rushes for a 'Lively Arts' programme on Robert Lowell, involving William Alfred, Seamus Heaney, Caroline Lowell, Eugene McCarthy, Frank Parker and Peter Taylor. The audio cassettes contain (a) discussions of Robert Lowell with Frank Bidart, Lillian Hellman, Cleanth Brooks, Gertrude Buckman, Blair Clark, Martha Ritter, Ann Dick, Grey Gowrie, Xandra Gowrie, Elizabeth Hardwick, Caroline Lowell, M. Heymann, William Meredith,

Robert Penn Warren, Charles Monteith, Frank Parker, Lesley Parker, Jonathan Raban, Robert Silvers, Peter Taylor, John Thompson and Helen Vendler, and (b) interviews with Peter Ackroyd, Gillon Aitken, Liz Calder, Anita Desai, Clarissa Luard, Pauline Melville, Sameen Momen, V.S. Naipaul, Keith Ravenscroft, Avril Ravenscroft, Philip Roth, and (c) BBC's 'Bookmark' programme on Salman Rushdie and BBC's 'Arena' programme on the life of Zola. This collection has yet to be catalogued, but it is open to the public. Details of the archive's listening service are to be found on its website:

http://www.bl.uk/collections/sound-archive/nsa.html

UNIVERSITY OF LEEDS, BROTHERTON COLLECTION

Letters from IH to Michael Hamburger, Alan Ross and others; manuscript and typescript material as well as correspondence relating to *The Review*. An itemised list of this correspondence – letters from some eighty correspondents to IH – can be found on the Brotherton Library's website:

http://brs.leeds.ac.uk/cgi-bin/brs_engine

UNIVERSITY OF HULL, BRYNMOR JONES LIBRARY, ARCHIVES AND SPECIAL COLLECTIONS

Typescript, proof, illustrations and correspondence relating to *The New Review*. A brief description of the collection is to be found on the university's website:

http://www.hull.ac.uk/lib/archives/litguide/review.html

UNIVERSITY OF TEXAS AT AUSTIN, HARRY RANSOM HUMANITIES RESEARCH CENTRE

ROBERT LOWELL COLLECTION, 1938-1983

Correspondence between IH and Blair Clark, as well as correspondence of others relating to *Robert Lowell: A Biography*. Further details can be found on the archive's website:

http://www.hrc.utexas.edu/fa/clark.html

THE CRITICS

THE REVIEW

'This small magazine of poetry and criticism makes a promising début. There are striking poems by Roy Fuller, Peter Redgrove and the Polish poet Zbigniew Herbert. The most interesting item, however, is a lengthy critical dialogue in which Anthony [sic] Alvarez argues for a new seriousness in poetry, a toughness of mind on the poet's part, which will enable him to confront the extremes of pain and ugliness in the modern world and still retain his sanity, while Donald Davie defends the importance of aestheticism, in the sense that the power of the medium, the poet's language, should be capable of transcending the self. The review section is limited in space but is principally interesting for a severe though discriminating notice of Thom Gunn's poetry by John Fuller.'

– Anonymous, *British Book News*, 1962

'Little magazines devoted to new poetry are frequent in their appearance and disappearance, but a little magazine, publishing new poems, yet mainly devoted to the really intelligent discussion and criticism of contemporary poetry, is a novelty. This is one reason for welcoming *The Review* (2s. 6d. every two months, edited by Mr Ian Hamilton, 99 Woodstock Road, Oxford). The first number contains some admirable poems and a number of unusually crisp and compact short reviews.'

– Anonymous, *Times Literary Supplement*, 1962

'R.I. Hamilton's little magazine from Oxford has made a good start, and this fourth issue is devoted to Mr Eliot. It has a good photograph and eight essays of fluctuating interest. F.W. Bateson on "Burbank" ("Burbank's modest hotel must 'really' be in Liverpool") and had previously housed Henry Adams and Henry James) and John Fuller on the "Five-Finger Exercises" (pioneering work) will have to be remembered and consulted. There are other exegetical pieces, some rather silly and over-assertive. I do not think it proper for a young critic to speak of this poet as "the sly old tom cat". John Bayley treats the "Collected Plays" as a tombstone and inscribes an elegant epitaph on the playwright.'

– Frank Kermode, *The Guardian*, 1962

'*The Review* is at last what we want from a little magazine, the conscious growing point of a new generation of talented writers ... For better or worse this is the voice we are going to hear.'

– Peter Levi, *Encounter*, 1962

'*The Review* is now in its second year. Its last number was given over entirely to T.S. Eliot's work, a number which very easily may become a collector's item.'

– Neville Braybrooke, *Time & Tide*, 1963

'There is widespread feeling now current that English poetry needs bucking up ... The one sign of hope is the foundation of a modern poetry magazine, *The Review*. This magazine is edited by Ian Hamilton and published outside London so that it may have, as near as possible, an objective point of view, unblurred by the camaraderie of literary London. Only by remaining outside the current groupings can it maintain its authority and right to reproach and castigate the literary slovenliness and amateurism of much present-day poetry.

Naturally, it does not know a definite answer, a universal solvent, to literary problems ... The important thing is that it is dedicated to attempt some sort of solution and it obviously intends to do this empirically rather than by abstraction and theory. Peter Levi said recently in *Encounter* that its critical standards were frighteningly high.

The importance of *The Review* ... is that it is the sole magazine in England that is trying to create taste, as opposed to the rigor-mortised journals such as *London Magazine* who lay in wait to snap up the edible when they have created the taste by which they are appreciated.'

– Peter Dale, *Isis*, 1963

'Of all the English little magazines now appearing regularly, *The Review* seems to be by far the most worthwhile. The unfussy manner adopted by many of the writers sometimes degenerates into a kind of licensed negligence or churlishness. Nevertheless, it has published some respectable poetry and stimulating criticism by people who aren't well-known; its most interesting numbers so far have perhaps been the special issues devoted to Eliot and Empson. Certainly the journal contains too much easy severity (the figure of the brilliant undergraduate seems to have been supplanted by the reproving undergraduate). But its best reviews have shown that it is possible to disapprove without being brutal or self-satisfied.'

– Anonymous, *New Statesman*, 1964

'[The Thirties] special number of *The Review* provides some excellent reading ...

– Cyril Connolly, *Sunday Times*, 1964

' ... *The Review* is by far the best of the British little magazines and seems to speak for a new crop of poets.'

– Walter Allen, *New York Times Book Review*, 1965

'The best poetry journal since Eliot's *Criterion*, Connolly's *Horizon* and Grigson's *New Verse*.'

– William Scammell, *Sunday Independent*, 1999

PRETENDING NOT TO SLEEP

'*The Review*, enterprising as always, produces for its thirteenth number three elegant pamphlets in one folder. The most interesting is that of the editor, Ian Hamilton, whose verse moves round a central core of uneasiness with a detached, pausing, almost Jamesian canniness. To use his own words, it is "edgy, poised", "elegant, perplexed".'

— Al Alvarez, *The Observer*, 1964

'Ian Hamilton is a discovery ... There is no complacent lingering over pain or pleasure, but the accuracy, the reticence we know to be the quality of high art.'

— Richard Howard, *Poetry* (Chicago), 1967

THE MODERN POET

'English little magazines concerned with poetry are today edited with an easy eclecticism which presupposes that all approaches to poetry have their merits. Any one of them might print the work of a Pop poet, or of Allen Ginsberg, or a newly-discovered poem by Edith Sitwell: any of them, that is, except *The Review*. Mr Hamilton knows what he does not like, and his magazine reflects not so much a personal taste as a personal distaste for what may loosely be called romantic, lyrical and rhetorical writing in the grand manner, and for all verse spun out of personal feelings that attempt to exclude the world outside the poet. A poem should not be but mean might be his motto ...

The quality and strictness of the editing give *The Review* its particular flavour, although Mr Hamilton's own contributions are comparatively few.'

— Anonymous, *The Times Literary Supplement*, 1969

THE VISIT

'The book as a whole is an undoubted and remarkable success because Ian Hamilton never deviates from his purpose: truth, respect for the language, respect for what it says. This is a distinguished first collection of poems.'

— Martin Dodsworth, *The Observer*, 1970

'Ian Hamilton's work marks an epoch in recent poetry. Writers have always celebrated the agonies due to passionate love or jealousy, and English poets of this century have often pitied themselves in verse either for their inadequacy in love or for the poverty of their attachments. A newer, more private theme has been the poet's inadequacy in handling his own painfully ambivalent emotions. Mr Hamilton follows such tendencies to an elevation on which he throws a glow of heroic virtue. In place of the struggle against sexual passion or one's own catastrophic ambivalence, he deals with the futility of tenderness, the poet's

incapacity to relieve the afflictions of those he loves.
   Mr Hamilton explores the situation until it becomes not narrowly pathetic but emblematic of human fate ...'

– Irvin Ehrenpreis, *The Times Literary Supplement*, 1970

'It is impossible to imagine a poetry more naked in its means or more lyrical in its essence. *The Visit* is a magnificent book, on a level with *Life Studies, Ariel* and *The Far Field*, and perhaps more exemplary than any of them.'

– Michael Fried, *The Spectator*, 1970

'The range of Hamilton's book is at the same time wider and narrower than some people have allowed; wider in subject-matter, narrower in success, perhaps. The subject-matter is not so strictly autobiographical as has been assumed but varies from intensely personal lyrics of love, marriage and death, through dramatic monologues of an aged mother, of a dying aesthete poet, of his mistress, to political comment and would-be epigram. The largest success is confined mainly to the first group. The book is thus less uniform, less 'minilithic' than has been assumed.
   ...
   When [Hamilton's] skills are truly keyed in, as they frequently are in the poems of marriage and mental disturbance, the poetry is very powerful and deeply moving. For a few of these poems I would trade in several fashionable American poets. Poems such as "Awakening", "Your Cry" and "Last Waltz" may appear brief but they have a power of feeling. One of their achievements is to re-introduce tenderness into English verse and to fend off defensive irony and emotional caution. Success outside this area is less assured. Hamilton has virtually only one style, so that, when he uses it for purposes other than an immediate impact of emotion, confusions and difficulties occur.
   ...
   It's difficult to see where Hamilton can develop after this book. The range of forms, diction, image and subject is refined and restricted to near repetitiousness. The ways out into dramatic monologue and reflection do not seem so successful. However, whichever way he moves from here he has *The Visit* behind him – no mean achievement.'

– Peter Dale, *Agenda*, 1971

A POETRY CHRONICLE

'Ian Hamilton has enviable gifts as a critic – intelligence, good taste, and an extensive vocabulary. He gives us the pleasure of judgements delivered without affectation or nonsense. Where so many hesitate it is a relief to hear him say, for example, that MacDiarmid fails to uncover in his poetry a mind of any real distinction, and that in praising "clear thought" he is "rather better at telling us what we need than he is at actually supplying it." That clears the air from our chests. We have needed this sharp man's reviews over the past few years. They made a space for disagreement in a blandly accepting world.
   Did we, however, need them in a book? The reviews, we might say, were part of a way

of thinking – were not, in themselves, thought. And indeed, boxed-up in this rather mean-looking volume, they do have an air both lifeless and vulnerable.
...
   A *Poetry Chronicle* has its interest, but, as the author says, it hardly presents an all-inclusive picture of what has been happening in poetry in the past decade. Is it even, as he claims "reasonably detailed"? Sylvia Plath is barely mentioned, Geoffrey Hill, Peter Porter and Charles Tomlinson are unmentioned, foreign poetry, even in translation, is ignored, and America is ill-served. The book too often displays an idle rhetoric out of keeping with serious literary criticism ("we have flicked through *The Golden Bough*", for example, not read it; Lowell is credited with a "tightly conversational tone", whatever that would be), and its judgements, though clear and challenging, do not have much to back them up. The evidence it offers is not only of Ian Hamilton's real gifts, but also of the way those gifts have been squandered, even in reviews for which we have been grateful: we needed more the critic of substance he might have been. As an omen for the health of our literary culture this book presents a dismal prospect.'

— Anonymous, *The Times Literary Supplement,* 1973

ROBERT LOWELL: A LIFE

'Ian Hamilton's biography, not only for the power of its story, but for the skill of its telling, puts in the shade those honourable but pale biographers who have written of poets lately. It is better than other recent biographies because it tells us how the poet wrote his poems. Ian Hamilton is himself a poet of edge and intelligence; and as editor of the now-defunct British magazine, *The New Review,* he had much to do with publishing Lowell's last work, that written during his "English period" (1970-77). But Hamilton is equally shrewd in his appraisal of the early years.
...
   Ian Hamilton has written a biography worthy of such terrible heroism as Lowell embodied.'

— Peter Davison, *Boston Globe,* 1982

'Ian Hamilton's comments on individual poems and volumes are sharp and acute. He commands an ironic wit and is not afraid to see shortcomings when they are there. Avoiding hero worship, he offers a steady understanding. It would be useful to have his judgement of Lowell's place in American poetry and modern literature, but he clearly believes that this is the moment for close inspection rather than large perspectives. If he does not do everything, it is chiefly because the tale he has to tell, and tells so well, is as complicated as it is compelling.'

— Richard Ellmann, *The New York Times,* 1982

'The biographer who would do [Robert Lowell's life] justice must possess extreme tact, lest he ... fall into oversimplification. The ideal biographer, of course, would be a divinely dispassionate creature, presenting all the germane information, interpreting the facts as perceptively as the works, but leaving ultimate judgement to the reader. Yet the great value of impartiality does not generate the kind of energy needed for an arduous biography such as Ian Hamilton's remarkable, nearly 500-page Robert Lowell, into which went extensive reading, tracking down, and interviewing. Such books can be motivated by passion: usually love, but sometimes hate. That Hamilton's book, on such a recent and pitfall-surrounded subject, can cleave so close to calm sympathy rather than to rowdy partisanship, to critical appreciation rather than to worship or envious malice, is no small achievement in itself.

... [T]he book is splendidly researched and documented, and its general knowledgeableness and subtlety are couched in a pleasingly perspicuous style.'

– John Simon, *The New Republic*, 1982

'Hamilton seems very conscious of the fact that he is writing biography, not criticism, and he rarely states his own views about Lowell's work, citing instead the judgements of reviewers made at the time when the works appeared, which Lowell read and sometimes suffered from. All the same, in his restrained way, Hamilton shows consistently firm and clear judgement.'

– Stephen Spender, *Washington Post Book World*, 1982

'The intellectual biography that will present the evolution of Lowell's mind will be written one day. But in the meantime, we have been given an unexpected gift by a foreign poet – the first account of the life of one of our American poets. We should perhaps be equally grateful to the people close to Lowell who have been willing to recall the life, joining themselves to Lowell's own long effort "to give / each figure in the photograph / his living name". Even so, Lowell's art, for all its intimate connection to lived event, seems finally to elude the tether of narrative. The fate of all literary biography is to remind us of the insufficiency of the life as an explanation of the art.'

– Helen Vendler, *New York Review of Books*, 1982

'Perhaps *Robert Lowell* reads like a chore because researching the book proved a laborious chore for Hamilton, and he's simply passing his fatigue on like a baton. (The only break in the glum cataloguing of detail comes when Hamilton quotes from Norman Mailer and Jean Stafford – their writing is so salty and shrewd that it perks up even this sluggish soiree.) It certainly can't be said that Hamilton's esteem for Lowell as a poet burns with a high tongue of flame ... It isn't that Hamilton is necessarily wrong in his appraisals, just that if enthusiasm for Lowell's work runs so thinly in his blood, then why do the book at all? Why not leave the spadework to someone who would more vigorously cherish the task?

Perhaps Hamilton was seduced by the notion of making a stamp on his time with a major biography. Robert Lowell, after all, was not only a writer of immense gifts and intelligence, but he had the look of a Great Poet – the shambling height, the brooding, tormented brow, the Ezra Pound glint of cracked brilliance in his eyes. And a Great Poet deserves a Great Biography, a sturdy monument where pigeons can convene. But though Hamilton says commending things about Lowell and his work, and ends his biography with a citation from King Lear ("We that are young / Shall never see so much, nor live so long"), you finally don't believe that Hamilton believes that Lowell was a figure of greatness. Instead, Lowell emerges as an unholy handful Hamilton can hardly wait to lateral into our laps.'

– James Wolcott, review of Robert Lowell: A Biography, Harper's, 1982

'Ian Hamilton is an elegant, sardonic stylist and an acute critic of poetry, more than willing to distinguish between the dross and the gold in Lowell's considerable output.

He is also a devoted sleuth who has put in an immense amount of leg-work, hunting up and interviewing everyone who knew Lowell ... The result is a searching evaluation of Lowell the poet as well as a detailed biography of the man.'

– Al Alvarez, Observer, 1983

'The book [Hamilton gives] us combines tough intelligence, tireless research, and a proper respect for the suffering it probes. The documentation – unpublished letters, interviews – is massive. Lowell's renowned public stands – his conscientious objection in World War II, his protest over Vietnam – lose their heroic simplicity and are seen for the first time in the context of his private morass. It is a remarkable addition to the annals of literature.'

– John Carey, The Sunday Times, 1983

'In Robert Lowell ... Ian Hamilton has written an extraordinarily careful and well-researched biography.

...

Hamilton's book deserves praise for many things, but I think chiefly for being astonishingly fair to all the major figures in the story he has set out to tell – not in itself an easy task, given a tale so congested with pain and cruelty, infidelity, wildness, and violence – but he is also to be congratulated on his respectful and intelligent dealings with the poetry. He is very keen, subtle, and knowing, for example, about Lowell's poem, "Home After Three Months Away", indicating with great care the stratified, geological layers of reference that work down through the poet's entire biography. He is even more helpful ... in the unravelling of an all but impenetrable poem, "The Misanthrope and the Painter", which seems otherwise defiantly hermetic and private ... In his honest dealings with his large cast of characters, and in his valuable comments on the poetry, Hamilton has done, I think, rather greater justice to Lowell than has been done to Byron by most of his biographers ... '

– Anthony Hecht, Grand Street, 1983

'This book lingers in the mind as much for its portrait of human loyalties as for its survey of a troubled and momentous career. Lowell's ultimate luck has been to inspire a biography that, like his best poetry, evokes not only his unique personality but the world in which he moved. It is a work of wit and intellect, feeling and imaginative depth.'

– Robert B. Shaw, Inquiry, 1983

'In an age in which the kind of people who used to be called "bookmen" commonly opt for the safety of the campus, Ian Hamilton has been an old-style adventurer. In the 1960s, apart from being an assistant editor of the *TLS*, he brilliantly edited the poetry magazine, *The Review*, a publication which between 1962 and 1972, in spite of being run on a shoestring, achieved a reputation well in excess of its small circulation. The champion of "intelligent lyricism", *The Review* was a pitiless critic of anything which it considered inflated, pretentious or modish ...

... After ten years of life, *The Review*, Hamilton felt, was settling into respectability; it was time to move on. *The New Review* was meant to be much wider in scope, to provide room for fiction, extended argument and drama scripts as well as poetry, yet without sacrificing the polemical edge of the old *Review*. The journal would seek to occupy the middle ground between the academic periodicals and the Sunday culture pages, eschewing the former's stuffiness and the latter's obligation to be brief. The order was nothing if not tall.

... [B]eyond a preference for hardness of tone, it is difficult to detect any particular editorial direction behind the collection ... And the truth is that, though it could be more challenging and polemical than this anthology suggests, *The New Review* was too miscellaneous in its interests ever to evolve the sharp, definite personality which marked out its predecessor. Nor, by way of compensation, could it claim an outstanding record as a talent-spotter. Ian McEwan was one of the few writers, relatively unknown at the time, whose work it promoted. The journal went, in the main, for familiar names ...

With this enjoyable anthology, Ian Hamilton has at least shown that *The New Review* did honourable work. He has erected, too, a monument to that quiet, if uneasy, period in Britain prior to the onset of the "winter of discontent" in 1978 – the year in which, undermined by financial problems, the journal suddenly folded.'

– Neil Berry, *The Times Literary Supplement,* 1985

IN SEARCH OF J.D. SALINGER

'Hamilton's book is as devious, as compelling, and in a covert way as violent, as a story by Chandler.'

– Victoria Glendinning, *The Times, 1988*

'A rich and subtly dramatic book ... a meticulous examination of Salinger's literary development.'

– Christopher Lehmann-Haupt, *New York Times,* 1988

'A sophisticated exploration of Salinger's life and writing and a sustained debate about the nature of literary biography, its ethical legitimacy, its aesthetic relevance to a serious reading of the writer's books.'

– Jonathan Raban, *The Observer,* 1988

'In the opening pages of his book, Ian Hamilton writes, "I had it in mind to attempt not a conventional biography – that would have been impossible – but a kind of Quest for Corvo, with Salinger as quarry." The analogy won't wash. A.J.A. Symons' book *The Quest for Corvo,* a fine and original work, happens to be about a literary scoundrel, Frederick Rolfe, a bizarre character whose squalid life was more fascinating than anything he wrote, while the obverse is true of J.D. Salinger, of whom Mr Hamilton justifiably observes, "The action for [him], was on the page."

There is another problem. Symons undertook his quest in 1925, 12 years after Rolfe's death, but Mr Salinger, happily, is still among the quick. At the risk of sounding stuffy, I think it indecently hasty to undertake a biography-cum-critical study of a still working writer and in highly questionable taste to pronounce him a perfect subject because, in Mr Hamilton's view, "he was, in any real-life sense, invisible, as good as dead." Invisible? Look here, we are talking about a writer whose only published novel, *The Catcher in the Rye,* which first appeared in 1951, was declared in 1968 to be one of America's 25 leading best sellers since the year 1895 and still sells something like a quarter of a million copies annually worldwide.

Ian Hamilton, to be fair, is no vulgarian: he has good credentials as a biographer, poet and critic.

– Mordecai Richler, *The New York Times,* 1988

'Canny and engaging ... impressively written, a tour de force.'

– R.Z. Sheppard, *Time, 1990*

FIFTY POEMS

'The best poems are those which let in more of "the world", and in the handful of pieces written since *The Visit* it is this slightly less cryptic, less sparing style that predominates. "Anniversary", "Returning", "Familiars", the symbolist perfection of "Rose" leave no doubts about the delicacy and strength of Hamilton's style at its best; but anyone might be forgiven for wishing that some sense of "what I got up to in those 'trashy years'" ("the booze, the jokes, the literary feuds, the almost-love-affairs, the cash, the somehow-getting-to-be-forty") had found a way into the poems of this time.'

– Alan Jenkins, *Observer,* 1988

'[Hamilton's] fifty poems inhabit sombre emotional territory, where few flowers bloom ...

The unadorned and modest poems, of delicate sadness, of small-scale character, are utterly controlled. They survive, luminous and beautiful in their precise nuances and grim atmospheres. A marriage that fails, a wife who has a major mental breakdown and a father who dies in middle age of cancer are the poem's abiding obsessions and inspirations ...

... [T]he value of the volume is the sense it gives of someone truthfully, rigorously recollecting pain in tranquillity, with quiet, white light clarity. Modest ambitions, thoroughly fulfilled.'

— Nicholas de Jongh, *Guardian*, 1988

'It is a great pity that shunting poetry aside has left [Hamilton] so little work to show, for he could have been a larger poet and a more skilful influence. The decision to live another kind of life may not have been easy, but it is not only Hamilton who has been impoverished by it.'

— Lachlan Mackinnon, *Times Literary Supplement*, 1988

' ... [F]ew slim volumes of poems contain so many powerful and memorable poems.
    Hamilton ... records that he is unable to judge the effectiveness of the most recent poems in the book but if the poems subsequent to this volume are anything to go on he has in fact extended his range and some of the humour and sardonicness of his prose has been used effectively to write a feelingful – to use one of his words – middle-aged poetry.'

— John Surple, *Agenda*, 1993

'The majority of the poems are generated by a wife's mental illness and a father's death from cancer. The few exceptions, just as sombre, are barely to be distinguished. There is something terrible and heroic in this narrow focus, in the way that these few poems, produced over many years, should have settled so close by one another, with their themes of break-up and breakdown, their shattered atmosphere, their identical reference points of hands and heads and hair and flowers and grass and snow and shadow ... Each individual poem is pruned back to an austere and beautiful knot of pain. Poetry, by his practice of it, is not craftsmanship or profession, but catastrophe. I can't, in general terms, think of any better way for a poem to be. Most poems have a hard time answering the question: "Is this really necessary?" Not his.
    ...
    Stood alongside *Fifty Poems*, most things just look impossibly trite, leisurely and overstuffed.

— Michael Hofmann, *London Review of Books*, 1994

WRITERS IN HOLLYWOOD 1915-1951

'There is little here in the way of original research, and at times the book seems padded, drifting into film history in general (as in the discussion of the talkies). Yet only occasionally is the narrative untrustworthy, or overly trusting.
    Elsewhere, though, wariness seems the book's chief virtue, as in the cool, sceptical scrutiny Hamilton brings to inflated claims and reputations, familiar (and suspiciously

well-tailored) anecdotes, schmaltz and hype.'

– Zachary Leader, *The Times Literary Supplement,* 1990

'... [A] well-researched and independent-minded book.
Writers in Hollywood is a thorough and properly sceptical history of the very peculiar practice of American screen-writing.'

– Lynne Truss, *The Listener,* 1990

'Ian Hamilton's intelligent, well-informed and often very funny book is a history of [the legend of the Hollywood script writer] and what lurks around it ...
However, *Writers in Hollywood* does take most of its information second-hand, and the narrative is a bit desultory, as if Hamilton didn't always know why he was retelling this anecdote rather than that ...
[T]he book, in spite of its alert irony, seems rather depressed and depressing, its last image the body of the drowned writer in a pool in *Sunset Boulevard.* Still, the story is depressing, perhaps more so than Hamilton thought when he began the book.'

– Michael Wood, *London Review of Books,* 1990

KEEPERS OF THE FLAME

'Hamilton could not, if he tried, write an unreadable book. *Keepers of the Flame* is that rarest of modern things, lit crit with laughs. Hamilton has an unfailingly good eye for an anecdote and a line in sarky parenthesis – on such things as William Davenant's pox-rotted nose – worthy of a stand-up comedian. Although it will find a home in that dreariest of Dewey Decimal deserts – the public reference section – this book is fun.'

– John Sutherland, *London Review of Books,* 1992

'... [An] absorbing and drily funny book ...
Hamilton himself is characteristically inquisitive and detached, humorous, knowledge-able and sympathetic. His book could do with fuller references and a bibliography ... But in a relatively small space, he manages to touch on a number of issues central to literary history: copyright law, for example, writers' attitude to fame ... and the roles of patrons, editors, relicts. All this involves some of the most intimate dilemmas which writers face: more intimate to them than to other famous people *because* they are writers, and under-stand particularly well the kinds of scrutiny they are, or will be, under. The section on the Carlyles is especially moving. Hamilton writes fair-mindedly about Sylvia Plath and Ted Hughes. And he is droll about Swinburne, and Theodore Watts-Dunton's nannying of the delinquent poet into a state of imaginative somnolence.'

– Jeremy Treglown, *Times Literary Supplement,* 1992

191

'Raymond Chandler once remarked that the English may not be the best prose writers in the world but they are unquestionably the best *dull* prose writers in the world. I thought of this statement from time to time while reading Ian Hamilton's *Keepers of the Flame: Literary Estates and the Rise of Biography*. It is a good, dull book – factual, solid, well-researched – about a hot subject, the ethics of literary biography, and it has its share of juicy anecdotes.

...

These are first-rate stories, and Hamilton presents them intelligently. He even states some of the major theoretical issues involved. For example, "the old insolubles: does poetic genius excuse or mitigate bad conduct; does / should knowing about the life have a bearing on how we read the work?" And there are other insolubles as well: when does the biographical imperative – and just what is that, exactly? – justify "contempt for old habits of decorum and respectfulness"? But Hamilton neglects to argue out the irreconcilable conflicts that face the biographer; he stands at a polite distance, though his own experience has involved him deeply in these very issues. *Keepers of the Flame* works as a sequence of chapters loosely linked by theme but without a provocative central thesis. American readers expect more excitement. English readers – from traditional regiments, at any rate – may enjoy the book nevertheless.'

– David Lehman, *New York Times Book Review*, 1994

WALKING POSSESSION

'Hamilton is ... one of the most scrupulous exponents of [reviewing]. Many of the pieces gathered here are not only witty and incisive, but carefully researched and argued. Like a hallmark of excellence, to see Hamilton's name on the cover of a literary paper always means that at least there will be something worth reading in it.'

– Mark Ford, *Times Literary Supplement*, 1994

'Of all the critics of his generation, none commands a prose so supple, pointed, icily laconic.'

– Clive James, jacket comment, 1994

THE OXFORD COMPANION TO TWENTIETH-CENTURY POETRY

'An *Oxford Companion* is, by its weight and apparent authority, likely to produce as many disputes as an anthology, where at least the editors are better placed to argue whatever corner they've painted themselves into ... The quality of the writing is, overall, very high, the range impressive, the approach as lively as the topic deserves. It is a handsome conversation piece, and should keep the passionate battles of the poetry world supplied with useful ammunition.'

– Robert Potts, *Times Literary Supplement*, 1994

'[G]enerously inclusive, [this book] will be seen in the future, I am certain, as a significant landmark of literary change. It documents the enormous burgeoning of English all over the world, a cultural fact bound to produce continuing poetic results.'

– Helen Vendler, *London Review of Books,* 1994

STEPS

'Here is the first book in a decade by a poet now fifty-eight who published when he was thirty-two a book that looked as though it should inaugurate the career of an important poet. But these ten short poems show how the edgy, baffled minimalism of his earlier work has crumbled into thinness and inconsequence ... There may be personal reasons for this but it's depressing to witness Hamilton's formidable literary intelligence (which has been evident enough in his activities as literary editor and biographer) failing to find a poetic outlet.'

– Ian Grigson, *Stand,* 1996

A GIFT IMPRISONED: THE POETIC LIFE OF MATTHEW ARNOLD

'Ian Hamilton is one of the best of contemporary poetry critics, so it is good to have this "poetic life" of Matthew Arnold with the emphasis centrally, though not wholly, on Arnold's verse. Hamilton treats both life and work with sympathy and discrimination, as well as with the humour that has always characterized his engagements with literature. Elegantly and economically argued throughout, *A Gift Imprisoned* provides further evidence that Arnold is very much alive for us today.'

– William Pritchard, jacket comment, 1998

'Hamilton's book vindicates literary biography by continually and persuasively illuminating Arnold's poems.'

– Edward Mendelsohn, jacket comment, 1998

'The best account yet of Matthew Arnold's mysterious hesitations and painful triumphs. Hamilton is everything a biographer should be.'

– James Wood, *The New Republic,* 1998

'Ian Hamilton's biography of Matthew Arnold is a small, sombre tragedy, an account of artistic suicide ... an aggrieved and moving report on the fate of literature in a society which can see no profit in it, and therefore condemns it to starve.'

– Peter Conrad, *The Observer,* 1998

'In the last couple of years there have been a long-awaited complete edition of Arnold's letters, a new biography, and now Ian Hamilton's absorbing biographical study of Arnold's poetic career. Out of all this a truer and more just picture of Arnold as poet and critic ought to emerge.

Hamilton's style is relaxed and informal, which makes this a highly readable book. It is not cluttered with academic references ... and the criticism is always biographical rather than formal but nonetheless acute.

... Hamilton succeeds in illuminating a subject that has clearly exercised his mind for many years. Readers of Arnold's poetry will find this book an essential companion, for it covers the years that matter in his poetic life.'

– Nicholas Murray, *Literary Review, 1998*

SIXTY POEMS

'Poetry is supposed to be, *par excellence*, the art in which deep emotions can be divulged and indulged; which is why the reserved British are thought to find it embarrassing.

Ian Hamilton first caught the public eye in the 1960s as a poetry reviewer who positively rejoiced in a culture of toughness, so he gave the impression that he shared the supposed national impatience with the art. Writing poetry might look a feeble kind of activity compared with, say, football or mountaineering. If you had to produce the stuff, it had better be good and genuine. Anything false, faked or overblown was out; the only true poetry was the least feigning.

But Hamilton was known to write poems himself, and poets treated severely in his magazine *The Review* waited with unpleasant eagerness to see what his first collection would be like. They were surprised. His terse and tender lyric poems showed an unfailing ear for cadence, and an eye for exact and poignant detail. Immensely touching, and done with unassailable emotional integrity, they went on only as long as was necessary to capture the grief, ambivalence, or ironic nostalgia in a scene of love, illness or dying.

... Hamilton is an original. David Harsent's phrase, in the tribute volume he has edited for Hamilton's 60th birthday [*Another Round at the Pillars: Essays, Poems and Reflections on Ian Hamilton*], about a "uniquely lyrical, passionate and sorrowing voice" is appropriate.'

– Alan Brownjohn, *The Sunday Times*, 1999

' ... *Sixty Poems* is sure to be one of the most affecting and satisfying collections we will see this year. One test of a good poem is how much it offers on re-reading. Does it still, as Emily Dickinson demanded, "take the top of your head off"? In this case, yes. Hamilton's small, bleak poems with their narrow range of detail, tone and subject are explosive.'

– Lavinia Greenlaw, *New Statesman*, 1999

'First, the mathematics. Sixty poems for sixty years, ten more than fifty poems ten years previously. The new *Sixty Poems* also embodies the entire text of Ian Hamilton's *The Visit*

(1970), barring some emendations (or further prunings) – though, ten years on, Faber omits to tell us this. And with all this discreet recycling going on it is a pity that Hamilton's wrily vestigial preface to *Fifty Poems* wasn't included again, as it's an important document, the nearest he was ever likely to come to a manifesto or ars poetica.
...
Hamilton ... is a very English poet, asserting the primacy of the quotidian, the empirical and the heartfelt in a traditional music. He is sparing with rhyme (though it occasionally creeps in) but not noticeably a formal innovator. The famous brevity is simply a desire to focus exclusively on the lyric moment, to honour a notion of the poem visiting the poet rather than being drummed up for the occasion. In the preface to *Fifty Poems*, Hamilton talks of having once wished to get more matter and clutter into the verse, but of having concluded that such things were better left to prose. "Why push and strain?" In the same place, he argues that, in some sense, he is still writing the poems of his youth, which spoke in "a voice made musical by a kind of anguished incredulity," the later poems being "bruised rewrites of what I'd done before." That, Hamilton argues, is the fate of "a lyric poet of the 'miraculous' persuasion," who will never grow up. "There won't be a middle period of worldliness and common sense."

This explains the uniformity of texture of the sixty poems, as well as the unusual force that comes from both the subject matter (madness and death) and from the utter authenticity of feelings belonging to poems that have not been unnaturally solicited. If Hamilton had written more he would have been more fêted. What he has written convinces us that it is *necessary*. In a poetry scene that is overcrowded, over-producing, and bereft of rigorous criticism, Hamilton's poetry looks more and more exemplary. And unlike Matthew Arnold, about whose earlier poetical years he has written so well, the late additions, few as they are do not represent a loss of performance and suggest, gratifyingly, that there will be more. Though not, in the nature of the case, all *that* much more.

– Nicholas Murray, *The Times Literary Supplement*, 1999

THE PENGUIN BOOK OF TWENTIETH-CENTURY ESSAYS

'Superb ... Excited by pretty well anything of human concern, interest and puzzlement, Hamilton has produced an immensely readable volume. He upholds the sterling virtue of good writing combined with emotional and intellectual engagement.'

– Ian Thomson, *Independent*, 1999

AGAINST OBLIVION: SOME LIVES OF THE TWENTIETH-CENTURY POETS

'The whole thing is crisp, sharp, opinionated, readable. But it is vulnerable too, as Hamilton must have realized, driven by an urgent sense of his own end. He was half-interested in some not-very-good (or awful) American poets: he includes H.D. (Hilda Doolittle), Conrad Aiken, Robinson Jeffers, Allen Tate, about all of whom he has almost nothing positive to say. He inexplicably excludes A.E. Housman (a contemporary of Kipling's), Siegfried Sassoon, Walter de la Mare, Andrew Young, John Crowe Ransom, Patrick Kavanagh, Edwin Muir,

George Barker, Gavin Ewart.

...

Because Hamilton was both highly intelligent and sensitive, as well as having a more developed and laconic sense of humour than most literary critics, there are many gems here: Robert Graves – with "nobody on hand to give him a hard time, he had to do it all by himself." But perhaps the poet who most resembles him is the American Randall Jarrell – "as he once testified, being a great poetry critic was a paltry sort of thing, involving a measure of self-relegation which, in the end, he maybe found impossible to bear." Knowing Ian Hamilton, loving him and admiring him as I did, I find this a sad testimony.'

– Anthony Thwaite, *Sunday Telegraph*, 2002

'Poets are biological throwbacks. Like children born with webbed feet or second sight, they were useful and revered in earlier, more primitive societies. But modern industrial culture has no use for them. Their art demands unsparing dedication, yet it earns, for the most part, neglect or contempt.

...

Hamilton's way of coping was characteristically tough and un-self-pitying. He was rigorously critical of poets and poetry, his own included. It was as though he thought that if he cleansed poetry of its delusions and posturings he would pre-empt or outflank its detractors. Sardonic, funny, with a steely intelligence, he was not immediately recognisable as a poet at all.

...

Stylish, gritty, often hilarious, *Against Oblivion* glitters with insights like flecks of mica. It gives precise expression to things you have noticed but not been able to formulate ... It is the cleverest, tersest introduction to 20th-century poetry you could hope to find, written by a man who has earned the right to be uncompromising. The buzz you get from reading it is tempered only by the thought that this is the last book we shall get from Hamilton, and there is absolutely nobody who can replace him.'

– John Carey, *Sunday Times*, 2002

'That Ian Hamilton's *Against Oblivion* should have ended up being published posthumously is an unfortunate coincidence that will be seen, journalistically, as an irony. It is his version of Samuel Johnson's *Lives of the English Poets* ...
Johnson's book was a commission; the list, for the most part, came from booksellers pushing their more successful poets. Hamilton's book was also a commission of sorts; the idea, he says, was "suggested to him" and "seemed a nice idea, if somewhat gimmicky, and I agreed to have a go." The result is a piece of light entertainment, close to hack work: risk-free speculation in the poetic futures market.'

– Robert Potts, *New Statesman*, 2002

'He takes Hardy, Yeats, Eliot and Auden as safe – but all the forty-five others in this gathering, from Kipling to Pound, from Bishop to Lowell, from Larkin to Plath, are argued for as if the ground might shift. With three or four pages of brisk critical analysis, plus a couple of poems representing each poet, the book is as much a lively anthology as an introduction to the humanely undeceived rigours of Hamilton's mind.'

– Michael Hulse, *Leviathan Quarterly*, 2002